MEDICAL DEVICES REGULATORY ASPECTS

A COMPREHENSIVE GUIDE

DR.MURALIDHAR RAO AKKALADEVI &
DR.K.HEMAMALINI

Made with ♥ on the Notion Press Platform
www.notionpress.com

Contents

Preface

The regulatory landscape for medical devices and in vitro diagnostics is as dynamic as it is complex. With rapid technological advancements and the continuous evolution of global health needs, the necessity for a comprehensive understanding of regulatory frameworks has never been more critical. This book, "Medical Devices Regulatory Aspects: A Comprehensive Guide," is crafted to serve as an essential resource for professionals navigating this intricate field. It offers an in-depth exploration of the regulatory processes, ethical considerations, and quality management systems that are fundamental to the successful introduction and maintenance of medical devices and diagnostics on a global scale.

The impetus for this book stems from a growing demand within the healthcare industry for clarity and guidance in the regulatory realm. As innovations drive the medical device sector forward, regulatory professionals, manufacturers, researchers, and healthcare providers must stay abreast of the latest standards, guidelines, and practices. This guide aims to bridge the gap between innovation and regulation, ensuring that advancements in medical technology are safely and efficiently translated into clinical practice.

Each chapter of this book is structured to provide a comprehensive overview of specific aspects of medical device regulation. From the foundational principles outlined in the initial chapters to more complex discussions on global regulatory strategies and case studies, the content is meticulously organized to cater to both newcomers and seasoned professionals in the field.

We begin with an introduction to medical devices and in vitro diagnostics, setting the stage for a deeper dive into the regulatory frameworks that govern these technologies. Subsequent chapters detail the specific regulatory environments of major markets, including the United States, the European Union, and key Asian jurisdictions. The book also addresses the ethical and quality considerations that are critical to the regulatory approval process and concludes with practical applications and a forward-looking perspective on harmonization initiatives.

This guide is not just a compilation of regulatory facts; it is a tool designed to foster understanding, enhance strategic planning, and encourage the effective implementation of regulatory principles. By providing case studies, real-world examples, and comprehensive analyses, we aim to equip readers with the knowledge and skills necessary to excel in the ever-evolving field of medical device regulation.

It is our hope that this book will serve as a valuable reference, aiding in the development of safe, effective, and innovative medical devices that meet today's global healthcare challenges. Whether you are a regulatory affairs veteran, a medical device developer, or an academic, the insights offered in these pages will help illuminate the path forward in the regulatory landscape.

Dr. Muralidhar Rao Akkaladevi

Dr.K.Hemamalini

12-05-2024

Medical Devices Regulatory Aspects

Dr. A. Muralidhar Rao, Professor & Principal

St.Mary's College of Pharmacy, Secunderabad

&

Dr.K.Hemamalini, Professor & Principal

Swami Vivekananda institute of Pharmaceutical Sciences, Hyderabad

Published by Notion Press

Notion Press, Inc.
800, West EI Camino Real #180,
California USA 94040

Notion Press Media Pvt Ltd,
#7, Red Cross Road,
Egmore, Chennai, Tamil Nadu 600008

Email ID: publish@notionpress.com

Phone Number: +91 44 46315631

CHAPTER ONE

INTRODUCTION TO MEDICAL DEVICES AND IN VITRO DIAGNOSTICS

1.1 Definition and Classification

1.1.1 Definition of Medical Devices and In Vitro Diagnostics (IVDs)

Medical devices and in vitro diagnostics (IVDs) are integral components of modern healthcare systems, playing pivotal roles in diagnosis, treatment, and monitoring of diseases. The definition of medical devices encompasses a broad spectrum of instruments, apparatuses, implants, reagents, software, and other related items intended for medical use. These devices are designed to exert therapeutic, diagnostic, or monitoring effects on patients, either alone or in combination with other medical products. In contrast, in vitro diagnostics (IVDs) specifically refer to medical devices utilized in the examination of specimens derived from the human body, such as blood, urine, or tissue samples, to provide diagnostic information. These diagnostic tools operate outside the body and are crucial in aiding clinical decision-making processes. IVDs encompass a wide range of products, including but not limited to, test kits, reagents, instruments, and software platforms, each serving distinct purposes in detecting, diagnosing, and monitoring various diseases and health conditions.

1.1.2 Classification of Medical Devices and IVDs

The classification of medical devices and IVDs is essential for regulatory and safety purposes, ensuring appropriate oversight and control measures are applied based on the inherent risks associated with their use. Regulatory authorities, such as the Food and Drug Administration (FDA) in the United States and the European Medicines Agency (EMA) in Europe, categorize medical devices and IVDs into different classes or categories based on their intended use, potential risks, and mode of action. In general, these classifications range from Class I, representing low-risk devices, to Class III or Class D, denoting high-risk devices requiring stringent regulatory scrutiny and evidence of safety and efficacy prior to market approval. This classification framework facilitates the establishment of regulatory pathways for pre-market approval, post-market surveillance, and quality management systems, ensuring that medical devices and IVDs meet predefined standards of safety, performance, and quality throughout their lifecycle. Additionally, classification systems often consider factors such as the duration of device contact with the body, invasiveness, mode of administration, and potential for harm in determining the appropriate regulatory pathway for market access. As medical technology continues to advance, the classification of devices and IVDs remains dynamic, evolving to address emerging technologies, novel applications, and evolving healthcare needs while maintaining the paramount importance of patient safety and public health.

1.1.2 Classification Systems

Medical devices and in vitro diagnostics (IVDs) are subject to classification systems established by regulatory authorities to ensure appropriate regulatory oversight and control based on the level of risk associated with their use. Two prominent classification systems are employed globally: the FDA Classes in the United States and the EU Classes in Europe.

FDA Classes: The U.S. Food and Drug Administration (FDA) employs a classification system consisting of three main classes: Class I, Class II, and Class III.

- **Class I:** This class includes low-risk devices that are subject to general controls, such as good manufacturing practices, labeling requirements, and adherence to performance standards. Examples of Class I devices include elastic bandages, examination gloves, and tongue depressors.
- **Class II:** Devices categorized as Class II are considered to pose moderate risks and require special controls in addition to general controls for ensuring safety and effectiveness. These may include special labeling requirements, mandatory performance standards, and post-market surveillance. Examples of Class II devices include powered wheelchairs, infusion pumps, and certain pregnancy test kits.

- **Class III:** High-risk devices fall under Class III, necessitating the highest level of regulatory control to ensure safety and efficacy. These devices often require premarket approval (PMA) or premarket notification (510(k)) before they can be marketed. Class III devices encompass implantable pacemakers, silicone gel-filled breast implants, and life-supporting or life-sustaining devices.

EU Classes: In the European Union (EU), medical devices are classified under four classes based on the level of risk and intended use, as outlined in the Medical Devices Regulation (MDR) and the In Vitro Diagnostic Medical Devices Regulation (IVDR).

- **Class I:** Devices with the lowest risk are categorized as Class I and are subject to general safety and performance requirements. Non-invasive devices, such as stethoscopes, dental floss, and walking aids, typically fall into this category.
- **Class IIa and IIb:** Class II devices are further subdivided into Class IIa and IIb based on increasing levels of risk. Class IIa devices pose moderate risks, while Class IIb devices pose higher risks and often require conformity assessment procedures involving notified bodies. Examples of Class II devices include contact lenses (IIa) and surgical lasers (IIb).
- **Class III:** High-risk devices, similar to the FDA classification, are designated as Class III in the EU. These devices require the involvement of a notified body for conformity assessment and are subject to stringent regulatory scrutiny. Class III devices include implantable defibrillators, joint replacement implants, and certain in vitro diagnostic devices.

These classification systems serve as critical frameworks for regulatory decision-making, ensuring that medical devices and IVDs are appropriately evaluated and controlled to safeguard public health and promote patient safety.

1.1.3 Differentiation Between Medical Devices and Pharmaceuticals

Medical devices and pharmaceuticals are distinct categories of healthcare products, each serving unique purposes and undergoing different regulatory pathways.

Medical Devices: Medical devices encompass a wide range of instruments, apparatuses, implants, reagents, software, and other related items intended for medical use. These products are designed to exert therapeutic, diagnostic, or monitoring effects on patients, either alone or in combination with other medical products. Medical devices operate through physical or mechanical means and are used externally or internally to diagnose, prevent, monitor, or treat diseases and health conditions. Examples of medical devices include diagnostic imaging equipment (e.g., MRI machines, X-ray machines), surgical instruments, prosthetic devices, infusion pumps, and glucose meters. The regulatory oversight of medical devices focuses on ensuring safety, performance, and quality throughout their lifecycle, encompassing pre-market approval, post-market surveillance, and quality management systems.

Pharmaceuticals: Pharmaceuticals, on the other hand, are chemical or biological substances intended for use in the diagnosis, cure, mitigation, treatment, or prevention of diseases. Unlike medical devices, pharmaceuticals exert their therapeutic effects through pharmacological mechanisms, such as biochemical interactions with biological targets in the body. Pharmaceuticals encompass a wide range of products, including small molecule drugs, biologics, vaccines, gene therapies, and cell therapies. These products may be administered orally, intravenously, topically, or via other routes of administration to achieve systemic or localized effects. Regulatory oversight of pharmaceuticals involves rigorous evaluation of safety, efficacy, and quality through preclinical studies, clinical trials, and post-market surveillance. Approval pathways for pharmaceuticals may vary depending on factors such as the therapeutic indication, the novelty of the product, and the regulatory jurisdiction.

Differentiation: The primary differentiation between medical devices and pharmaceuticals lies in their mode of action and intended use. Medical devices operate through physical or mechanical means to diagnose, treat, or monitor diseases, while pharmaceuticals exert their effects through chemical or biological mechanisms to cure, mitigate, or prevent diseases. Additionally, medical devices are often tangible, hardware-based products, whereas pharmaceuticals are chemical or biological substances typically administered as medications. Despite these differences, both medical devices and pharmaceuticals play crucial roles in modern healthcare systems, working synergistically to diagnose, treat, and manage diseases, thereby improving patient outcomes and quality of life.

1.2 Essential Principles

1.2.1 Safety and Performance Requirements

Safety and performance requirements constitute fundamental principles governing the design, development, manufacturing, and use of medical devices and in vitro diagnostics (IVDs). These principles are essential to ensure that devices meet stringent standards of safety, efficacy, and quality throughout their lifecycle, thereby safeguarding the health and well-being of patients and users.

Safety Requirements: Safety requirements encompass measures aimed at mitigating risks associated with the use of medical devices and IVDs, including potential hazards to patients, operators, and other stakeholders. These requirements necessitate the identification, assessment, and mitigation of risks throughout the device's lifecycle, from initial concept and design to manufacturing, distribution, and post-market surveillance. Manufacturers are obligated to conduct thorough risk assessments and implement appropriate risk control measures to minimize or eliminate potential hazards. Safety requirements also encompass considerations such as biocompatibility, electrical safety, mechanical safety, software safety, and usability to ensure that devices are safe for their intended use environments and populations.

Performance Requirements: Performance requirements dictate the capabilities, functionality, and effectiveness of medical devices and IVDs in achieving their intended purposes. These requirements encompass specifications related to accuracy, precision, sensitivity, specificity, reliability, and performance consistency under varying conditions. Manufacturers are tasked with demonstrating that their devices meet predetermined performance criteria through rigorous testing, validation, and verification procedures. Performance requirements also extend to factors such as device interoperability, compatibility with ancillary equipment or software, and adherence to relevant performance standards and guidelines. Additionally, performance requirements may evolve over time to reflect advancements in technology, changes in clinical practice, and emerging regulatory expectations, necessitating ongoing monitoring and reassessment by manufacturers.

Harmonization and Compliance: Harmonization of safety and performance requirements across regulatory jurisdictions is essential to facilitate global market access and ensure consistent standards of device quality and safety. Regulatory authorities collaborate with international standards organizations and industry stakeholders to develop and harmonize requirements, such as those outlined in ISO standards and regional regulatory frameworks. Manufacturers must demonstrate compliance with applicable regulations and standards by conducting comprehensive testing, documentation, and quality management practices. Non-compliance with safety and performance requirements can result in regulatory sanctions, product recalls, and reputational damage, underscoring the importance of adherence to these essential principles in the medical device and IVD industry.

In summary, safety and performance requirements are integral components of the regulatory framework governing medical devices and IVDs, emphasizing the paramount importance of patient safety, device effectiveness, and quality assurance in healthcare delivery. Compliance with these principles ensures that devices meet stringent standards of safety, efficacy, and performance, ultimately benefiting patients, healthcare providers, and society as a whole.

1.2.2 Risk Management and Risk Analysis

Risk management and risk analysis are integral components of the regulatory framework governing medical devices and in vitro diagnostics (IVDs), aimed at identifying, assessing, mitigating, and monitoring risks associated with the use of these products throughout their lifecycle.

Risk Management: Risk management entails a systematic approach to identifying, assessing, controlling, and monitoring risks associated with medical devices and IVDs to ensure their safety and effectiveness. Manufacturers are responsible for implementing risk management processes in accordance with international standards, such as ISO 14971, which provide guidelines for risk management in medical device development. The risk management process involves several key steps, including:

1. **Risk Identification:** Manufacturers identify potential hazards associated with the device's use, including biological, chemical, mechanical, and usability hazards.
2. **Risk Assessment:** The identified risks are evaluated in terms of severity, probability of occurrence, and detectability to prioritize them for further analysis and control.
3. **Risk Control:** Risk control measures are implemented to mitigate or eliminate identified risks, including design modifications, protective mechanisms, warnings, and instructions for use.

4. **Risk Evaluation:** The effectiveness of risk control measures is evaluated to ensure that residual risks are reduced to acceptable levels.
5. **Risk Monitoring:** Ongoing monitoring and assessment of risks are conducted throughout the device's lifecycle, including post-market surveillance, to identify and address emerging risks or changes in risk profiles.

Risk Analysis: Risk analysis is a critical component of the risk management process, focusing on the systematic identification and evaluation of potential hazards, their associated risks, and the effectiveness of risk control measures. Risk analysis involves several methodologies and techniques, including:

1. **Hazard Analysis:** Identification of potential hazards associated with the device's design, materials, components, and intended use.
2. **Failure Mode and Effects Analysis (FMEA):** Systematic evaluation of potential failure modes, their causes, effects on device performance, and likelihood of occurrence.
3. **Fault Tree Analysis (FTA):** Analyzing potential system failures by tracing backward from undesirable outcomes to identify contributing factors and root causes.
4. **Risk Estimation:** Quantitative or qualitative assessment of risks based on factors such as severity, probability, and detectability.
5. **Benefit-Risk Assessment:** Evaluation of the balance between the benefits and risks associated with device use to support informed decision-making by regulators, healthcare providers, and patients.

By integrating risk management and risk analysis into the product development process, manufacturers can proactively identify and address potential risks, enhance device safety and effectiveness, and demonstrate compliance with regulatory requirements. Effective risk management practices contribute to the overall quality and reliability of medical devices and IVDs, ultimately benefiting patients and healthcare providers by minimizing the potential for harm and maximizing the potential for therapeutic benefit.

1.2.3 Clinical Evaluation and Performance Studies

Clinical evaluation and performance studies are essential components of the regulatory process for medical devices and in vitro diagnostics (IVDs), aimed at assessing their safety, efficacy, and performance in real-world clinical settings.

Clinical Evaluation: Clinical evaluation involves the systematic assessment of clinical data and scientific evidence to demonstrate the safety, performance, and clinical benefits of a medical device or IVD throughout its lifecycle. This process is essential for obtaining regulatory approval or clearance and for ensuring ongoing compliance with regulatory requirements. Key aspects of clinical evaluation include:

1. **Literature Review:** Gathering and analyzing existing scientific literature, clinical studies, and post-market surveillance data relevant to the device, its intended use, and similar products.
2. **Clinical Data Collection:** Collecting clinical data from various sources, including clinical investigations, post-market surveillance, registries, and published literature, to support the device's safety and effectiveness.
3. **Data Analysis:** Analyzing and synthesizing clinical data to evaluate the device's performance, safety profile, clinical outcomes, and potential risks.
4. **Clinical Evidence Generation:** Generating new clinical data through clinical investigations or studies, if necessary, to address gaps in the existing evidence base or to confirm the device's safety and efficacy.
5. **Risk-Benefit Assessment:** Assessing the balance between the device's clinical benefits and potential risks to determine its overall risk-benefit profile and suitability for clinical use.

Clinical evaluation is an iterative process that continues throughout the device's lifecycle, incorporating new data, insights, and regulatory requirements to ensure ongoing assurance of device safety and effectiveness.

Performance Studies: Performance studies are specific clinical studies or evaluations conducted to assess the device's performance characteristics, technical specifications, and functional capabilities under real-world conditions. These studies are designed to demonstrate the device's ability to achieve its intended purpose and to meet predefined performance criteria. Key elements of performance studies include:

1. **Study Design:** Developing study protocols and methodologies tailored to assess the device's performance parameters, such as accuracy, precision,

sensitivity, specificity, and reliability.

2. **Participant Selection:** Recruiting appropriate study participants representing the target population or patient group for whom the device is intended.
3. **Data Collection:** Collecting relevant data and measurements to evaluate the device's performance outcomes, including comparative assessments against standard-of-care methods or predicate devices.
4. **Data Analysis:** Analyzing study data to assess the device's performance characteristics, identify any limitations or areas for improvement, and validate its technical specifications.
5. **Regulatory Compliance:** Ensuring that performance studies comply with applicable regulatory requirements, standards, and guidelines, including ethical considerations, data integrity, and patient safety.

Performance studies provide critical evidence of the device's technical capabilities and functional performance under real-world conditions, complementing the clinical evaluation process and supporting regulatory submissions and market approvals.

Overall, clinical evaluation and performance studies are essential components of the evidence-based regulatory pathway for medical devices and IVDs, enabling manufacturers to demonstrate the safety, efficacy, and performance of their products and to facilitate their introduction into clinical practice for the benefit of patients and healthcare providers.

1.2.4 Quality Management Systems (QMS)

Quality Management Systems (QMS) are integral to the design, manufacturing, and distribution processes of medical devices and in vitro diagnostics (IVDs), ensuring that products consistently meet regulatory requirements and fulfill user expectations for safety, efficacy, and performance.

Purpose of QMS: The primary purpose of a QMS is to establish a systematic framework for managing quality throughout the entire lifecycle of a medical device or IVD, from initial concept and design to post-market surveillance and product discontinuation. QMS aims to:

1. **Ensure Compliance:** Ensure compliance with regulatory requirements, standards, and guidelines established by regulatory authorities, such as the FDA, EMA, and ISO.

2. **Enhance Product Quality:** Foster a culture of quality and continuous improvement to enhance product quality, reliability, and performance.
3. **Mitigate Risks:** Identify, assess, and mitigate risks associated with the design, manufacturing, and use of medical devices and IVDs to ensure patient safety and product effectiveness.
4. **Facilitate Traceability:** Establish mechanisms for traceability and documentation of product development, manufacturing processes, component suppliers, and distribution channels to enable accountability and transparency.
5. **Support Decision-Making:** Provide data-driven insights and metrics to support informed decision-making by management, regulatory authorities, and other stakeholders.
6. **Promote Customer Satisfaction:** Meet or exceed customer expectations for product quality, performance, and reliability to enhance customer satisfaction and loyalty.

Components of QMS: A robust QMS typically comprises several interrelated components designed to address key aspects of quality management throughout the product lifecycle. These components may include:

1. **Quality Policy and Objectives:** Clearly defined quality policy and objectives established by senior management to communicate the organization's commitment to quality and continuous improvement.
2. **Quality Planning:** Development of quality plans, procedures, and processes to ensure that quality objectives are achieved and maintained.
3. **Document Control:** Implementation of document control procedures to manage the creation, approval, distribution, and revision of documents related to product design, manufacturing, and quality assurance.
4. **Risk Management:** Integration of risk management processes, such as hazard analysis and risk assessment, into product development and lifecycle management activities to mitigate potential risks to patient safety and product quality.
5. **Design Control:** Implementation of design control processes to manage the design and development of medical devices and IVDs, ensuring that they meet specified requirements and regulatory standards.
6. **Supplier Management:** Establishment of supplier evaluation, qualification, and oversight processes to ensure the quality and

reliability of components, materials, and services sourced from external suppliers.

7. **Production and Process Control:** Implementation of production and process control procedures to ensure consistency, reproducibility, and reliability in manufacturing operations, including equipment calibration, process validation, and product inspection.
8. **Corrective and Preventive Action (CAPA):** Implementation of CAPA procedures to systematically investigate, address, and prevent non-conformities, deviations, and quality issues identified during product development, manufacturing, or post-market surveillance.
9. **Change Management:** Establishment of change management processes to control and document changes to product designs, manufacturing processes, or quality management procedures to ensure regulatory compliance and product integrity.
10. **Training and Competence:** Provision of training programs and competency assessments for personnel involved in product design, manufacturing, quality assurance, and regulatory compliance to ensure adequate skills and knowledge.
11. **Audits and Inspections:** Conducting internal audits and inspections, as well as participating in external audits by regulatory authorities or certification bodies, to assess compliance with regulatory requirements and QMS effectiveness.

Benefits of QMS: Implementing a QMS offers several benefits to organizations involved in the development, manufacturing, and distribution of medical devices and IVDs, including:

1. **Enhanced Product Quality:** Improving product quality, reliability, and performance through systematic quality management practices.
2. **Compliance Assurance:** Ensuring compliance with regulatory requirements, standards, and guidelines to minimize regulatory risks and facilitate market approvals.
3. **Risk Mitigation:** Identifying, assessing, and mitigating risks associated with product development, manufacturing, and use to enhance patient safety and product effectiveness.
4. **Operational Efficiency:** Streamlining processes, reducing waste, and optimizing resource utilization to improve operational efficiency and productivity.

5. **Customer Satisfaction:** Meeting or exceeding customer expectations for product quality, performance, and reliability to enhance customer satisfaction and loyalty.
6. **Continuous Improvement:** Fostering a culture of continuous improvement and innovation to drive organizational growth and competitiveness in the marketplace.

In summary, Quality Management Systems (QMS) play a crucial role in ensuring the safety, efficacy, and reliability of medical devices and in vitro diagnostics (IVDs) throughout their lifecycle. By implementing a robust QMS, organizations can achieve compliance with regulatory requirements, enhance product quality, mitigate risks, improve operational efficiency, and ultimately deliver value to patients, healthcare providers, and other stakeholders.

1.3 Product Lifecycle

1.3.1 Development and Design Controls

Development and design controls are critical components of the product lifecycle for medical devices and in vitro diagnostics (IVDs), ensuring that products are designed, developed, and manufactured in accordance with regulatory requirements and quality standards to meet user needs and ensure safety and efficacy.

Development Process: The development process encompasses the activities involved in transforming conceptual ideas into tangible medical devices or IVDs. Key stages of the development process include:

1. **Conceptualization:** Generating ideas and concepts for new products or improvements to existing ones based on market needs, user feedback, technological advancements, and regulatory requirements.
2. **Feasibility Assessment:** Evaluating the technical feasibility, market potential, regulatory requirements, and resource requirements for potential product concepts to determine their viability.
3. **Requirements Definition:** Defining user needs, product specifications, design inputs, and performance criteria based on input from stakeholders, including healthcare professionals, patients, regulatory authorities, and marketing teams.
4. **Design and Development:** Iteratively designing and developing prototypes or product iterations based on defined requirements, incorporating feedback from design reviews, usability studies, and risk

assessments.

5. **Verification and Validation:** Conducting verification and validation activities to ensure that the product meets specified requirements and performs as intended under simulated or real-world conditions.
6. **Regulatory Compliance:** Ensuring compliance with applicable regulatory requirements, standards, and guidelines throughout the development process, including design controls, risk management, and documentation requirements.

Design Controls: Design controls are a set of systematic procedures and processes implemented throughout the product development process to ensure that devices are designed and developed in accordance with predefined requirements and specifications. Key elements of design controls include:

1. **Design and Development Planning:** Developing a comprehensive plan outlining the design and development activities, milestones, responsibilities, and resources required to bring the product to market.
2. **Design Input:** Defining the inputs, requirements, and specifications for the product based on user needs, intended use, regulatory requirements, and risk management considerations.
3. **Design Output:** Documenting the results of the design and development process, including design drawings, specifications, prototypes, and other technical documentation.
4. **Design Review:** Conducting formal design reviews at key stages of the development process to evaluate progress, identify issues, and ensure compliance with design inputs and regulatory requirements.
5. **Design Verification:** Performing verification activities to demonstrate that the product meets specified design requirements and performs as intended under controlled conditions.
6. **Design Validation:** Conducting validation activities to demonstrate that the product meets user needs and intended use requirements under simulated or real-world conditions.
7. **Design Transfer:** Transferring the design to manufacturing and ensuring that all design outputs, specifications, and documentation are accurately communicated to manufacturing personnel.
8. **Design Changes:** Implementing procedures for managing changes to the product design, including documentation, review, approval, and

verification of design changes to maintain product integrity and regulatory compliance.

By implementing robust development and design controls, manufacturers can ensure that medical devices and IVDs are designed, developed, and manufactured in a systematic and controlled manner, resulting in products that meet user needs, regulatory requirements, and quality standards. This approach helps to minimize risks, ensure product safety and efficacy, and facilitate regulatory approvals and market access throughout the product lifecycle.

1.3.2 Preclinical Testing and Verification

Preclinical testing and verification are crucial stages in the development lifecycle of medical devices and in vitro diagnostics (IVDs), aimed at assessing the safety, performance, and efficacy of products prior to clinical trials and regulatory submissions.

Preclinical Testing: Preclinical testing involves the evaluation of medical devices and IVDs in laboratory settings and preclinical animal models to assess their safety profile, biocompatibility, and initial performance characteristics. Key aspects of preclinical testing include:

1. **Biocompatibility Testing:** Assessing the compatibility of the device materials with biological systems to ensure that they do not cause adverse reactions or toxicity when in contact with the body.
2. **Mechanical Testing:** Evaluating the mechanical properties of the device, such as strength, durability, and wear resistance, to ensure its reliability and performance under simulated physiological conditions.
3. **Functional Testing:** Testing the device's functionality, including its ability to perform intended tasks, deliver therapeutic effects, or produce accurate diagnostic results.
4. **Performance Testing:** Assessing the device's performance characteristics, such as accuracy, precision, sensitivity, specificity, and reproducibility, to ensure its reliability and effectiveness in clinical use.
5. **Safety Testing:** Conducting safety assessments to identify potential risks associated with device use, including electrical safety, thermal safety, and other potential hazards.
6. **Validation Testing:** Validating the performance of the device against established standards, guidelines, or predicate devices to demonstrate its suitability for intended use.

Verification: Verification involves the confirmation that the design outputs of the device meet the specified design inputs and requirements. It ensures that the device has been designed and developed correctly according to predetermined criteria. Key aspects of verification include:

1. **Design Verification Testing:** Conducting testing and analysis to demonstrate that the device meets the specified design requirements, including functional specifications, performance criteria, and regulatory standards.
2. **Prototyping and Testing:** Building prototypes or representative models of the device and subjecting them to rigorous testing to verify their functionality, reliability, and performance under simulated or real-world conditions.
3. **Software Verification:** Verifying the functionality, accuracy, and reliability of any software components or algorithms embedded within the device, including verification of inputs, outputs, and software validation protocols.
4. **Risk Mitigation:** Identifying and addressing any design deficiencies, discrepancies, or non-conformities through iterative design modifications, corrective actions, or risk mitigation measures.
5. **Documentation and Traceability:** Documenting the results of verification activities, including test protocols, test reports, and verification records, to demonstrate compliance with regulatory requirements and facilitate traceability throughout the product lifecycle.

By conducting thorough preclinical testing and verification, manufacturers can identify and address potential design flaws, performance issues, and safety concerns early in the development process, minimizing risks and optimizing the likelihood of successful clinical trials and regulatory approvals. These activities also help to ensure that medical devices and IVDs arc safe, effective, and reliable when used in clinical settings, ultimately benefiting patients and healthcare providers.

1.3.3 Clinical Trials and Regulatory Approval

Clinical trials and regulatory approval are integral components of the product lifecycle for medical devices and in vitro diagnostics (IVDs), essential for demonstrating safety, efficacy, and performance before market entry.

Clinical Trials:

Clinical trials are systematic investigations conducted to evaluate the safety and effectiveness of medical devices or IVDs in human subjects. Key elements of clinical trials include:

1. **Study Design:** Designing protocols outlining study objectives, inclusion/exclusion criteria, endpoints, treatment arms, and statistical analyses.
2. **Participant Recruitment:** Recruiting eligible participants who meet specific criteria and obtaining informed consent prior to enrollment.
3. **Data Collection:** Collecting clinical data, including patient demographics, medical history, treatment outcomes, and adverse events, according to the trial protocol.
4. **Data Analysis:** Analyzing trial data to assess safety, efficacy, and statistical significance of outcomes.
5. **Adverse Event Reporting:** Reporting and documenting adverse events and device malfunctions occurring during the trial in compliance with regulatory requirements.
6. **Ethical Considerations:** Obtaining approval from Institutional Review Boards (IRBs) or Ethics Committees to ensure participant safety and ethical conduct of the trial.

Regulatory Approval:

Regulatory approval involves obtaining authorization from regulatory agencies such as the FDA in the US or the EMA in Europe to market and distribute medical devices or IVDs. Key aspects of regulatory approval include:

1. **Regulatory Submission:** Compiling comprehensive data on device safety, efficacy, and performance to submit regulatory applications such as Premarket Notifications (510(k)), Premarket Approvals (PMA), or CE Marking applications in Europe.
2. **Review Process:** Regulatory agencies review submitted data, clinical trial results, and supporting documentation to evaluate compliance with regulatory standards and guidelines.
3. **Decision-Making:** Based on the review, regulatory authorities decide whether to approve, clear, or request additional information regarding the device.
4. **Post-Market Surveillance:** Manufacturers conduct post-market surveillance activities to monitor device performance, collect adverse

event reports, and ensure ongoing compliance with regulatory requirements.

5. **Labeling and Marketing:** Upon approval, manufacturers develop labeling and promotional materials compliant with regulatory requirements for accurate communication of device indications, contraindications, and risks.

Clinical trials and regulatory approval are critical stages in ensuring that medical devices and IVDs meet safety and efficacy standards before being introduced to the market. These processes require adherence to rigorous scientific and regulatory standards to protect patient safety and promote public health.

1.3.4 Manufacturing and Post-Market Surveillance

Manufacturing and post-market surveillance are essential phases in the product lifecycle of medical devices and in vitro diagnostics (IVDs), ensuring ongoing quality, safety, and performance after regulatory approval and commercialization.

Manufacturing:

Manufacturing involves the production of medical devices and IVDs in accordance with established quality standards and regulatory requirements. Key aspects of manufacturing include:

1. **Quality Management Systems (QMS):** Implementing QMS processes to ensure that manufacturing operations adhere to regulatory requirements, standards, and specifications.
2. **Production Processes:** Operating manufacturing facilities and equipment to produce devices consistently and reliably, following validated processes and procedures.
3. **Component Sourcing:** Sourcing raw materials, components, and sub-assemblies from approved suppliers and maintaining supply chain integrity and traceability.
4. **Quality Control:** Conducting inspections, testing, and validation activities to verify the quality, performance, and compliance of manufactured devices with established specifications.
5. **Good Manufacturing Practices (GMP):** Adhering to GMP guidelines to ensure the cleanliness, sterility, and overall quality of manufacturing facilities and processes.

6. **Process Validation:** Validating manufacturing processes to ensure that they consistently produce devices that meet predetermined specifications and regulatory requirements.
7. **Documentation and Record-Keeping:** Maintaining comprehensive documentation and records of manufacturing activities, including batch records, device history records, and quality control reports.

Post-Market Surveillance:

Post-market surveillance involves monitoring the safety, performance, and effectiveness of medical devices and IVDs after they have been commercialized and introduced into clinical practice. Key elements of post-market surveillance include:

1. **Adverse Event Reporting:** Collecting, documenting, and investigating adverse events, device malfunctions, and other safety-related issues reported by healthcare providers, patients, or other stakeholders.
2. **Complaint Handling:** Managing and addressing complaints received from users regarding device performance, usability, or safety concerns, and implementing corrective and preventive actions as necessary.
3. **Field Safety Corrective Actions (FSCA):** Implementing FSCA procedures to address safety issues or defects identified in marketed devices, including recalls, field corrections, and product notifications.
4. **Periodic Safety Updates:** Compiling and submitting periodic safety update reports to regulatory authorities, summarizing post-market surveillance data and device performance trends.
5. **Trend Analysis:** Analyzing post-market surveillance data to identify patterns, trends, or signals of potential safety or performance issues and taking appropriate corrective actions.
6. **Registry Studies:** Conducting registry studies or post-market clinical studies to monitor long-term device performance, patient outcomes, and real-world utilization.
7. **Labeling Updates:** Updating device labeling, instructions for use, and promotional materials as necessary to communicate new safety information, warnings, or precautions to users.

Manufacturing and post-market surveillance are critical phases in ensuring the ongoing quality, safety, and effectiveness of medical devices and IVDs throughout their lifecycle. By maintaining robust manufacturing processes and implementing effective post-market surveillance programs, manufacturers can identify and address safety concerns, optimize device performance, and maintain compliance with regulatory requirements to safeguard patient health and public safety.

1.4 Regulatory Landscape

1.4.1 FDA Regulations in the United States

The Food and Drug Administration (FDA) in the United States plays a pivotal role in regulating medical devices and in vitro diagnostics (IVDs), ensuring their safety, effectiveness, and quality. FDA regulations establish rigorous standards and requirements for product development, manufacturing, marketing, and post-market surveillance to protect public health and promote innovation in the healthcare industry.

Classification System: The FDA classifies medical devices into three main classes based on the level of risk they pose to patients and users:

1. **Class I:** Low-risk devices that are subject to general controls, such as labeling requirements, registration, and good manufacturing practices (GMP), but do not require premarket approval or clearance.
2. **Class II:** Moderate-risk devices that are subject to special controls, such as performance standards, post-market surveillance, and premarket notification (510(k)) or premarket approval (PMA) requirements to demonstrate safety and effectiveness.
3. **Class III:** High-risk devices that are subject to premarket approval (PMA) requirements, involving comprehensive scientific evidence of safety and effectiveness, as well as stringent post-market surveillance and quality assurance measures.

Premarket Pathways: The FDA offers several pathways for premarket review and approval of medical devices and IVDs:

1. **510(k) Premarket Notification:** Submission of a 510(k) notification to demonstrate that the device is substantially equivalent to a legally marketed predicate device and does not raise new questions of safety or effectiveness.
2. **Premarket Approval (PMA):** Submission of a PMA application containing comprehensive scientific evidence, including clinical data, to demonstrate the safety and effectiveness of high-risk Class III devices.

3. **De Novo Classification:** Submission of a de novo request for novel devices that do not have a predicate device, requiring the FDA to establish a new risk-based classification and regulatory requirements.

Quality System Regulation (QSR): The FDA's Quality System Regulation (QSR), outlined in 21 CFR Part 820, establishes comprehensive requirements for manufacturers to implement quality management systems (QMS) and ensure the quality, safety, and effectiveness of medical devices throughout their lifecycle. Key elements of the QSR include:

1. **Design Controls:** Implementation of design and development controls to ensure that devices are designed, developed, and manufactured in accordance with predefined specifications and requirements.
2. **Device Labeling:** Compliance with labeling requirements to provide accurate and clear information to users regarding device indications, contraindications, warnings, and instructions for use.
3. **Good Manufacturing Practices (GMP):** Adherence to GMP guidelines to ensure the cleanliness, sterility, and overall quality of manufacturing facilities, processes, and equipment.
4. **Complaint Handling:** Establishment of procedures for handling and investigating complaints received from users regarding device performance, safety, or quality issues.
5. **Adverse Event Reporting:** Reporting and documenting adverse events, device malfunctions, and other safety-related incidents in compliance with regulatory reporting requirements.

Post-Market Surveillance: The FDA requires manufacturers to conduct post-market surveillance activities to monitor device performance, collect adverse event reports, and address safety concerns after commercialization. Manufacturers are also required to submit periodic reports, including Annual Reports, Post-Approval Studies, and Postmarket Surveillance Plans, to provide updates on device safety and effectiveness.

In summary, FDA regulations in the United States establish stringent standards and requirements for the development, manufacturing, marketing, and post-market surveillance of medical devices and IVDs, aiming to ensure their safety, effectiveness, and quality throughout their lifecycle. Compliance with FDA regulations is essential for manufacturers to obtain market approval, maintain regulatory compliance, and safeguard public health.

1.4.1.1 510(k) Premarket Notification

The 510(k) premarket notification process is a regulatory pathway overseen by the Food and Drug Administration (FDA) in the United States for certain medical devices. Key aspects of the 510(k) process include:

1. **Demonstration of Substantial Equivalence:** Manufacturers submit a 510(k) notification to demonstrate that their device is substantially equivalent to a legally marketed predicate device in terms of intended use, technological characteristics, and performance.
2. **Predicate Device Selection:** Manufacturers select a predicate device that is already cleared or approved by the FDA and share similarities with their own device to establish substantial equivalence.
3. **Comparison with Predicate:** Manufacturers provide detailed comparisons between their device and the predicate device, highlighting similarities and differences in design, materials, indications, and performance characteristics.
4. **Risk Assessment:** Manufacturers conduct a risk assessment to identify and evaluate potential risks associated with the device and demonstrate that any differences between their device and the predicate do not raise new questions of safety or effectiveness.
5. **Regulatory Review:** The FDA reviews the 510(k) submission to determine whether the device is substantially equivalent to the predicate device and whether it meets applicable regulatory requirements and standards.
6. **Decision-Making:** Based on the review, the FDA issues a clearance letter if the device is found to be substantially equivalent and meets regulatory requirements, allowing the device to be marketed and sold in the United States.

1.4.1.2 Premarket Approval (PMA)

Premarket Approval (PMA) is a regulatory pathway overseen by the Food and Drug Administration (FDA) in the United States for high-risk medical devices. Key aspects of the PMA process include:

1. **Comprehensive Review:** Manufacturers submit a PMA application containing comprehensive scientific evidence, including preclinical and clinical data, to demonstrate the safety and effectiveness of the device.

2. **Clinical Trials:** Manufacturers conduct clinical trials to generate clinical data supporting the safety and effectiveness of the device in intended patient populations, with appropriate endpoints and statistical analyses.
3. **Risk Assessment:** Manufacturers conduct a thorough risk assessment to identify and mitigate potential risks associated with the device's use, including biological, chemical, mechanical, and usability hazards.
4. **Regulatory Review:** The FDA reviews the PMA application and supporting data to assess the device's safety, efficacy, and performance, as well as compliance with regulatory requirements and standards.
5. **Panel Review:** Some PMA applications may undergo review by an FDA advisory panel composed of experts in relevant fields to provide independent evaluation and recommendations to the FDA.
6. **Decision-Making:** Based on the review, the FDA makes a decision regarding the approval of the PMA application, either granting approval if the device meets regulatory requirements or issuing a request for additional information or clarification.

1.4.2 European Union (EU) Regulations

1.4.2.1 Medical Device Regulation (MDR)

The Medical Device Regulation (MDR) is a regulatory framework established by the European Union (EU) for medical devices, aiming to enhance safety and effectiveness while promoting innovation and market access. Key aspects of the MDR include:

1. **Scope:** The MDR applies to a wide range of medical devices, including active implantable devices, medical software, and accessories, and introduces new classification rules based on risk.
2. **Conformity Assessment:** Manufacturers must undergo a conformity assessment process, involving conformity assessment procedures, notified bodies, and technical documentation, to demonstrate compliance with regulatory requirements.
3. **Clinical Evaluation:** Manufacturers are required to conduct clinical evaluations to assess the safety and performance of their devices, with a focus on clinical evidence, equivalence, and post-market surveillance.
4. **Unique Device Identification (UDI):** The MDR mandates the use of a Unique Device Identification (UDI) system to enhance traceability and identification of medical devices throughout their lifecycle.

5. **Post-Market Surveillance:** Manufacturers must establish post-market surveillance systems to monitor device performance, collect adverse event reports, and implement corrective and preventive actions to address safety concerns.

1.4.2.2 In Vitro Diagnostic Regulation (IVDR)

The In Vitro Diagnostic Regulation (IVDR) is a regulatory framework established by the European Union (EU) for in vitro diagnostic devices, aiming to ensure their safety, reliability, and performance. Key aspects of the IVDR include:

1. **Scope:** The IVDR applies to in vitro diagnostic devices intended for clinical use, including reagents, instruments, software, and accessories, and introduces new risk-based classification rules.
2. **Conformity Assessment:** Manufacturers must undergo a conformity assessment process, involving notified bodies and technical documentation, to demonstrate compliance with regulatory requirements.
3. **Performance Evaluation:** Manufacturers are required to perform performance evaluations to demonstrate the analytical and clinical performance of their in vitro diagnostic devices, with a focus on clinical validity and utility.
4. **Quality Management Systems:** The IVDR mandates the implementation of quality management systems (QMS) to ensure the quality, safety, and reliability of in vitro diagnostic devices throughout their lifecycle.
5. **Unique Device Identification (UDI):** Similar to the MDR, the IVDR requires the use of a Unique Device Identification (UDI) system for in vitro diagnostic devices to enhance traceability and identification.

1.4.3 International Standards and Harmonization

International standards and harmonization efforts play a crucial role in aligning regulatory requirements, facilitating market access, and promoting global harmonization of medical device regulations. Key aspects of international standards and harmonization include:

1. **ISO Standards:** The International Organization for Standardization (ISO) develops and publishes international standards for medical devices, including standards for quality management systems (e.g., ISO

13485) and risk management (e.g., ISO 14971).

2. **Harmonization Initiatives:** Regulatory authorities participate in harmonization initiatives, such as the International Medical Device Regulators Forum (IMDRF), to harmonize regulatory requirements, promote convergence, and facilitate mutual recognition of regulatory decisions.
3. **Mutual Recognition Agreements (MRAs):** Some countries or regions establish mutual recognition agreements (MRAs) to facilitate the acceptance of regulatory approvals, certifications, and conformity assessment results from other jurisdictions, reducing duplication of efforts and streamlining market access.
4. **Collaborative Partnerships:** Regulatory authorities collaborate with industry stakeholders, professional organizations, and other regulatory agencies to exchange information, share best practices, and address emerging challenges in medical device regulation.

International standards and harmonization initiatives contribute to the development of consistent, transparent, and science-based regulatory frameworks, promoting innovation, patient safety, and public health on a global scale.

1.5 Importance of Understanding Medical Device Regulation

Medical device regulation plays a crucial role in safeguarding patient safety, promoting public health, and ensuring the quality and effectiveness of medical devices and in vitro diagnostics (IVDs). Understanding medical device regulation is essential for various stakeholders, including manufacturers, healthcare professionals, regulatory authorities, and patients.

1.5.1 Patient Safety and Public Health

The foremost importance of understanding medical device regulation lies in its direct impact on patient safety and public health. Regulatory frameworks establish standards and requirements to ensure that medical devices and IVDs are safe, effective, and reliable when used in clinical practice. Key aspects include:

1. **Risk Mitigation:** Regulations mandate manufacturers to conduct risk assessments and implement measures to mitigate potential risks associated with device use, including biological, chemical, mechanical, and usability hazards. By addressing these risks, regulatory frameworks

aim to minimize adverse events and protect patient safety.

2. **Quality Assurance:** Medical device regulations establish quality management systems (QMS) and manufacturing standards to ensure that devices are produced consistently and meet predefined specifications and performance criteria. Quality assurance measures promote the reliability and effectiveness of medical devices, reducing the likelihood of device failures and patient harm.
3. **Clinical Evidence:** Regulatory approval processes, such as premarket review and post-market surveillance, require manufacturers to provide comprehensive clinical data demonstrating the safety and effectiveness of their devices. By evaluating clinical evidence, regulatory authorities assess the benefits and risks of medical devices, guiding healthcare providers and patients in making informed treatment decisions.
4. **Post-Market Surveillance:** Regulatory frameworks mandate post-market surveillance activities to monitor device performance, collect adverse event reports, and address safety concerns after market commercialization. By identifying and addressing emerging safety issues, post-market surveillance enhances the ongoing safety and effectiveness of medical devices, contributing to public health protection.
5. **Public Trust:** Compliance with medical device regulations instills public trust and confidence in the healthcare system by demonstrating a commitment to patient safety and quality. Patients and healthcare providers rely on regulatory oversight to ensure that medical devices meet rigorous standards and undergo thorough evaluation before entering the market.

In summary, understanding medical device regulation is essential for upholding patient safety, promoting public health, and maintaining confidence in the healthcare system. By adhering to regulatory requirements, stakeholders contribute to the development, manufacturing, and utilization of safe, effective, and reliable medical devices and IVDs, ultimately benefiting patients and society as a whole.

1.5.2 Market Access and Commercialization

Understanding medical device regulation is paramount for ensuring market access and successful commercialization of medical devices and in vitro diagnostics (IVDs). Regulatory compliance is essential for manufacturers seeking to introduce their products into the global market.

Key aspects of market access and commercialization include:

1. **Regulatory Approval:** Compliance with regulatory requirements is necessary to obtain market approval or clearance from regulatory authorities such as the Food and Drug Administration (FDA) in the United States or the European Medicines Agency (EMA) in Europe. Understanding the regulatory pathways, submission requirements, and review processes is crucial for manufacturers to navigate the approval process efficiently.
2. **Premarket Submissions:** Manufacturers must prepare and submit comprehensive premarket submissions, such as premarket notifications (510(k)), premarket approvals (PMA), or CE marking applications, containing detailed information on device safety, efficacy, performance, and manufacturing processes. Understanding the specific requirements for each type of submission is essential for successful regulatory approval.
3. **Conformity Assessment:** Compliance with conformity assessment procedures, including testing, certification, and quality management system (QMS) audits, is necessary to demonstrate that medical devices meet applicable regulatory standards and requirements. Understanding the conformity assessment process helps manufacturers ensure that their devices adhere to regulatory expectations.
4. **Labeling and Packaging:** Regulatory agencies impose labeling and packaging requirements to provide users with accurate and comprehensive information about medical devices, including indications for use, contraindications, warnings, and instructions for use. Understanding labeling and packaging regulations is essential for manufacturers to develop compliant labeling materials that facilitate safe and effective device use.
5. **Post-Market Obligations:** Manufacturers have post-market obligations, including post-market surveillance, adverse event reporting, and quality system maintenance, to ensure ongoing compliance with regulatory requirements after commercialization. Understanding post-market obligations helps manufacturers establish robust post-market surveillance systems and implement appropriate corrective and preventive actions to address safety concerns.
6. **Global Harmonization:** Harmonization of regulatory requirements and standards facilitates market access by streamlining regulatory processes

and reducing duplication of efforts for manufacturers seeking to enter multiple markets. Understanding international standards and harmonization initiatives enables manufacturers to develop strategies for global market entry and expansion.

In summary, understanding medical device regulation is essential for achieving market access and successful commercialization of medical devices and IVDs. By ensuring regulatory compliance, manufacturers can navigate the complex regulatory landscape, obtain market approvals efficiently, and bring safe and effective products to market, ultimately benefiting patients, healthcare providers, and society as a whole.

1.5.3 Innovation and Product Development

Understanding medical device regulation is crucial for fostering innovation and facilitating product development in the healthcare industry. Regulatory frameworks provide guidance and requirements for manufacturers to ensure that innovative medical devices and in vitro diagnostics (IVDs) meet safety, efficacy, and quality standards. Key aspects of innovation and product development include:

1. **Regulatory Compliance:** Regulatory requirements influence the design, development, and commercialization of medical devices, shaping the innovation process to prioritize patient safety and public health. Manufacturers must understand regulatory expectations to incorporate compliance considerations into their product development strategies.
2. **Design Controls:** Regulatory frameworks mandate the implementation of design controls to ensure that medical devices are designed, developed, and manufactured in accordance with predefined specifications and requirements. Design controls help manufacturers systematically manage risks, address user needs, and ensure device performance throughout the product lifecycle.
3. **Clinical Evidence:** Regulatory approval processes require manufacturers to provide comprehensive clinical data demonstrating the safety and effectiveness of their devices. Conducting clinical studies and generating robust clinical evidence are essential components of the product development process, guiding regulatory submissions and informing healthcare decision-making.
4. **Quality Management Systems (QMS):** Regulatory compliance necessitates the implementation of quality management systems (QMS)

to ensure the quality, safety, and reliability of medical devices. QMS principles, such as risk management, design controls, and post-market surveillance, support innovation by providing a framework for systematic product development and continuous improvement.

5. **Emerging Technologies:** Regulatory frameworks adapt to accommodate advancements in technology, including digital health, artificial intelligence, and personalized medicine. Manufacturers developing innovative technologies must navigate evolving regulatory landscapes and collaborate with regulatory authorities to address novel regulatory challenges and opportunities.
6. **Global Market Access:** Understanding international regulations and harmonization initiatives is essential for manufacturers seeking to enter global markets and expand their product portfolios. Harmonized standards and mutual recognition agreements facilitate market access by reducing regulatory barriers and promoting consistency in regulatory requirements across jurisdictions.

In summary, understanding medical device regulation is integral to fostering innovation and driving product development in the healthcare industry. Regulatory compliance provides a framework for manufacturers to develop safe, effective, and high-quality medical devices and IVDs, ultimately advancing patient care and improving public health outcomes.

1.5.4 Legal and Ethical Considerations

Understanding medical device regulation encompasses legal and ethical considerations that are essential for ensuring compliance, protecting patient rights, and upholding ethical principles in healthcare. Key aspects of legal and ethical considerations include:

1. **Patient Rights:** Regulatory frameworks prioritize patient safety and rights, requiring manufacturers to design and develop medical devices that meet safety, efficacy, and quality standards. Upholding patient rights, including the right to safety, privacy, and informed consent, is paramount throughout the product lifecycle.
2. **Informed Consent:** Ethical considerations mandate obtaining informed consent from patients participating in clinical trials or receiving medical treatments involving devices. Informed consent involves providing patients with clear and comprehensive information about the risks, benefits, and alternatives to treatment, empowering them to make

autonomous decisions regarding their healthcare.

3. **Data Privacy and Security:** Regulatory compliance entails protecting patient data privacy and security in accordance with applicable laws and regulations, such as the Health Insurance Portability and Accountability Act (HIPAA) in the United States or the General Data Protection Regulation (GDPR) in the European Union. Safeguarding patient information from unauthorized access, disclosure, or misuse is essential for maintaining trust and confidence in healthcare.
4. **Product Liability:** Legal considerations include product liability laws governing manufacturers‘ responsibility for injuries or damages caused by defective medical devices. Manufacturers must ensure that their devices are safe, reliable, and free from defects, and they may be held liable for damages resulting from design flaws, manufacturing defects, or inadequate warnings or instructions.
5. **Regulatory Compliance:** Compliance with medical device regulations is a legal requirement for manufacturers seeking to market and distribute their products. Non-compliance can result in regulatory sanctions, fines, or legal consequences, jeopardizing market access and reputational integrity.
6. **Ethical Marketing Practices:** Ethical considerations extend to marketing and promotional activities, requiring manufacturers to provide accurate and truthful information about their products and refrain from misleading or deceptive practices. Ethical marketing ensures that healthcare providers and patients receive transparent and reliable information to make informed decisions about device utilization.

In summary, understanding medical device regulation involves navigating legal and ethical considerations to ensure compliance, protect patient rights, and uphold ethical standards in healthcare. By adhering to legal requirements and ethical principles, manufacturers contribute to patient safety, public trust, and the integrity of the healthcare system.

1.6 Future Trends and Emerging Technologies

As the healthcare landscape continues to evolve, several trends and emerging technologies are poised to transform the medical device and in vitro diagnostics (IVD) industry. These advancements hold the potential to enhance patient care, improve clinical outcomes, and revolutionize healthcare delivery. Key areas of focus include the impact of artificial intelligence and machine learning, advances in remote monitoring and telemedicine, and regulatory challenges associated with personalized medicine and digital health.

1.6.1 Impact of Artificial Intelligence and Machine Learning

Artificial intelligence (AI) and machine learning (ML) have emerged as powerful tools in medical device development, diagnosis, and treatment planning. These technologies enable the analysis of large datasets, identification of patterns and trends, and generation of actionable insights to support clinical decision-making. AI-driven medical devices and algorithms have the potential to improve diagnostic accuracy, personalize treatment approaches, and streamline healthcare delivery processes. However, integrating AI and ML into medical devices raises unique regulatory challenges related to data privacy, algorithm transparency, and clinical validation, necessitating collaboration between regulatory authorities, industry stakeholders, and healthcare professionals to establish robust regulatory frameworks and standards.

1.6.2 Advances in Remote Monitoring and Telemedicine

The adoption of remote monitoring and telemedicine technologies has accelerated in response to the COVID-19 pandemic and the growing demand for virtual healthcare solutions. Remote monitoring devices, wearable sensors, and telehealth platforms enable real-time monitoring of patient health metrics, remote consultations, and virtual care delivery, facilitating access to healthcare services and improving patient engagement and adherence. However, regulatory challenges, such as interoperability, data security, and reimbursement policies, pose barriers to widespread adoption and integration of remote monitoring and telemedicine technologies into routine clinical practice. Addressing these challenges requires collaboration among regulatory agencies, healthcare providers, technology developers, and policymakers to develop flexible regulatory frameworks and reimbursement models that support innovation and promote equitable access to telehealth services.

1.6.3 Regulatory Challenges with Personalized Medicine and Digital Health

Personalized medicine and digital health technologies hold promise for optimizing healthcare delivery, tailoring treatments to individual patients' genetic makeup, lifestyle factors, and disease characteristics. Personalized medical devices, genetic tests, and digital health applications enable precision diagnosis, treatment selection, and monitoring, leading to improved patient outcomes and reduced healthcare costs. However, regulatory challenges, such as the interpretation of genetic test results, data privacy concerns, and the validation of digital health algorithms, present obstacles to the adoption and integration of personalized medicine and digital health technologies into clinical practice. Regulatory agencies must collaborate with industry stakeholders, healthcare professionals, and patient advocacy groups to develop guidelines, standards, and evidence-based regulatory pathways that support the safe and effective use of personalized medicine and digital health technologies while protecting patient safety and privacy.

1.7 Conclusion

1.7.1 Recap of Key Concepts and Takeaways

In conclusion, understanding medical device regulation is essential for ensuring patient safety, promoting innovation, and facilitating market access in the healthcare industry. Key concepts discussed in this overview include the classification of medical devices, essential principles such as safety and performance requirements, the product lifecycle from development to post-market surveillance, and the regulatory landscape in different regions, including the United States and the European Union. Additionally, emerging trends and technologies, such as artificial intelligence, remote monitoring, telemedicine, personalized medicine, and digital health, present both opportunities and challenges for regulatory agencies, industry stakeholders, and healthcare professionals.

1.7.2 Implications for Industry and Healthcare Professionals

For industry stakeholders, understanding medical device regulation is critical for navigating regulatory pathways, obtaining market approvals, and ensuring compliance with quality and safety standards. Healthcare professionals must stay informed about regulatory requirements to make informed decisions about device selection, utilization, and patient care. Collaboration between industry, regulatory agencies, healthcare providers, and patients is essential to address emerging challenges, promote innovation, and improve patient outcomes.

1.7.3 Call to Action: Importance of Adhering to Regulatory Standards and Best Practices

As the healthcare landscape continues to evolve, adherence to regulatory standards and best practices is paramount for ensuring patient safety, maintaining public trust, and advancing innovation in the medical device and IVD industry. Industry stakeholders and healthcare professionals must prioritize regulatory compliance, transparency, and ethical conduct to promote the development and utilization of safe, effective, and high-quality medical devices and diagnostics. By working together, we can navigate regulatory challenges, harness the potential of emerging technologies, and contribute to the delivery of patient-centered healthcare worldwide.

CHAPTER TWO

REGULATORY FRAMEWORKS : IMDRF/ GHTF AND GLOBAL STANDARDS

2.1 Overview of IMDRF/GHTF

2.1.1 Evolution and Background of IMDRF/GHTF

The International Medical Device Regulators Forum (IMDRF), formerly known as the Global Harmonization Task Force (GHTF), emerged from a collaborative effort among regulatory authorities and industry stakeholders to streamline and harmonize medical device regulations globally. Its evolution can be traced back to the early 1990s when concerns over the increasing complexity and diversity of medical device regulations prompted regulatory bodies to seek avenues for cooperation. The GHTF, established in 1992, served as a pivotal platform for fostering collaboration and convergence among regulatory authorities from different regions, including Europe, the United States, Japan, Canada, and Australia. Over time, the GHTF evolved into the IMDRF, reflecting a broader international scope and a more inclusive approach to regulatory harmonization. This transition underscored the commitment of participating nations to align regulatory practices and facilitate the global availability of safe and effective medical devices.

2.1.2 Objectives and Mission Statement

The IMDRF operates with the primary objective of enhancing patient safety and promoting global public health by harmonizing regulatory practices related to medical devices. Its mission is encapsulated in a comprehensive mission statement that outlines the organization's core principles and strategic goals. At the forefront of IMDRF's objectives is the facilitation of regulatory convergence through the development of internationally recognized guidelines, standards, and best practices. By fostering alignment among regulatory authorities, the IMDRF aims to minimize regulatory barriers, streamline market access, and expedite the introduction of innovative medical technologies. Furthermore, the IMDRF is committed to promoting transparency, consistency, and predictability in regulatory processes, thereby fostering trust and confidence among stakeholders. Central to its mission is the recognition of the dynamic nature of the medical device industry and the need for adaptive regulatory frameworks that can accommodate technological advancements and emerging challenges. Through ongoing collaboration and engagement with stakeholders, the IMDRF endeavors to maintain relevance and effectiveness in an ever-evolving regulatory landscape.

2.1.3 Key Initiatives and Collaborations

Within the framework of the IMDRF, several key initiatives and collaborations play a pivotal role in advancing regulatory harmonization and promoting global public health. One notable initiative is the development of harmonized regulatory guidelines and principles aimed at standardizing regulatory requirements across different jurisdictions. These guidelines cover various aspects of medical device regulation, including quality management systems, clinical evaluations, and post-market surveillance, among others. By establishing common principles and expectations, these guidelines facilitate a more consistent and efficient regulatory review process, thereby reducing the burden on manufacturers and regulatory authorities alike.

In addition to guideline development, the IMDRF fosters collaboration through information sharing and capacity-building activities. Through workshops, seminars, and training programs, regulatory authorities exchange knowledge and expertise, enhancing their ability to effectively regulate medical devices in accordance with international standards. Moreover, the IMDRF facilitates the exchange of regulatory information and best practices through its online platform and working groups, enabling regulatory authorities to stay abreast of emerging trends and developments in the field.

Furthermore, the IMDRF engages in strategic collaborations with other international organizations and stakeholders to address global challenges and promote convergence in regulatory approaches. Collaborative efforts with organizations such as the World Health Organization (WHO), the International Organization for Standardization (ISO), and the International Electrotechnical Commission (IEC) allow for the alignment of regulatory requirements with international standards and norms. By leveraging collective expertise and resources, these partnerships contribute to the development of robust and effective regulatory frameworks that prioritize patient safety and public health.

2.2 Organizational Structure and Functions

2.2.1 Steering Committee and Working Groups

The organizational structure of the International Medical Device Regulators Forum (IMDRF) comprises a Steering Committee and various Working Groups, each playing distinct roles in advancing the organization's objectives and initiatives. At the apex of the organizational hierarchy is the Steering Committee, which serves as the governing body responsible for setting strategic priorities, overseeing the implementation of key initiatives, and providing guidance on policy matters. Comprised of representatives from participating regulatory authorities and observer organizations, the Steering Committee ensures that the IMDRF operates in accordance with its mission and principles, fostering consensus-building and collaboration among stakeholders.

Working Groups form the backbone of the IMDRF's operational framework, focusing on specific areas of regulatory harmonization and standards development. These groups, composed of subject matter experts nominated by regulatory authorities and industry stakeholders, undertake in-depth discussions and research to address key challenges and develop consensus-based guidance documents. Working Groups are established based on identified priorities and may evolve over time to reflect emerging issues and technological advancements in the medical device field.

The Steering Committee provides oversight and direction to Working Groups, guiding their activities and ensuring alignment with the IMDRF's strategic objectives. Working Groups operate through a transparent and inclusive process, soliciting input from relevant stakeholders and conducting consultations to gather diverse perspectives. By fostering collaboration and knowledge exchange, Working Groups facilitate the development of harmonized regulatory guidelines and best practices that promote patient safety and facilitate market access for medical devices.

Overall, the collaborative efforts of the Steering Committee and Working Groups within the IMDRF's organizational structure contribute to the development of robust and effective regulatory frameworks that support innovation while safeguarding public health. Through their respective functions, these entities play a critical role in advancing regulatory convergence and promoting global harmonization of medical device regulations.

2.2.2 Role of Participating Regulatory Authorities

Participating regulatory authorities play a crucial role within the organizational framework of the International Medical Device Regulators Forum (IMDRF), contributing to the development and implementation of harmonized regulatory standards and practices. These regulatory authorities, representing different regions and jurisdictions, collaborate closely with other stakeholders to achieve consensus on key issues and priorities. Their involvement ensures that regulatory perspectives from diverse contexts are taken into account, enhancing the relevance and applicability of IMDRF guidance documents and initiatives.

Participating regulatory authorities contribute to the work of the IMDRF through various channels, including membership in the Steering Committee and active participation in Working Groups. By sharing their regulatory expertise and insights, these authorities contribute to the development of consensus-based guidelines and recommendations that reflect international best practices and standards. Moreover, participating regulatory authorities play a critical role in promoting the adoption and implementation of IMDRF guidance within their respective jurisdictions, thereby fostering regulatory convergence and alignment at the national level.

Furthermore, participating regulatory authorities serve as conduits for stakeholder engagement and feedback, facilitating communication between the IMDRF and various industry stakeholders, healthcare professionals, and patient advocacy groups. Through their outreach efforts, regulatory authorities promote transparency and inclusivity in the regulatory process, ensuring that diverse perspectives are considered in decision-making. Overall, the active involvement of participating regulatory authorities is essential for the success and effectiveness of the IMDRF, as it ensures broad-based support and adoption of harmonized regulatory approaches across different regions and jurisdictions.

2.2.3 Stakeholder Engagement and Public Consultation

Stakeholder engagement and public consultation are integral components of the International Medical Device Regulators Forum (IMDRF) process, ensuring transparency, inclusivity, and accountability in the development of regulatory standards and guidance documents. The IMDRF recognizes the importance of soliciting input from a wide range of stakeholders, including industry representatives, healthcare professionals, patient advocacy groups, and academia, to ensure that regulatory decisions reflect diverse perspectives and address the needs of all stakeholders.

Through public consultation processes, the IMDRF invites stakeholders to provide feedback on draft guidance documents, proposals, and initiatives before they are finalized. This open and transparent approach allows stakeholders to contribute their expertise, insights, and concerns, enabling the IMDRF to make informed decisions that are responsive to the needs of the medical device community. Public consultations typically involve the dissemination of draft documents through the IMDRF website or other relevant channels, followed by a specified period for stakeholders to submit comments and suggestions for consideration.

Stakeholder engagement goes beyond formal public consultations and encompasses a range of activities aimed at fostering dialogue, collaboration, and partnership between the IMDRF and various stakeholder groups. These activities may include workshops, webinars, stakeholder meetings, and outreach events designed to facilitate information sharing, capacity building, and networking opportunities. By actively engaging with stakeholders throughout the regulatory process, the IMDRF promotes transparency, builds trust, and strengthens its credibility as a global regulatory forum committed to advancing patient safety and public health.

2.3 Regulatory Guidelines

2.3.1 Harmonization of Regulatory Requirements

The harmonization of regulatory requirements is a fundamental objective of the International Medical Device Regulators Forum (IMDRF), aimed at facilitating the global availability of safe and effective medical devices while minimizing unnecessary regulatory burdens. At the core of this endeavor is the development of consensus-based regulatory guidelines that establish common principles, expectations, and standards for the assessment and approval of medical devices across different jurisdictions.

The IMDRF works collaboratively with participating regulatory authorities and stakeholders to develop and harmonize regulatory guidelines that address key aspects of medical device regulation, including premarket assessment, post-market surveillance, quality management systems, and clinical evaluations, among others. These guidelines draw upon international best practices, scientific evidence, and regulatory expertise to provide practical recommendations and standards that promote regulatory convergence and consistency.

Central to the harmonization process is the recognition of regulatory diversity and the need to balance harmonization efforts with the unique regulatory context and requirements of individual jurisdictions. While striving for alignment and convergence, the IMDRF acknowledges the importance of flexibility and adaptation to accommodate regional variations in regulatory frameworks, market dynamics, and healthcare systems.

The harmonization of regulatory requirements is not a one-time event but an ongoing process that requires continuous dialogue, collaboration, and refinement. The IMDRF regularly reviews and updates its guidance documents in response to emerging technologies, scientific advancements, and evolving regulatory challenges. Through periodic revisions and consultations, the IMDRF ensures that its regulatory guidelines remain current, relevant, and effective in safeguarding patient safety and public health while promoting innovation and market access for medical devices.

Overall, the harmonization of regulatory requirements within the IMDRF framework contributes to a more efficient, predictable, and transparent regulatory environment, benefiting patients, healthcare providers, manufacturers, and regulatory authorities alike. By fostering regulatory convergence and alignment, the IMDRF promotes confidence and trust in the safety and performance of medical devices, ultimately improving access to innovative healthcare technologies and enhancing public health outcomes on a global scale.

2.3.2 Development of Essential Principles and Standards

The development of essential principles and standards constitutes a cornerstone of the regulatory guidance framework within the International Medical Device Regulators Forum (IMDRF). These principles serve as foundational pillars guiding the assessment, evaluation, and regulation of medical devices across participating jurisdictions. Essential principles encompass fundamental criteria related to safety, efficacy, performance, and quality, which are essential for ensuring the safety and effectiveness of medical devices throughout their lifecycle.

The IMDRF, in collaboration with regulatory authorities and stakeholders, develops and refines essential principles and standards through a consensus-driven process that integrates scientific evidence, regulatory expertise, and input from diverse stakeholders. These essential principles provide a common framework for regulatory authorities to evaluate and assess medical devices, irrespective of geographical boundaries or regulatory differences. By establishing clear and transparent criteria, essential principles promote regulatory convergence, consistency, and predictability, thereby facilitating market access and promoting public health.

Furthermore, the development of standards within the IMDRF framework complements essential principles by providing technical specifications, guidelines, and methodologies for implementing regulatory requirements in practice. These standards cover various aspects of medical device regulation, including quality management systems, risk management, clinical evaluations, and post-market surveillance, among others. By harmonizing standards and aligning them with international best practices, the IMDRF promotes interoperability, facilitates compliance, and enhances the efficiency of regulatory processes for medical devices.

The ongoing development and refinement of essential principles and standards within the IMDRF framework reflect a commitment to continuous improvement and adaptation to meet evolving regulatory challenges and technological advancements. By leveraging collective expertise and collaboration, the IMDRF contributes to the development of robust and effective regulatory frameworks that prioritize patient safety, promote innovation, and facilitate access to high-quality medical devices on a global scale.

2.3.3 Alignment with International Regulatory Frameworks (e.g., FDA, EU)

Alignment with international regulatory frameworks, such as those established by the U.S. Food and Drug Administration (FDA) and the European Union (EU), is a key priority within the International Medical Device Regulators Forum (IMDRF). Recognizing the importance of regulatory convergence and harmonization, the IMDRF works collaboratively with regulatory authorities and stakeholders to ensure consistency and compatibility between its guidance documents and international regulatory standards.

The IMDRF engages in dialogue and consultation with regulatory counterparts, including the FDA and the EU regulatory agencies, to promote mutual understanding, identify areas of convergence, and facilitate the alignment of regulatory requirements. Through regular communication and information exchange, the IMDRF seeks to harmonize regulatory approaches, streamline processes, and minimize regulatory barriers to market access for medical devices.

Moreover, the IMDRF actively monitors and assesses developments in international regulatory frameworks, including changes in legislation, guidelines, and standards, to ensure that its own guidance remains current, relevant, and aligned with global best practices. By staying abreast of international regulatory trends and developments, the IMDRF can anticipate emerging challenges and proactively address them through collaborative efforts with regulatory authorities and stakeholders.

Alignment with international regulatory frameworks enhances the efficiency and effectiveness of regulatory processes, reduces duplication of efforts, and facilitates the global availability of safe and effective medical devices. By fostering regulatory convergence and compatibility, the IMDRF promotes confidence and trust in the safety and performance of medical devices, ultimately benefiting patients, healthcare providers, manufacturers, and regulatory authorities worldwide.

2.4 Summary Technical Document (STED)

2.4.1 Purpose and Scope of STED

The Summary Technical Document (STED) serves as a standardized format for the preparation of regulatory submissions related to medical devices within the International Medical Device Regulators Forum (IMDRF). The primary purpose of the STED is to streamline the regulatory review process by providing a structured and comprehensive overview of essential technical information related to the design, development, manufacturing, and performance of medical devices. By adhering to a common format and content framework, the STED facilitates efficient assessment and evaluation by regulatory authorities, thereby expediting market approval and promoting timely access to innovative medical technologies.

The scope of the STED encompasses a wide range of technical and scientific data relevant to the regulatory review of medical devices. This includes information on device description and classification, design and manufacturing processes, performance characteristics, risk management, biocompatibility, clinical evidence, and labeling, among other aspects. By consolidating key technical information into a standardized format, the STED enables regulatory authorities to systematically assess the safety, efficacy, and quality of medical devices in a structured and transparent manner.

Furthermore, the STED is designed to accommodate the needs and requirements of regulatory authorities from different regions and jurisdictions, promoting consistency and harmonization in regulatory practices. By providing a common language and format for regulatory submissions, the STED facilitates communication and collaboration among regulatory authorities and stakeholders, enhancing efficiency and transparency throughout the regulatory review process. Overall, the purpose and scope of the STED underscore its importance as a valuable tool for optimizing regulatory processes and promoting global harmonization of medical device regulations.

2.4.2 Content and Format Requirements

The content and format requirements of the STED are designed to ensure consistency, clarity, and completeness in regulatory submissions related to medical devices. The STED provides detailed guidance on the organization and presentation of technical information, outlining specific sections and subsections that should be included in the document. Key content requirements of the STED include:

1. Device Description: Comprehensive description of the medical device, including its intended use, design specifications, materials, and components.
2. Device Classification: Classification of the device according to regulatory requirements, including identification of applicable standards and regulations.
3. Design and Manufacturing Information: Detailed information on the design and manufacturing processes, including specifications, drawings, and quality assurance measures.
4. Performance Characteristics: Data on the performance characteristics of the device, including technical specifications, testing methods, and validation studies.
5. Risk Management: Assessment of device risks and mitigation measures, including identification of hazards, risk analysis, and risk control strategies.
6. Biocompatibility: Evaluation of the device's biocompatibility, including testing results and compliance with relevant standards and guidelines.

7. Clinical Evidence: Summary of clinical data and evidence supporting the safety and efficacy of the device, including clinical study reports and post-market surveillance data.
8. Labeling and Instructions for Use: Description of labeling requirements and instructions for use, including packaging, labeling, and user manuals.

In addition to content requirements, the STED specifies formatting guidelines for document structure, layout, and presentation. This includes standardized section headings, numbering, font styles, and referencing conventions to ensure consistency and readability. By adhering to these content and format requirements, regulatory submissions prepared in accordance with the STED facilitate efficient review and assessment by regulatory authorities, contributing to the timely approval and market access of medical devices.

2.4.3 Use of STED in Regulatory Submissions and Reviews

The Summary Technical Document (STED) serves as a valuable tool in regulatory submissions and reviews within the International Medical Device Regulators Forum (IMDRF), facilitating a structured and efficient approach to the assessment and evaluation of medical devices. The use of STED in regulatory submissions streamlines the process for both manufacturers and regulatory authorities, providing a standardized format for organizing and presenting essential technical information related to the design, development, and performance of medical devices.

Manufacturers preparing regulatory submissions can leverage the STED to ensure that their submissions are comprehensive, consistent, and compliant with regulatory requirements. By following the content and format guidelines outlined in the STED, manufacturers can systematically compile and present technical data in a manner that aligns with the expectations of regulatory authorities. This not only expedites the preparation of regulatory submissions but also enhances the clarity and transparency of the information provided, facilitating the regulatory review process.

Regulatory authorities, in turn, rely on the STED as a structured framework for evaluating the safety, efficacy, and quality of medical devices during the review process. The standardized format of the STED enables regulatory reviewers to efficiently access and assess relevant technical information, ensuring a thorough and systematic evaluation of key aspects such as device design, manufacturing, performance characteristics, and risk management. By providing a common language and structure for regulatory submissions, the STED promotes consistency and comparability in regulatory reviews across different regions and jurisdictions.

Moreover, the use of STED in regulatory submissions and reviews enhances communication and collaboration between manufacturers and regulatory authorities. By adhering to a common format and content framework, both parties can facilitate mutual understanding and alignment of expectations throughout the regulatory process. Manufacturers can proactively address regulatory requirements and provide comprehensive information, while regulatory authorities can conduct more efficient and effective reviews, leading to timely market approvals and improved access to innovative medical technologies.

Overall, the use of STED in regulatory submissions and reviews underscores its significance as a standardized tool for optimizing regulatory processes and promoting global harmonization of medical device regulations. By fostering consistency, transparency, and efficiency, the STED contributes to the advancement of patient safety, public health, and innovation in the medical device industry.

2.5 Global Medical Device Nomenclature (GMDN)

2.5.1 Introduction to GMDN System

The Global Medical Device Nomenclature (GMDN) system represents a standardized classification system for medical devices, designed to facilitate international communication, regulatory harmonization, and information exchange across the healthcare sector. Developed collaboratively by regulatory authorities, industry stakeholders, and standards organizations, the GMDN system provides a common language and framework for categorizing and identifying medical devices based on their intended use, function, and characteristics.

At its core, the GMDN system aims to address the challenges associated with the diverse and complex landscape of medical device terminology and classification. With thousands of different types of medical devices on the market, each with its own unique attributes and specifications, achieving consistency and interoperability in terminology is essential for regulatory oversight, market surveillance, and patient safety.

The GMDN system achieves this by assigning a unique numeric code to each medical device, along with a standardized term describing its generic category and characteristics. These codes and terms are organized hierarchically within the GMDN database, allowing users to navigate and search for specific devices based on various criteria, such as therapeutic area, technology type, or regulatory classification. This standardized classification system enables regulatory authorities, healthcare providers, manufacturers, and other stakeholders to communicate effectively and accurately about medical devices, regardless of geographical location or regulatory jurisdiction.

Moreover, the GMDN system plays a critical role in regulatory harmonization and convergence efforts, facilitating the alignment of regulatory requirements and standards across different regions and jurisdictions. By providing a common reference point for device classification and terminology, the GMDN system promotes consistency and comparability in regulatory submissions, reviews, and decision-making processes. This, in turn, helps to streamline market access for medical devices, reduce regulatory barriers, and enhance patient safety by ensuring that devices are properly categorized and regulated based on their intended use and risk profile.

In summary, the introduction of the GMDN system represents a significant milestone in the standardization and harmonization of medical device nomenclature worldwide. By providing a common language and framework for classification, the GMDN system promotes interoperability, transparency, and efficiency across the healthcare ecosystem, ultimately contributing to improved regulatory oversight, patient outcomes, and public health on a global scale.

2.5.2 Structure and Components of GMDN Codes

The structure of Global Medical Device Nomenclature (GMDN) codes is designed to provide a systematic and standardized method for categorizing and identifying medical devices based on their intended use, function, and characteristics. GMDN codes consist of a series of alphanumeric characters that convey specific information about the device, including its generic category, technology type, and other relevant attributes. Understanding the structure and components of GMDN codes is essential for accurately classifying and communicating information about medical devices within the healthcare ecosystem.

The components of GMDN codes typically include:

1. **Device Group**: The first segment of the GMDN code represents the highest level of classification, indicating the broad category or group to which the device belongs. Device groups are organized hierarchically

within the GMDN system and encompass a wide range of medical devices, such as implants, diagnostic equipment, surgical instruments, and therapeutic devices.

2. **Generic Descriptor**: Following the device group, the GMDN code includes a generic descriptor that provides additional detail about the specific type or function of the device. This descriptor helps to further refine the classification of the device within its broader category and distinguish it from other devices with similar characteristics.
3. **GMDN Term**: The GMDN term corresponds to the generic descriptor and provides a standardized description of the device's intended use, technology, and features. The GMDN term is aligned with the International Medical Device Regulators Forum (IMDRF) terminology and serves as the official reference for identifying and communicating about medical devices within the GMDN system.
4. **Additional Segments**: In some cases, GMDN codes may include additional segments or qualifiers to provide further detail or specificity about the device. These segments may include information such as device size, configuration, or intended patient population, depending on the complexity and variability of the device category.

Overall, the structure and components of GMDN codes enable users to systematically classify and identify medical devices based on their key attributes and characteristics. By providing a standardized framework for device classification and terminology, the GMDN system promotes interoperability, consistency, and transparency in regulatory processes, market surveillance, and healthcare communication.

2.5.3 Benefits of GMDN for Regulatory Compliance and Market Access

The Global Medical Device Nomenclature (GMDN) system offers numerous benefits for regulatory compliance and market access, contributing to streamlined processes, enhanced communication, and improved patient safety within the healthcare industry.

1. **Standardization and Consistency**: GMDN provides a standardized classification system for medical devices, ensuring consistency in terminology and categorization across different regions and regulatory jurisdictions. By adhering to a common language and framework, manufacturers, regulatory authorities, and other stakeholders can

communicate effectively and accurately about medical devices, facilitating regulatory compliance and market access.

2. **Facilitated Regulatory Submissions**: GMDN codes streamline the preparation and submission of regulatory documentation by providing a systematic method for categorizing and identifying medical devices. Manufacturers can use GMDN codes to accurately classify their devices and ensure compliance with regulatory requirements, reducing the risk of errors and delays in the regulatory review process.
3. **Harmonized Regulatory Reviews**: GMDN promotes regulatory harmonization and convergence by providing a common reference point for device classification and terminology. Regulatory authorities can use GMDN codes to streamline the review and assessment of medical devices, facilitating efficient decision-making and alignment of regulatory requirements across different regions.
4. **Enhanced Market Access**: GMDN codes facilitate market access for medical devices by providing a standardized language for communicating device information to regulatory authorities, healthcare providers, and other stakeholders. Manufacturers can use GMDN codes to demonstrate compliance with regulatory requirements and facilitate product registration and market approval in multiple jurisdictions.
5. **Improved Patient Safety**: GMDN enhances patient safety by enabling accurate and transparent communication about medical devices throughout their lifecycle. Healthcare providers can use GMDN codes to access standardized information about device characteristics, indications for use, and safety considerations, ensuring informed decision-making and appropriate patient care.
6. **Efficient Post-Market Surveillance**: GMDN supports post-market surveillance activities by enabling the tracking and monitoring of medical devices based on standardized codes and terminology. Regulatory authorities can use GMDN codes to identify and track devices within their jurisdiction, facilitating timely detection of adverse events, recalls, and other safety concerns.

Overall, the adoption of GMDN for regulatory compliance and market access offers significant advantages for manufacturers, regulatory authorities, healthcare providers, and patients alike. By providing a standardized framework for device classification and communication, GMDN promotes efficiency, transparency, and safety throughout the healthcare ecosystem, ultimately contributing to improved public health outcomes on a global scale.

2.6 Importance of IMDRF/GHTF and Global Standards

The International Medical Device Regulators Forum (IMDRF), formerly known as the Global Harmonization Task Force (GHTF), and global standards play a pivotal role in shaping the regulatory landscape and advancing public health outcomes in the medical device industry. Their importance can be understood through several key factors:

1. **Facilitating Regulatory Convergence**: IMDRF/GHTF and global standards facilitate regulatory convergence by harmonizing regulatory requirements, guidelines, and practices across different regions and jurisdictions. By aligning regulatory frameworks, these initiatives reduce barriers to market access, promote consistency in regulatory decision-making, and enhance the efficiency of regulatory processes. This fosters innovation and ensures that patients have timely access to safe and effective medical devices worldwide.
2. **Enhancing Patient Safety**: Central to the mission of IMDRF/GHTF and global standards is the promotion of patient safety. By establishing internationally recognized standards for device safety, performance, and quality, these initiatives help ensure that medical devices meet stringent regulatory requirements and undergo rigorous evaluation before entering the market. This protects patients from potential risks and adverse events associated with the use of medical devices, thereby improving overall public health outcomes.
3. **Streamlining Regulatory Processes**: IMDRF/GHTF and global standards streamline regulatory processes by providing a common language and framework for regulatory submissions, reviews, and approvals. Standardized guidelines and documentation requirements simplify the regulatory compliance process for manufacturers, reducing administrative burdens and accelerating market access for innovative medical technologies. This enables manufacturers to bring new products to market more quickly, benefiting both patients and industry stakeholders.
4. **Promoting Innovation and Market Access**: By harmonizing regulatory requirements and fostering a predictable regulatory environment, IMDRF/GHTF and global standards promote innovation and market access for medical devices. Manufacturers can navigate regulatory

complexities more effectively, enabling them to invest in research and development, introduce new technologies, and expand their market presence. This stimulates competition, drives technological advancements, and ultimately improves patient care through the availability of cutting-edge medical devices.

5. **Fostering International Collaboration**: IMDRF/GHTF and global standards foster international collaboration among regulatory authorities, industry stakeholders, and other key players in the medical device ecosystem. By bringing together expertise from diverse regions and disciplines, these initiatives facilitate knowledge exchange, capacity-building, and best practice sharing. This collaborative approach strengthens regulatory oversight, enhances regulatory harmonization efforts, and promotes mutual recognition of regulatory decisions, benefiting all stakeholders involved.

In summary, IMDRF/GHTF and global standards play a crucial role in promoting regulatory convergence, enhancing patient safety, streamlining regulatory processes, fostering innovation, and facilitating international collaboration in the medical device industry. Their continued importance underscores the need for ongoing cooperation and commitment to advancing global health outcomes through harmonized regulatory approaches.

2.6.1 Facilitating International Trade and Market Access

Standards play a fundamental role in facilitating international trade and market access for medical devices by providing a common framework for regulatory compliance and product acceptance across different countries and regions. Several key ways in which standards facilitate international trade and market access include:

1. **Harmonization of Technical Requirements**: Standards harmonization ensures that technical requirements for medical devices are aligned across multiple jurisdictions. This alignment reduces trade barriers by enabling manufacturers to develop products that meet a single set of standards accepted internationally, rather than having to comply with divergent requirements in each market. Harmonized standards promote efficiency, reduce duplication of effort, and facilitate the global acceptance of medical devices, thereby enhancing market access for manufacturers.

2. **Mutual Recognition Agreements (MRAs)**: Standards contribute to the development of mutual recognition agreements (MRAs) between countries or regions, whereby regulatory authorities agree to accept conformity assessments conducted in accordance with recognized standards from other jurisdictions. MRAs streamline market access by eliminating the need for redundant testing and certification processes, thereby reducing costs and time to market for manufacturers. By relying on standardized assessments, regulatory authorities can maintain confidence in the safety and quality of medical devices while facilitating trade and market access.
3. **Enhanced Transparency and Predictability**: Standards provide transparency and predictability in regulatory requirements and expectations, which are essential for manufacturers seeking to enter new markets. By adhering to internationally recognized standards, manufacturers can anticipate regulatory requirements and ensure that their products meet the necessary criteria for market acceptance. This clarity and predictability reduce regulatory uncertainty and enable manufacturers to make informed decisions regarding market entry strategies and investment in product development.
4. **Market Confidence and Consumer Protection**: Standards contribute to market confidence and consumer protection by establishing clear requirements for the safety, performance, and quality of medical devices. Compliance with recognized standards demonstrates a manufacturer's commitment to product quality and regulatory compliance, enhancing confidence among regulatory authorities, healthcare providers, and end-users. This confidence promotes market acceptance and facilitates market access for medical devices, ultimately benefiting public health outcomes.
5. **Facilitated Access to Global Supply Chains**: Standards facilitate access to global supply chains by ensuring interoperability and compatibility between different components, materials, and systems used in the manufacture of medical devices. By adhering to standardized specifications and requirements, manufacturers can seamlessly integrate their products into global supply chains, source components from multiple suppliers, and collaborate with partners across borders. This facilitates innovation, reduces costs, and enhances efficiency in the production and distribution of medical devices, ultimately improving market access and availability for end-users worldwide.

In conclusion, standards play a critical role in facilitating international trade and market access for medical devices by harmonizing technical requirements, supporting mutual recognition agreements, enhancing transparency and predictability, promoting market confidence, and facilitating access to global supply chains. By providing a common framework for regulatory compliance and product acceptance, standards contribute to the growth and sustainability of the medical device industry while ensuring the safety and quality of products available in global markets.

2.6.2 Enhancing Regulatory Efficiency and Effectiveness

Standards play a crucial role in enhancing regulatory efficiency and effectiveness in the medical device industry by providing a common language and framework for regulatory processes, streamlining procedures, and promoting consistency and transparency. Several key ways in which standards enhance regulatory efficiency and effectiveness include:

1. **Streamlined Regulatory Processes:** Standards provide clear and standardized guidelines for regulatory processes, including product testing, certification, and market approval. By adhering to recognized standards, manufacturers can navigate regulatory requirements more efficiently, reducing the time and resources required to bring products to market. This streamlining of regulatory processes accelerates market access for medical devices, promoting innovation and improving patient access to new technologies.
2. **Consistency and Predictability**: Standards promote consistency and predictability in regulatory decision-making by establishing uniform criteria and requirements for assessing the safety, efficacy, and quality of medical devices. Regulatory authorities can rely on recognized standards as benchmarks for evaluating compliance, ensuring that similar devices are subject to consistent scrutiny regardless of geographical location or regulatory jurisdiction. This consistency enhances regulatory predictability and fosters confidence among manufacturers, investors, and healthcare providers, ultimately benefiting patient care and public health outcomes.
3. **Facilitated Compliance and Conformity Assessment**: Standards facilitate compliance and conformity assessment by providing clear benchmarks for manufacturers to demonstrate compliance with regulatory requirements. By aligning their products with recognized

standards, manufacturers can streamline the certification process, reduce the need for redundant testing, and expedite market approval. This facilitates market access for medical devices while ensuring that products meet stringent quality and safety standards, thereby safeguarding patient health and well-being.

4. **Promotion of Good Manufacturing Practices (GMP)**: Standards promote the adoption of good manufacturing practices (GMP) by establishing guidelines and best practices for the design, production, and quality control of medical devices. Compliance with GMP standards ensures that manufacturers adhere to rigorous quality standards throughout the manufacturing process, reducing the risk of defects, contamination, and adverse events. This enhances product quality, reliability, and safety, ultimately improving patient outcomes and public confidence in medical devices.
5. **Continuous Improvement and Innovation**: Standards drive continuous improvement and innovation in the medical device industry by providing a framework for benchmarking best practices, integrating new technologies, and addressing emerging regulatory challenges. As standards evolve to reflect advances in science, technology, and regulatory requirements, manufacturers are encouraged to innovate and improve their products to meet evolving standards and market demands. This fosters a culture of innovation and excellence within the industry, leading to the development of safer, more effective, and higher-quality medical devices that benefit patients and healthcare providers worldwide.

In summary, standards enhance regulatory efficiency and effectiveness in the medical device industry by streamlining processes, promoting consistency and predictability, facilitating compliance and conformity assessment, promoting good manufacturing practices, and driving continuous improvement and innovation. By providing a common framework for regulatory compliance and quality assurance, standards contribute to the safety, efficacy, and accessibility of medical devices, ultimately improving patient outcomes and public health on a global scale.

2.6.3 Promoting Patient Safety and Public Health

Standards play a critical role in promoting patient safety and public health in the medical device industry by establishing rigorous quality and safety requirements, facilitating regulatory oversight, and fostering a culture of continuous improvement and innovation. Several key ways in which standards promote patient safety and public health include:

1. **Establishing Safety and Performance Requirements**: Standards define safety and performance requirements for medical devices, ensuring that products meet stringent quality and safety standards before entering the market. By adhering to recognized standards, manufacturers demonstrate their commitment to producing safe and effective devices that meet the needs of patients and healthcare providers.
2. **Enhancing Regulatory Oversight**: Standards support regulatory oversight by providing clear benchmarks for assessing compliance with regulatory requirements. Regulatory authorities rely on recognized standards as reference points for evaluating product safety, efficacy, and quality, enabling them to make informed regulatory decisions and take appropriate enforcement actions when necessary. This ensures that medical devices meet rigorous regulatory standards and undergo thorough evaluation before reaching patients.
3. **Facilitating Post-Market Surveillance**: Standards facilitate post-market surveillance activities by providing criteria for monitoring the safety and performance of medical devices throughout their lifecycle. By establishing requirements for adverse event reporting, post-market monitoring, and quality management systems, standards enable manufacturers and regulatory authorities to detect and respond to potential safety issues in a timely manner, minimizing risks to patients and public health.
4. **Supporting Interoperability and Compatibility**: Standards promote interoperability and compatibility between different medical devices and healthcare systems, ensuring seamless integration and communication across the healthcare ecosystem. By adhering to standardized specifications and protocols, manufacturers can develop devices that work reliably with other products and technologies, reducing the risk of errors, interoperability issues, and adverse events that could compromise patient safety.
5. **Encouraging Continuous Improvement and Innovation**: Standards encourage continuous improvement and innovation by providing a framework for benchmarking best practices, integrating new technologies, and addressing emerging regulatory challenges. As standards evolve to reflect advances in science, technology, and patient

care, manufacturers are motivated to innovate and improve their products to meet evolving standards and market demands. This fosters a culture of innovation and excellence within the industry, leading to the development of safer, more effective, and higher-quality medical devices that benefit patients and public health.

In summary, standards play a vital role in promoting patient safety and public health in the medical device industry by establishing safety and performance requirements, enhancing regulatory oversight, facilitating post-market surveillance, supporting interoperability and compatibility, and encouraging continuous improvement and innovation. By providing a common framework for quality assurance and regulatory compliance, standards contribute to the delivery of safe, effective, and high-quality medical devices that improve patient outcomes and protect public health on a global scale.

2.7 Future Directions and Challenges

2.7.1 Expansion of IMDRF/GHTF Membership and Participation

The future direction of the International Medical Device Regulators Forum (IMDRF), formerly known as the Global Harmonization Task Force (GHTF), involves expanding membership and participation to further promote regulatory convergence, enhance collaboration, and address global challenges in medical device regulation. Key strategies for achieving this expansion include:

- **Increasing Membership**: IMDRF/GHTF aims to expand its membership to include regulatory authorities from additional countries and regions, particularly those with emerging medical device markets or unique regulatory challenges. By welcoming new members, IMDRF/GHTF can foster greater diversity of perspectives and expertise, enhancing its capacity to develop globally relevant guidance and standards.
- **Engaging Stakeholders**: IMDRF/GHTF seeks to engage a broader range of stakeholders, including industry representatives, healthcare providers, patients, and advocacy groups, in its activities and decision-making processes. By involving stakeholders in discussions and consultations, IMDRF/GHTF can ensure that its initiatives reflect the needs and priorities of all stakeholders, promoting transparency, inclusivity, and accountability.

- **Promoting Capacity Building**: IMDRF/GHTF aims to promote capacity building and knowledge sharing among regulatory authorities, particularly those from low- and middle-income countries with limited resources and expertise in medical device regulation. By providing training, technical assistance, and mentorship programs, IMDRF/GHTF can empower regulatory authorities to enhance their regulatory systems and participate more actively in international collaboration efforts.
- **Facilitating Regional Partnerships**: IMDRF/GHTF collaborates with regional regulatory harmonization initiatives, such as the Association of Southeast Asian Nations (ASEAN) Medical Device Directive, to promote convergence and alignment of regulatory requirements at the regional level. By fostering partnerships with regional initiatives, IMDRF/GHTF can leverage synergies, share best practices, and support harmonization efforts across multiple jurisdictions.
- **Enhancing Communication and Outreach**: IMDRF/GHTF prioritizes communication and outreach efforts to raise awareness of its activities, engage stakeholders, and disseminate information about regulatory developments and best practices. By leveraging communication channels such as conferences, workshops, webinars, and online platforms, IMDRF/GHTF can reach a wider audience and facilitate dialogue and collaboration on global regulatory issues.

In addressing these challenges, IMDRF/GHTF aims to strengthen its role as a leading international forum for regulatory harmonization and collaboration in the medical device industry, advancing public health and patient safety on a global scale.

2.7.2 Addressing Emerging Technologies and Novel Devices

The rapid advancement of technology presents both opportunities and challenges for medical device regulation. As new technologies emerge and novel devices are developed, regulatory authorities face the challenge of ensuring that regulatory frameworks remain flexible, adaptive, and capable of addressing evolving risks and uncertainties. Key strategies for addressing emerging technologies and novel devices include:

- **Proactive Regulation**: Regulatory authorities must adopt a proactive approach to regulation that anticipates and responds to emerging technologies and novel devices. This involves engaging with stakeholders, monitoring technological developments, and updating regulatory frameworks to accommodate new risks and challenges.

- **Risk-Based Approach**: A risk-based approach to regulation is essential for evaluating emerging technologies and novel devices, as it enables regulatory authorities to prioritize resources and focus regulatory oversight on products with the greatest potential impact on patient safety and public health. By assessing risks and benefits in a systematic and transparent manner, regulatory authorities can make informed decisions about regulatory requirements and market access.
- **Collaboration and Engagement**: Collaboration and engagement with industry, academia, healthcare providers, and other stakeholders are critical for understanding the capabilities, limitations, and implications of emerging technologies and novel devices. By fostering dialogue and collaboration, regulatory authorities can leverage external expertise, share information, and develop consensus-based approaches to addressing regulatory challenges.
- **Regulatory Science and Innovation**: Investment in regulatory science and innovation is essential for advancing the science and methodologies used in regulatory decision-making for emerging technologies and novel devices. By supporting research, development, and validation of new regulatory tools and techniques, regulatory authorities can enhance their capacity to evaluate the safety, efficacy, and quality of innovative medical devices.
- **International Collaboration**: Given the global nature of emerging technologies and novel devices, international collaboration and harmonization are essential for promoting consistency, efficiency, and interoperability in regulatory processes. Regulatory authorities should collaborate through initiatives such as IMDRF/GHTF to harmonize regulatory requirements, share best practices, and facilitate mutual recognition of regulatory decisions.

In addressing these challenges, regulatory authorities can promote innovation, protect patient safety, and support the development and adoption of emerging technologies and novel devices that have the potential to transform healthcare and improve patient outcomes.

2.7.3 Overcoming Barriers to Global Harmonization and Standardization

Global harmonization and standardization in medical device regulation face several barriers that must be addressed to promote consistency, efficiency, and transparency in regulatory processes. Key challenges include:

- **Divergent Regulatory Requirements**: Variations in regulatory requirements across different countries and regions create complexity and uncertainty for manufacturers seeking to market medical devices globally. Regulatory authorities must work collaboratively through initiatives such as IMDRF/GHTF to harmonize requirements, align standards, and promote mutual recognition of regulatory decisions.
- **Resource Constraints**: Many regulatory authorities, particularly those from low- and middle-income countries, face resource constraints in terms of funding, expertise, and infrastructure. Capacity building and technical assistance programs are essential for empowering regulatory authorities to participate in international harmonization efforts and enhance their regulatory systems.
- **Lack of Consensus and Alignment**: Achieving consensus and alignment among diverse stakeholders, including regulatory authorities, industry representatives, healthcare providers, and patients, can be challenging due to differing priorities, perspectives, and interests. Effective communication, engagement, and collaboration are essential for building consensus and fostering trust among stakeholders.
- **Pace of Technological Innovation**: The rapid pace of technological innovation in the medical device industry presents challenges for regulatory authorities in terms of evaluating safety, efficacy, and quality. Regulatory frameworks must be flexible, adaptive, and responsive to technological advancements, while also ensuring that regulatory standards keep pace with innovation.
- **Legal and Regulatory Barriers**: Legal and regulatory barriers, such as intellectual property rights, trade agreements, and market access restrictions, can impede global harmonization and standardization efforts. Regulatory authorities must address these barriers through dialogue, negotiation, and advocacy to promote a more conducive regulatory environment for international collaboration.

2.8 Conclusion

2.8.1 Recap of Key Concepts and Takeaways

In conclusion, the regulatory frameworks established by the International Medical Device Regulators Forum (IMDRF), formerly known as the Global Harmonization Task Force (GHTF), and global standards play a critical role in shaping the medical device industry and promoting public health outcomes worldwide. Key concepts and takeaways from this discussion include:

- **Regulatory Convergence**: IMDRF/GHTF facilitates regulatory convergence by harmonizing standards, guidelines, and practices across different regions and jurisdictions, promoting consistency, efficiency, and transparency in regulatory processes.
- **Global Standards**: Global standards provide a common framework for regulatory compliance and product acceptance, facilitating international trade, market access, and interoperability while ensuring patient safety and public health.
- **Challenges and Opportunities**: Despite the progress made in regulatory harmonization and standardization, challenges remain, including the need to address emerging technologies, overcome barriers to global harmonization, and enhance collaboration among regulatory agencies and industry stakeholders.

2.8.2 Implications for Regulatory Agencies and Industry Stakeholders

For regulatory agencies, the implications of global standards and regulatory convergence include the need to adopt a proactive approach to regulation, engage stakeholders, invest in regulatory science and innovation, and promote capacity building and collaboration at the international level.

For industry stakeholders, adherence to global standards and regulatory requirements is essential for ensuring compliance, promoting market access, and safeguarding patient safety. Industry must also prioritize innovation, quality, and transparency in product development and regulatory submissions to meet evolving regulatory expectations.

2.8.3 Call to Action: Commitment to Collaboration and Compliance with Global Standards

As we move forward, a commitment to collaboration and compliance with global standards is essential for advancing regulatory convergence, promoting patient safety, and fostering innovation in the medical device industry. Regulatory agencies, industry stakeholders, and other key players must work together collaboratively to address emerging challenges, overcome barriers to global harmonization, and ensure that medical devices meet the highest standards of safety, efficacy, and quality for the benefit of patients worldwide. By embracing this call to action, we can collectively contribute to the advancement of public health and the delivery of safe, effective, and accessible medical technologies for all.

CHAPTER THREE

ETHICS AND QUALITY CONSIDERATIONS

3.1.1 Definition and Importance of Clinical Investigation Ethics

Clinical investigation ethics encompasses the moral principles and guidelines that govern the conduct of research involving human participants. Its primary purpose is to ensure the dignity, rights, safety, and well-being of the research participants. The cornerstone of ethical clinical research is the respect for individuals, which translates into several key requirements: informed consent, confidentiality, minimization of harm, and maximization of benefits.

Informed consent is crucial; it means that participants must receive comprehensive information about the research, including its objectives, potential risks, benefits, and alternatives. They should understand this information and voluntarily agree to participate without any coercion. Confidentiality protects the privacy of participants by ensuring that personal information is not disclosed without consent.

Furthermore, ethical guidelines require that the risks to participants are minimized. This involves using procedures that follow sound scientific principles and ensuring that the potential benefits justify the risks. The principle of beneficence not only obligates researchers to prevent harm but also compels them to contribute to the welfare of the participant.

Another critical aspect is the fair selection of participants. This involves ensuring that the selection process is equitable and inclusive, avoiding vulnerable populations unless the research is directly beneficial to them.

The significance of clinical investigation ethics lies not only in protecting participants but also in preserving the integrity of the scientific process. Ethical research is more likely to be legally compliant, socially acceptable, and respected by the public, which ultimately supports the advancement of medical knowledge and the improvement of health outcomes.

By adhering to these ethical principles, researchers uphold the highest standards of quality and integrity, fostering trust between the scientific community and the public. This trust is essential for the ongoing collaboration and participation necessary for clinical research and the broader field of medical science.

3.1.2 Historical Development of Ethical Guidelines in Clinical Research

The historical development of ethical guidelines in clinical research is marked by several key milestones that have shaped current practices and policies. These guidelines have evolved primarily in response to past abuses in research, leading to a greater emphasis on the protection of human subjects.

One of the earliest documented instances of ethical guidelines for medical research is the Nuremberg Code, developed in 1947 as a result of the Nuremberg trials, where the inhumane and unethical experiments conducted by Nazi doctors during World War II were brought to light. The Nuremberg Code emphasized voluntary consent as absolutely essential and required that experiments should yield fruitful results for the good of society, unprocurable by other methods or means of study.

Following the Nuremberg Code, the Declaration of Helsinki was formulated by the World Medical Association in 1964. This set of guidelines further refined ethical standards for clinical research, stressing the importance of considering the risks and benefits of research, the necessity of informed consent, and special protections for research subjects who are in a vulnerable position.

In the United States, the National Research Act of 1974 established the National Commission for the Protection of Human Subjects of Biomedical and Behavioral Research. This commission developed the Belmont Report in 1979, which outlined three fundamental ethical principles: respect for persons (involving recognition of personal autonomy and the protection of those with diminished autonomy), beneficence (maximizing benefits and minimizing harms and risks), and justice (ensuring reasonable, non-exploitative, and well-considered procedures administered fairly).

Another significant development was the introduction of Good Clinical Practice (GCP) guidelines in the 1990s, an international ethical and scientific quality standard for designing, conducting, recording, and reporting trials that involve the participation of human subjects.

Compliance with GCP provides public assurance that the rights, safety, and well-being of trial participants are protected and that the clinical trial data are credible.

These historical developments reflect a growing global consensus on the fundamental ethical principles that should guide clinical research. They emphasize a commitment to respecting individual rights and ensuring the welfare of research participants. This evolution of ethical guidelines not only helps to protect individuals but also builds public trust in clinical research, which is essential for its continued viability and success.

3.1.3 Key Principles of Ethical Clinical Investigations

Ethical clinical investigations are governed by several fundamental principles that ensure the protection and dignity of research participants. These principles are universally recognized and form the backbone of ethical guidelines across various research disciplines. Understanding these key principles is essential for any researcher involved in clinical studies.

Respect for Persons

This principle involves acknowledging the autonomy of individuals and protecting those with diminished autonomy. It requires that participants enter into research voluntarily and with adequate information. Informed consent is a critical element of respecting individuals‘ autonomy. It ensures that participants are adequately informed about the nature and risks of the research, understand the information, and consent without any form of coercion.

Beneficence

The principle of beneficence obligates researchers to minimize harm and maximize benefits. It requires that researchers undertake efforts to ensure the well-being of participants by carefully assessing the risks and benefits involved in the research. This principle is not limited to protecting participants from harm but also encompasses efforts to secure their well-being throughout the research process.

Non-Maleficence

Closely related to beneficence, non-maleficence is the duty to do no harm. Researchers must not only aim to maximize benefits but also have an obligation to minimize the risk of harm. This involves using safe research methods and ensuring that any potential risks are clearly communicated to the participants.

Justice

Justice in clinical investigations concerns the fair distribution of the burdens and benefits of research. This principle requires that individuals and groups be treated fairly and equitably in terms of their participation in research. It also implies the fair selection of subjects, ensuring that no group is unduly burdened or unjustly excluded from the potential benefits of research.

Integrity

Integrity in clinical research involves adherence to the highest standards of objectivity and professionalism. Researchers are expected to conduct their studies honestly and report their findings transparently. This principle ensures that the research is conducted without bias and that the results contribute effectively to scientific knowledge.

Confidentiality

Participants in clinical research entrust researchers with sensitive personal information. The principle of confidentiality obligates researchers to protect this information and use it only in ways that have been consented to by the participants. Maintaining confidentiality is essential for respecting participants' privacy and maintaining trust.

Together, these principles ensure ethical conduct in clinical investigations, fostering trust between researchers and participants and enhancing the scientific and ethical integrity of the research process. By adhering to these principles, researchers uphold the dignity and rights of participants while contributing valuable knowledge to the scientific community.

3.1.4 Ethical Review Processes and Institutional Review Boards (IRBs)

Ethical review processes are a fundamental component of clinical research, designed to ensure that studies are conducted in accordance with ethical standards that protect participants and maintain the integrity of the research. The Institutional Review Board (IRB) plays a central role in this process.

Role of Institutional Review Boards (IRBs)

An IRB is a committee established to review and approve the initiation and conduct of clinical trials involving human subjects. The primary purpose of the IRB is to ensure that the rights, safety, and welfare of participants are protected. This is achieved by reviewing the research protocols, informed consent documents, and any other materials related to the study. IRBs are composed of a diverse group of individuals, which can include physicians, scientists, and non-scientists, as well as members from the community, ensuring a comprehensive review of the ethical aspects of the research.

IRB Review Process

The review process begins when a researcher submits a detailed research proposal to the IRB. This proposal includes the study's objectives, methodology, potential risks, benefits, and the mechanisms for obtaining informed consent. The IRB evaluates the proposal to ensure compliance with ethical standards:

1. **Risk-Benefit Analysis:** IRBs assess whether the risks to participants are minimized and are reasonable in relation to the anticipated benefits. They ensure that the research has a sound scientific basis and that the benefits justify the risks.
2. **Informed Consent:** The IRB reviews the informed consent process and documents to ensure that they are clear, comprehensive, and that they truly inform participants about the study's nature, risks, and benefits.
3. **Participant Selection:** The board ensures that the selection criteria are fair and equitable, and that there is no potential for exploitation of vulnerable groups.
4. **Privacy and Confidentiality:** IRBs also ensure that adequate measures are in place to protect the confidentiality and privacy of participants.

Continuing Review

Once the research is approved, IRBs are also responsible for ongoing oversight of the study. This includes reviewing any proposed modifications to the research and conducting periodic reviews to ensure that the study remains compliant with ethical standards.

Importance of IRBs

The importance of IRBs cannot be overstated. They not only protect participants but also enhance the credibility and validity of the research. By ensuring that studies are ethically conducted, IRBs maintain public trust in scientific research, which is crucial for the advancement of medical knowledge and the development of new therapies.

In conclusion, IRBs and ethical review processes are vital for upholding ethical standards in clinical investigations. They ensure that research is conducted responsibly, with a firm commitment to the protection of human subjects and the integrity of the scientific process.

3.1.5 Challenges and Ethical Dilemmas in Clinical Investigations

Clinical investigations often present complex ethical challenges and dilemmas that can be difficult to navigate. These challenges arise from conflicts between the principles of ethical research and the practical realities of conducting studies involving human subjects. Addressing these dilemmas requires careful consideration and a balanced approach to ethical decision-making.

Informed Consent Complexities

One of the primary ethical challenges in clinical research is obtaining genuine informed consent. Researchers must ensure that participants fully understand the risks, benefits, and alternatives to the study. However, complexities can arise due to participants' varying levels of education, language barriers, or medical literacy. Additionally, there may be concerns about whether consent is truly voluntary, especially in populations that may feel coerced by financial incentives or healthcare dependencies.

Risk-Benefit Analysis

Determining the acceptable balance between risks and benefits can be particularly challenging. While researchers aim to minimize risk, some level of risk is inherent in many studies, especially those testing new drugs or procedures. The ethical dilemma lies in deciding when the potential benefits justify these risks, particularly in studies involving vulnerable populations or those with terminal illnesses.

Privacy and Confidentiality

Maintaining privacy and confidentiality in clinical research is crucial but challenging. The dilemma arises when the public interest in knowledge and the need for scientific transparency must be balanced against individual rights to privacy. This is especially pertinent in genetic research or studies involving sensitive health data, where the unauthorized disclosure of personal information could lead to discrimination or stigmatization.

Use of Placebo

The use of placebo in clinical trials poses ethical questions, particularly when effective treatments are already available. Assigning participants to placebo groups where effective therapies exist can be seen as denying them potentially beneficial treatment. However, placebos are often necessary to establish the efficacy of new treatments, creating a conflict between scientific validity and patient care.

Vulnerable Populations

Research involving vulnerable groups (such as children, pregnant women, or economically disadvantaged individuals) is fraught with ethical complexities. These populations are at greater risk of exploitation and may have limited capacity to give informed consent. Ensuring their protection while also considering the potential benefits of research is a persistent ethical challenge.

Globalization of Clinical Trials

The globalization of clinical trials introduces additional ethical concerns, such as the potential for "ethics dumping"—where research is conducted in lower-income countries to avoid stringent ethical standards. Ensuring that participants in all regions receive equal protection and benefits poses significant challenges, particularly when navigating varying cultural norms and regulatory environments.

Addressing these ethical dilemmas requires a multidisciplinary approach involving ethicists, researchers, regulatory bodies, and community representatives. It is essential to continually assess and evolve ethical standards and review mechanisms to respond to new challenges as medical science advances. By doing so, the research community can uphold the integrity of clinical investigations and ensure the protection of all participants.

3.1.6 Case Studies Illustrating Ethical Issues in Clinical Research

Case studies are a valuable tool for understanding the practical applications of ethical principles in clinical research. They illustrate the complexities of real-world situations and help researchers and ethicists explore the implications of their decisions. Here are a few notable cases that highlight different ethical issues:

Case Study 1: The Tuskegee Syphilis Study

This infamous clinical study conducted between 1932 and 1972 by the U.S. Public Health Service involved 399 poor African-American men diagnosed with syphilis, who were never told they had the disease. The researchers did not provide them with the proper treatment needed to cure their illness even after penicillin became the drug of choice for syphilis in 1947. The ethical violations in this study included deception, lack of informed consent, and exploitation of a vulnerable population. The Tuskegee study led to major changes in U.S. law and regulation on the protection of participants in clinical studies, including the requirement for informed consent.

Case Study 2: The Willowbrook Hepatitis Experiments

From 1956 to 1970, researchers at Willowbrook State School, a facility for children with intellectual disabilities in New York, intentionally infected new arrivals with hepatitis in an attempt to discover a vaccine. The ethical issues here included the informed consent process, as consent was often coerced by implying that admission to the overcrowded institution depended on participation in the study. This case raised significant concerns about the ethical treatment of vulnerable populations in research.

Case Study 3: Henrietta Lacks and the HeLa Cells

Henrietta Lacks was a poor African-American woman whose cancer cells were taken without her knowledge or consent in 1951 while she was receiving treatment at Johns Hopkins Hospital. Her cells led to significant medical breakthroughs, including the development of the polio vaccine. The ethical issues involve the use of her cells without consent and the subsequent commercialization of research based on her cells without compensation to her family. This case has prompted discussions about privacy, consent, and the fair use of biological materials.

Case Study 4: The AZT Trials in Pregnant Women in Developing Countries

In the 1990s, trials in developing countries tested the efficacy of AZT in preventing mother-to-child transmission of HIV. Despite knowing that short-course AZT could reduce transmission rates, placebo controls were used in populations where no treatment was available, raising ethical concerns. The primary issues involved the use of a placebo when an effective treatment existed and the implications of conducting research in low-income countries that might not otherwise have access to such medications.

Case Study 5: A Clinical Trial for Stroke in Italy

A recent controversial clinical trial in Italy tested the efficacy of a stem cell therapy for stroke patients. Concerns were raised about the premature approval and implementation of the trial, the potential biases in patient selection, and the adequacy of the informed consent process, especially given the desperate condition of the patients and their families. This case illustrates the complexities involved in emerging therapies and the need for rigorous regulatory standards.

These case studies highlight the necessity for stringent ethical standards and robust oversight mechanisms in clinical research. They also demonstrate the evolving nature of ethical considerations in response to new scientific developments and societal values, emphasizing the need for continual education and dialogue among researchers, ethicists, and the public to address these challenges effectively.

3.2.1 Overview and Evolution of GCP Guidelines

Good Clinical Practice (GCP) guidelines are a set of internationally recognized ethical and scientific quality standards for designing, conducting, recording, and reporting trials that involve the participation of human subjects. Compliance with these guidelines is crucial for ensuring that the rights, safety, and well-being of trial participants are protected, and that the data generated are credible and accurate.

Overview of GCP Guidelines

The core principles of GCP guidelines include the protection of human rights for the participants in clinical trials, the assurance of the integrity of scientific data, and the adherence to regulatory requirements. These guidelines are used globally by pharmaceutical companies, research institutions, and clinicians to ensure that the standards of clinical research are consistently high. GCP guidelines cover a broad range of considerations, including protocol development, trial design, ethical considerations, participant recruitment, informed consent, data handling, and reporting.

Evolution of GCP Guidelines

The evolution of GCP guidelines has been shaped by a series of declarations and regulations, each building upon the last to refine practices and respond to new ethical challenges and scientific advancements.

1. **Nuremberg Code (1947):** After World War II, the Nuremberg Code was established to address ethical misconduct in research. Although not directly a part of GCP, it laid the foundational ethical principles, such as voluntary consent and the requirement for prior animal work before human testing.
2. **Declaration of Helsinki (1964):** Developed by the World Medical Association, this was a significant step forward in creating ethical guidelines specifically for medical research involving human subjects. It emphasized informed consent, the risks versus benefits assessment, and the necessity for scientifically valid research protocols.
3. **Belmont Report (1979):** The Belmont Report further defined key ethical principles, which include respect for persons, beneficence, and justice. These principles have become integral to GCP guidelines.
4. **FDA Adoption of GCP (1980s):** The U.S. Food and Drug Administration (FDA) adopted GCP regulations that required all clinical trials in the U.S. seeking FDA approval for marketing to adhere to these guidelines. This marked a pivotal point in standardizing clinical research practices in the U.S.

5. **International Conference on Harmonisation (ICH) Guidelines for GCP (E6, 1996):** The ICH GCP guidelines were a milestone in harmonizing the regulatory requirements for clinical trials among Europe, Japan, and the US. These guidelines have been widely adopted globally and detail the responsibilities of all parties involved in clinical trials, including sponsors, investigators, and ethics committees.
6. **ISO 14155:2011 for Medical Device Trials:** This international standard addresses the requirements specific to clinical trials of medical devices. It emphasizes the clinical investigation plan, the ethical conduct of the trial, and the safety of subjects. It aligns with the principles of GCP and adapts them to the specific context of medical devices.

The evolution of GCP guidelines reflects the growing complexities and global nature of clinical research. As science advances, these guidelines are periodically revised and updated to address new ethical challenges, incorporate technological advancements, and improve the reliability and safety of clinical trial practices. This ongoing development ensures that GCP remains a dynamic tool, critical to the conduct of ethical and scientifically sound clinical research.

3.2.2 Key Principles and Objectives of GCP Guidelines

Good Clinical Practice (GCP) guidelines are central to the conduct of clinical research, ensuring that studies are designed, conducted, and reported in accordance with universally accepted ethical and scientific standards. These guidelines serve to protect the rights, safety, and well-being of trial participants, as well as to ensure the integrity and credibility of the data collected.

Key Principles of GCP Guidelines

1. **Rights, Safety, and Well-Being of Trial Subjects:** The foremost principle of GCP is to prioritize the rights, safety, and well-being of the trial subjects above all other considerations. This principle ensures that ethical and humanitarian concerns govern medical science and research.
2. **Informed Consent:** Each participant must be fully informed about the objectives, risks, benefits, and any alternative procedures available before participating in the trial. Informed consent must be obtained in writing before the person participates in the study, ensuring that it is given voluntarily, without any coercion.

3. **Scientific Validity:** All clinical trials must be scientifically justified and based on a thorough knowledge of the scientific literature. The research must follow a clear, detailed protocol that meets the standards of scientific integrity.
4. **Risk-Benefit Assessment:** Before any trial is conducted, there must be a careful assessment of risks and benefits, both known and potential. The expected benefits must justify the risks involved in the study.
5. **Independent Review:** GCP requires that an independent review board (IRB) or ethics committee (EC) review and approve the protocol and conduct of the trial to ensure compliance with ethical norms. This review helps safeguard the interests of the trial participants.
6. **Compliance with Regulations:** All clinical trials must be conducted in compliance with the regulatory requirements that govern the conduct of clinical research in the respective country or region.
7. **Qualified Personnel:** Everyone involved in conducting a clinical trial must be adequately qualified by education, training, and experience to perform their respective tasks.
8. **Accurate Record Keeping and Reporting:** GCP guidelines mandate that all clinical trial information and data be recorded, handled, and stored in a way that allows for accurate reporting, interpretation, and verification. This is essential for maintaining the integrity of the clinical trial data.
9. **Confidentiality:** The confidentiality of records that could identify subjects must be protected, respecting the privacy and confidentiality rules in accordance with the applicable regulatory requirements.
10. **Systems with Procedures that Assure Quality:** Every aspect of the trial should be supported by systems and procedures that operate according to the principle of quality assurance.

Objectives of GCP Guidelines

- **To Provide Assurance:** That the data and reported results are credible and accurate, and that the rights, integrity, and confidentiality of trial subjects are protected.
- **To Harmonize Regulations:** GCP aims to provide a single standard for the design, conduct, performance, monitoring, auditing, recording, analyses, and reporting of clinical trials. This helps to facilitate mutual acceptance of clinical data by regulatory authorities worldwide.

- **To Facilitate International Collaboration:** By standardizing ethical and scientific standards, GCP facilitates collaboration across borders, helping to streamline the process of drug and device approval across different countries.

The implementation of these principles ensures that clinical research is carried out in a way that respects all participants and generates reliable data, thereby contributing effectively to global health knowledge.

3.2.3 Application of GCP in Clinical Trials: Responsibilities of Investigators, Sponsors, and Monitors

Good Clinical Practice (GCP) guidelines outline specific responsibilities for key players in clinical trials, including investigators, sponsors, and monitors. These responsibilities ensure that the trials are conducted ethically and scientifically, and that data integrity and participant safety are maintained throughout the research process.

Responsibilities of Investigators

Investigators are primarily responsible for the conduct of the trial at the trial site. Their responsibilities include:

1. **Protecting the Rights and Welfare of Participants:** Ensuring that the trial is conducted ethically as per the approved protocol and that participants' rights, safety, and well-being are prioritized throughout the study.
2. **Informed Consent:** Ensuring that informed consent is obtained from each participant before their enrollment in the trial. This must be done in accordance with the GCP guidelines and the applicable regulatory requirements.
3. **Adherence to Protocol:** Conducting the study strictly in accordance with the trial protocol, and not deviating from it unless necessary to protect the safety, rights, or welfare of participants.
4. **Medical Care:** Providing medical care to participants for any adverse events, including those related to the trial, and making decisions about a participant's continued participation in the trial.
5. **Record Keeping and Documentation:** Maintaining accurate, complete, and timely records to document the trial procedures and results.

Responsibilities of Sponsors

Sponsors are usually pharmaceutical companies, academic institutions, or government agencies that initiate, manage, and finance the clinical trial. Their responsibilities include:

1. **Trial Management, Data Handling, and Record Keeping:** Ensuring that the trials are managed, the data handled, and the records kept as per the GCP guidelines to safeguard the accuracy and reliability of the trial results.
2. **Protocol Development:** Developing a detailed protocol for the conduct of the trial, including the rationale, objectives, design, methodology, statistical considerations, and organization.
3. **Safety Monitoring:** Implementing and maintaining systems for monitoring the safety of participants throughout the trial.
4. **Selection of Investigators and Sites:** Choosing qualified investigators and ensuring that they have adequate resources to properly conduct the trial.
5. **Ensuring Compliance:** Ensuring compliance with the regulatory requirements and GCP standards across all aspects of the trial.

Responsibilities of Monitors

Monitors are appointed by the sponsor and are tasked with overseeing the progress of a clinical trial. Their responsibilities include:

1. **Site Monitoring:** Regularly visiting the trial sites to ensure that the trial is being conducted according to the protocol and GCP guidelines.
2. **Verification of Data:** Ensuring that the data reported by investigators are accurate, complete, and verifiable from source documents.
3. **Communication:** Serving as the main line of communication between the sponsor and the site investigators.
4. **Reporting:** Reporting any deviations from the protocol or other issues at the trial site to the sponsor immediately.
5. **Ensuring Proper Informed Consent Procedures:** Checking that the informed consent process is being conducted properly and that all participants have provided consent before participating in the trial.

By fulfilling these responsibilities, investigators, sponsors, and monitors play crucial roles in ensuring that clinical trials are conducted in a manner that adheres to both ethical and scientific standards. This collaborative effort is essential for the success of clinical research, safeguarding participant welfare, and ensuring the validity and integrity of the data collected.

3.2.4 Compliance with GCP: Training, Documentation, and Audit Trails

Compliance with Good Clinical Practice (GCP) guidelines is essential for the conduct of clinical trials. It ensures that the data generated are reliable and that the rights, safety, and well-being of trial participants are protected. Key elements of GCP compliance include thorough training for all personnel involved in the trial, meticulous documentation practices, and the maintenance of robust audit trails.

Training

Training is a fundamental requirement under GCP to ensure that all personnel involved in a clinical trial are knowledgeable about the principles and practices of GCP, as well as their specific responsibilities within the trial. The aspects of training typically include:

1. **Initial and Ongoing Training:** All individuals involved in the trial must receive training prior to the commencement of the study and periodically as needed throughout the duration of the trial. This training often includes updates on new regulations or changes to existing guidelines.
2. **Role-Specific Training:** Training is tailored according to the roles of the personnel, ensuring that investigators, study coordinators, monitors, and other staff understand their specific duties and responsibilities.
3. **Documentation of Training:** It is crucial to document all training activities, including topics covered and the individuals trained, to provide evidence of compliance and readiness for audits.

Documentation

Accurate and thorough documentation is crucial in clinical trials to ensure traceability of actions, decisions, and data. This includes:

1. **Trial Protocol:** A detailed plan that describes the objective(s), design, methodology, statistical considerations, and organization of a trial.
2. **Informed Consent Forms:** Documentation that ensures all participants have been informed about the trial's risks, benefits, and alternatives, and have consented to participate.

3. **Case Report Forms (CRFs):** Standardized forms used to record data collected from each trial participant, which are submitted to the sponsor for analysis.
4. **Investigator's Brochure:** A compilation of the clinical and non-clinical data on the investigational product(s) that is relevant to the study of the product(s) in human subjects.

Audit Trails

An audit trail is a secure, computer-generated, time-stamped electronic record that allows the reconstruction and examination of the sequence of environments and activities surrounding or leading to each event in any electronic data record. Key considerations include:

1. **Creation and Maintenance:** Audit trails are created for actions related to clinical data (e.g., data changes, record access) to ensure that any data creation, modification, or deletion can be fully reconstructed.
2. **Security:** Access to audit trails must be controlled, and they must be preserved in a manner that protects them from unauthorized access or alterations.
3. **Inspection and Review:** Regular inspections and reviews of the audit trails are essential to ensure compliance with GCP and to identify and rectify any irregularities or deviations from the protocol.

Regulatory Inspections and Internal Audits

1. **Regulatory Inspections:** Regulatory authorities may conduct inspections to verify compliance with GCP and other regulations. These inspections can be planned or unannounced.
2. **Internal Audits:** Sponsors often conduct internal audits as part of their quality assurance procedures. These audits help to identify any non-compliance issues before regulatory inspections.

Compliance with GCP through effective training, meticulous documentation, and maintenance of audit trails ensures the reliability of trial results and the protection of trial participants. This comprehensive approach to compliance not only upholds ethical standards but also bolsters the scientific integrity of the clinical research.

3.2.5 Challenges and Limitations in Implementing GCP Guidelines

Implementing Good Clinical Practice (GCP) guidelines effectively across diverse clinical trial settings presents several challenges and limitations. These challenges stem from a variety of factors including regulatory diversity, resource limitations, and logistical complexities. Addressing these challenges is crucial for ensuring the integrity of clinical trials and the safety of participants.

Regulatory and Cultural Diversity

1. **Varying Regulatory Requirements:** GCP guidelines are intended to be international, but each country may have its own regulatory nuances. This diversity can create challenges for multinational trials where a one-size-fits-all approach may not work. Adapting protocols to meet different national regulations can be time-consuming and costly.
2. **Cultural Differences:** Cultural variations can affect participant recruitment, the informed consent process, and the implementation of protocols. For example, in some cultures, community leaders or family heads might need to be consulted as part of the consent process, which can complicate adherence to standard GCP procedures.

Resource Limitations

1. **Economic Constraints:** In resource-limited settings, the infrastructure may not be adequate to meet the high standards required by GCP. This includes limitations in technology, personnel, and facilities which can hinder the conduct of trials according to GCP standards.
2. **Training and Expertise:** Continuous training is essential for maintaining GCP compliance, but it can be a significant challenge in regions with a shortage of qualified trainers or limited access to training resources. Ensuring that all staff are up-to-date with GCP and related regulatory changes is critical but often difficult to achieve consistently.

Logistical and Operational Challenges

1. **Data Management:** Ensuring the integrity of clinical data in an environment of increasingly complex data collection and storage solutions is challenging. Effective implementation of GCP requires robust systems to manage, store, and verify large volumes of data, which may not always be available, especially in smaller or less-funded research

settings.

2. **Patient Recruitment and Retention:** Recruiting and retaining participants in compliance with GCP can be challenging, especially for trials that require long-term commitments or involve invasive procedures. Factors such as patient motivation, transportation issues, and socioeconomic factors can significantly impact participant retention.

Ethical Concerns

1. **Informed Consent:** Ensuring truly informed consent, especially in trials involving complex technologies or treatments, can be challenging. Participants must fully understand the implications of their involvement, which requires clear communication that can be impeded by language barriers, literacy levels, and medical jargon.
2. **Exploitation Risks:** There's a risk of exploiting vulnerable populations in clinical trials, especially in lower-income countries. Ensuring that trials are ethical and not just a means of easier regulatory pathways is a constant concern.

Adaptation to Emerging Technologies and Treatments

1. **Keeping Pace with Innovation:** As medical science advances rapidly, keeping regulatory standards and GCP guidelines up to date with emerging technologies and treatments can be challenging. This includes adapting guidelines to cover new areas like gene therapy, personalized medicine, and digital health interventions.

Solutions and Improvements

Addressing these challenges requires a multifaceted approach:

- **Global Collaboration:** Enhanced cooperation between regulatory bodies worldwide can help harmonize standards and share best practices.
- **Capacity Building:** Investing in infrastructure and training in under-resourced areas to improve compliance capabilities.
- **Adaptive Regulations:** Updating and refining GCP guidelines regularly to keep pace with scientific advancements and societal changes.

Overcoming the challenges in implementing GCP guidelines is essential for maintaining the integrity and effectiveness of clinical trials globally, ensuring that research outcomes are reliable and that participant rights are protected irrespective of geographic location.

3.2.6 Strategies for Ensuring GCP Compliance and Quality Assurance

Ensuring compliance with Good Clinical Practice (GCP) guidelines is critical for the success of clinical trials, safeguarding the rights and safety of participants, and ensuring the integrity of data. Various strategies can be employed by organizations and trial sponsors to enhance GCP compliance and overall quality assurance in clinical research.

Comprehensive Training Programs

1. **Regular Training and Re-certification:** Implementing regular and comprehensive GCP training for all staff involved in clinical trials is essential. This includes initial training for new employees and ongoing training to keep existing staff updated on any changes or updates in GCP guidelines and regulations.
2. **Role-Specific Training:** Tailoring training programs to specific roles within the clinical trial team ensures that each member understands their responsibilities and how they relate to GCP compliance.

Robust Quality Management Systems

1. **Standard Operating Procedures (SOPs):** Developing and maintaining detailed SOPs that align with GCP standards helps standardize processes across all trial sites and ensures consistency in how trials are conducted.
2. **Quality Control and Quality Assurance:** Implementing rigorous quality control measures and regular quality assurance audits ensures that clinical trial processes are continuously monitored and improved.

Effective Data Management Practices

1. **Secure and Compliant Data Systems:** Utilizing data management systems that comply with regulatory requirements for data protection and security helps prevent data breaches and ensures the integrity of trial data.
2. **Regular Data Monitoring:** Conducting regular monitoring visits and data audits to ensure accuracy and completeness of data collection, and

to verify that data are being managed according to the protocol and GCP.

Ethics and Independent Review

1. **Use of Independent Ethics Committees:** Ensuring that all clinical trial protocols are reviewed and approved by an independent ethics committee, which can provide an unbiased assessment of the trial's ethical considerations.
2. **Continuous Ethical Oversight:** Maintaining ongoing communication with ethics committees and responding promptly to any issues they raise during the trial.

Proactive Risk Management

1. **Risk Assessment:** Conducting thorough risk assessments during the planning stages of a trial and throughout its execution to identify potential risks to GCP compliance.
2. **Mitigation Strategies:** Developing strategies to mitigate identified risks, such as additional training, enhanced monitoring, or revising protocols.

Strengthening Investigator and Site Selection

1. **Thorough Vetting Process:** Carefully selecting investigators and clinical trial sites based on past performance, GCP compliance history, and the ability to meet the specific needs of the trial.
2. **Support and Oversight:** Providing ongoing support and oversight to trial sites to ensure they have the resources and knowledge necessary to comply with GCP guidelines.

Adherence to Regulatory Requirements

1. **Keeping Updated on Regulations:** Staying informed about current and emerging regulatory requirements and integrating these into training programs and trial protocols.
2. **Regulatory Liaison:** Establishing roles within the organization specifically designed to manage regulatory compliance and to act as a liaison with regulatory authorities.

By employing these strategies, organizations can enhance their GCP compliance, ensuring that clinical trials are conducted responsibly and effectively. This not only protects participants but also ensures the validity and reliability of the trial results, facilitating smoother regulatory approvals and advancements in healthcare.

3.3.1 Introduction to Quality System Regulations (QSR)

Quality System Regulations (QSR) are essential frameworks that govern the manufacturing processes, design, and distribution of medical devices. The goal of QSR is to ensure that medical devices are safe, effective, and of high quality. ISO 13485 is one of the key international standards for establishing a Quality Management System (QMS) for the medical device industry.

Overview of ISO 13485

ISO 13485 specifies requirements for a QMS where an organization needs to demonstrate its ability to provide medical devices and related services that consistently meet customer and applicable regulatory requirements. It is designed to be used by organizations involved in the design, production, installation, and servicing of medical devices and related services. Importantly, ISO 13485 is harmonized with the Quality System Regulation 21 CFR Part 820 of the U.S. Food and Drug Administration (FDA), making it widely accepted as a global standard.

Key Features of ISO 13485

1. **Customer Focus:** Ensuring that customer requirements are understood and met is a central focus of the standard, aligning with the broader goal of ensuring that medical devices meet user needs and intended uses.
2. **Leadership and Commitment:** The standard emphasizes the need for top management's commitment to the development and implementation of the QMS and continual improvement of its effectiveness.
3. **Risk Management:** ISO 13485 incorporates specific requirements for risk management throughout the product lifecycle, from design to delivery and post-market activities.
4. **Regulatory Requirements:** The standard requires that organizations meet applicable regulatory requirements for medical devices in the markets where they operate. This includes compliance with laws and regulations specific to medical device safety and performance.
5. **Resource Management:** ISO 13485 specifies the need for adequate resources, including human resources, specialized skills, infrastructure,

and work environment, to maintain the QMS and meet product and regulatory demands.

6. **Product Realization:** The standard outlines a detailed process for product realization, including planning, design, development, production, and delivery. This process ensures that the product consistently meets the requirements and is produced under controlled conditions.
7. **Measurement, Analysis, and Improvement:** ISO 13485 requires organizations to monitor, measure, analyze, and improve their processes to demonstrate conformity of the product, ensure conformity of the QMS, and ensure product safety and effectiveness.

Purpose and Benefits of Implementing ISO 13485

The implementation of ISO 13485 helps organizations align their processes with the stringent requirements of the medical device industry. Benefits include:

- **Enhanced Product Quality:** By adhering to standardized processes, companies can ensure higher quality products that are safer and more effective.
- **Increased Customer Trust:** Certification to ISO 13485 demonstrates a commitment to quality, which can increase trust from customers and end-users.
- **Regulatory Compliance:** Compliance with ISO 13485 can facilitate easier navigation of global regulatory requirements for medical devices, aiding in obtaining approvals from regulatory bodies.
- **Operational Efficiency:** By standardizing processes and focusing on quality, organizations can reduce costs through efficiencies and improved reliability of production processes.

3.3.2 Scope and Application of ISO 13485

ISO 13485 is designed to be a comprehensive Quality Management System (QMS) standard specifically for the medical device industry. Its scope and application are broad, covering various aspects of a medical device's lifecycle, from initial conception to delivery and post-market activities. This standard is applicable to organizations regardless of their size or type except where explicitly stated.

Scope of ISO 13485

ISO 13485 applies to organizations involved in one or more stages of the lifecycle of a medical device, including design and development, production, storage and distribution, installation, or servicing of a medical device, and the design and development or provision of associated activities (e.g., technical support). The standard can also be used by suppliers or external parties that provide product, including quality management system-related services to such organizations.

Key Areas Covered by ISO 13485

1. **Design and Development:** Ensuring that medical devices are designed and developed in a way that meets both regulatory requirements and customer needs.
2. **Production and Service Provision:** Managing and controlling the means of production and service provision in controlled conditions designed to ensure product quality and conformity to regulatory requirements.
3. **Customer and Regulatory Requirements:** Ensuring continuous compliance with customer needs and the stringent regulatory requirements applicable in the medical device industry.
4. **Risk Management:** Emphasizing the importance of risk management in the medical device field and integrating specific requirements for risk analysis throughout the product realization processes.

Application of ISO 13485

The application of ISO 13485 is intended to be flexible and can be tailored to the nature of the medical device, the size and structure of the organization, and the regulatory environment. Here's how different types of organizations might use ISO 13485:

1. **Medical Device Manufacturers:** For manufacturers, ISO 13485 is often a regulatory requirement. Implementing ISO 13485 helps in ensuring consistent design, development, production, installation, and delivery of medical devices that are safe and perform as intended.
2. **Suppliers and External Parties:** Suppliers of materials, components, or services related to the quality management system can adopt ISO 13485 to align their operations with the quality requirements of the medical device manufacturers they serve.
3. **Subcontractors and Partners:** Organizations that perform work on behalf of medical device companies can implement ISO 13485 to ensure

their processes meet the necessary quality standards.

4. **Regulatory Bodies and Certifiers:** These entities use ISO 13485 to assess an organization's ability to meet the standard's requirements and to ensure consistent regulatory compliance.

Benefits of Applying ISO 13485

- **Facilitates Market Access:** Compliance with ISO 13485 is often seen as a first step towards complying with regulatory requirements in various countries, facilitating global market access for medical device products.
- **Enhances Organizational Efficiency:** By standardizing processes and emphasizing quality control, ISO 13485 can lead to improvements in efficiency and consistency, reducing errors and increasing profitability.
- **Improves Product Quality and Safety:** The standard helps ensure that medical devices are consistently produced and controlled according to high quality standards, enhancing their safety and performance.
- **Builds Credibility with Stakeholders:** Achieving ISO 13485 certification can enhance an organization's credibility with regulatory authorities, suppliers, and customers by demonstrating a commitment to quality and safety.

3.3.3 Structure and Requirements of ISO 13485: Documentation, Management Responsibility, Resource Management, Product Realization, and Measurement, Analysis, and Improvement

ISO 13485 outlines a framework for a Quality Management System (QMS) specific to the medical device industry. This standard is structured to ensure comprehensive management of all aspects of design, development, production, and delivery of medical devices. The structure includes specific requirements in areas such as documentation, management responsibility, resource management, product realization, and measurement, analysis, and improvement.

Documentation

1. **General Documentation Requirements:** Organizations must establish and maintain a QMS documentation system that includes quality policy and objectives, a quality manual, documented procedures and records, and documents necessary for the planning, operation, and control of processes.

2. **Control of Documents:** Documents required by the QMS must be controlled. Revisions must be reviewed and approved by appropriate personnel. The organization must ensure documents remain legible, readily identifiable, and retrievable.
3. **Control of Records:** Records must be established and maintained to provide evidence of conformity to requirements and the effective operation of the QMS. Records must be legible, identifiable, and retrievable.

Management Responsibility

1. **Management Commitment:** Top management must demonstrate their commitment to the development and implementation of the QMS and the continual improvement of its effectiveness.
2. **Customer Focus:** Management must ensure that customer requirements are determined and met, aiming to enhance customer satisfaction.
3. **Quality Policy and Planning:** Organizations must define a quality policy that is appropriate to the purpose of the organization, and commit to meeting applicable regulatory and customer requirements. Quality objectives must be set and quality planning must be carried out to ensure the maintenance of the QMS.
4. **Responsibility and Authority:** Clear responsibilities and authorities must be defined and communicated within the organization.
5. **Management Review:** Top management must periodically review the QMS to ensure its continuing suitability, adequacy, effectiveness, and alignment with the strategic direction of the organization.

Resource Management

1. **Provision of Resources:** Adequate resources, including human resources, infrastructure, and work environment, must be provided to implement and maintain the QMS and to support the design, development, production, and delivery of medical devices.
2. **Human Resources:** Personnel performing work affecting product quality must be competent based on appropriate education, training, skills, and experience.
3. **Infrastructure and Work Environment:** The organization must manage the infrastructure (buildings, workspace, associated utilities, equipment)

and work environment needed to achieve conformity to product requirements.

Product Realization

1. **Planning of Product Realization:** Organizations must plan and develop the processes needed for product realization, including setting quality objectives and requirements for the product.
2. **Design and Development:** There must be systematic controls in the stages of design and development, including planning, inputs, outputs, review, verification, and validation.
3. **Purchasing:** The organization must ensure that purchased products conform to specified purchase requirements. The type and extent of control applied to suppliers and purchased products must be dependent on the effect of the purchased product on subsequent product realization or the final product.
4. **Production and Service Provision:** Production and service provision must be controlled, and must include the availability of information that describes the characteristics of the product, the availability of work instructions, the use of suitable equipment, and the monitoring and control of suitable process parameters and product characteristics.

Measurement, Analysis, and Improvement

1. **Monitoring and Measurement:** Methods for monitoring and measuring the QMS performance and the product must be defined. This includes feedback mechanisms, internal audits, and monitoring of production and service processes.
2. **Control of Nonconforming Product:** The organization must ensure that product which does not conform to product requirements is identified and controlled to prevent unintended use or delivery.
3. **Analysis of Data:** Data derived from monitoring and measurement must be analyzed to demonstrate the suitability and effectiveness of the QMS.
4. **Improvement:** The organization must continually improve the effectiveness of the QMS through the use of quality policy, quality objectives, audit results, analysis of data, corrective and preventive actions, and management review.

Implementing these structured requirements of ISO 13485 ensures that medical devices are produced in accordance with the highest standards, aligning with regulatory requirements and meeting customer expectations. This systematic approach to quality management facilitates the achievement of consistency, effectiveness, and efficiency in the production of safe and reliable medical devices.

3.3.5 Benefits of ISO 13485 Certification: Improving Product Quality and Regulatory Compliance

ISO 13485 certification provides numerous benefits for organizations involved in the design, manufacture, and distribution of medical devices. The standard is globally recognized and specifically designed to promote best practices in quality management systems and ensure compliance with regulatory requirements. The primary benefits focus on enhancing product quality and facilitating regulatory compliance, which are critical factors in the medical device industry.

Improving Product Quality

1. **Consistent Quality Standards:** ISO 13485 provides a framework for establishing quality management processes that ensure consistency in the design, development, and production of medical devices. This consistency helps in reducing the likelihood of product defects or failures, which can be costly and damaging to the reputation of the company.
2. **Enhanced Product Reliability:** By adhering to stringent quality management practices, companies can enhance the reliability of their medical devices. Reliable products perform as expected in clinical settings, which is crucial for the safety and well-being of patients.
3. **Customer Satisfaction:** Improved product quality directly contributes to higher customer satisfaction. Medical devices that meet high-quality standards are less likely to cause complications or require recalls, thus enhancing customer trust and satisfaction.
4. **Competitive Advantage:** High product quality can differentiate a manufacturer in the competitive medical device market. ISO 13485 certification can provide a competitive edge by demonstrating a commitment to quality to customers and stakeholders.

Facilitating Regulatory Compliance

1. **Streamlined Compliance Processes:** ISO 13485 is aligned with global regulatory requirements, including those set by the European Union, the United States Food and Drug Administration (FDA), and other regulatory bodies. This alignment helps streamline compliance processes, making it easier for companies to meet diverse regulatory requirements across different markets.
2. **Smoother Market Entry:** Certification to ISO 13485 is often a prerequisite or a favorable factor in product approvals and market access in various countries. This can expedite the regulatory approval process and facilitate smoother entry into new markets.
3. **Reduced Legal and Regulatory Risks:** By ensuring compliance with recognized standards, ISO 13485 certification helps reduce the risk of legal issues and regulatory sanctions. This can protect companies from costly litigation and fines, as well as damage to reputation.
4. **Audit Preparedness:** Regular audits required for ISO 13485 certification ensure that the company is always prepared for external audits by regulatory bodies. This ongoing readiness can reduce the stress and disruption typically associated with compliance inspections.

Operational Improvements

1. **Increased Efficiency and Cost Savings:** ISO 13485 encourages organizations to optimize their production processes and improve efficiency. This can lead to significant cost savings by reducing waste, minimizing errors, and decreasing the need for rework.
2. **Employee Engagement and Training:** The standard emphasizes the importance of adequate training and the involvement of employees in quality management processes. This can lead to better employee engagement, improved morale, and increased productivity.
3. **Continuous Improvement:** ISO 13485 establishes a framework for continuous improvement, encouraging companies to constantly seek ways to enhance their quality management systems, processes, and outcomes. This focus on continuous improvement drives innovation and helps companies adapt to changes in technology and market demands.

3.3.6 Continuous Improvement and Maintenance of ISO 13485 Certification

Achieving ISO 13485 certification is not just about meeting a set of criteria at a particular point in time; it's about committing to an ongoing process of improvement that ensures the quality management system (QMS) continually evolves and improves. This continuous improvement is crucial for maintaining certification and for ensuring that the processes remain effective and efficient in producing high-quality medical devices.

Key Strategies for Continuous Improvement

1. **Internal Audits:** Regular internal audits are vital for assessing the QMS against the ISO 13485 standards. These audits help identify areas for improvement and ensure compliance with the established procedures. They also prepare the organization for external audits by regulatory authorities.
2. **Management Reviews:** Top management should regularly review the performance of the QMS to ensure its continuing suitability, adequacy, and effectiveness. These reviews should be based on input from various data sources, including audit results, customer feedback, and process performance.
3. **Corrective and Preventive Actions (CAPA):** An effective CAPA system is essential for addressing non-conformities and potential non-conformities. This system should be proactive, aiming not only to correct issues but to prevent their recurrence by addressing the root cause.
4. **Training and Development:** Ongoing training and development programs for employees are critical in maintaining a high level of competency and ensuring that all personnel are aware of the latest quality requirements and techniques.
5. **Supplier Management:** Continuously monitoring and evaluating suppliers to ensure they meet the required quality standards is crucial. This may involve regular audits and assessments of suppliers' processes and output.
6. **Customer Feedback and Complaint Handling:** Actively seeking, monitoring, and analyzing customer feedback and complaints can provide insights into areas needing improvement and help in assessing the effectiveness of the QMS.

Maintenance of ISO 13485 Certification

1. **Surveillance Audits:** Certification bodies conduct periodic surveillance audits to ensure ongoing compliance with ISO 13485 standards. These audits are typically annual and are essential for the maintenance of certification.
2. **Recertification:** Every three years, a full recertification audit is conducted to reevaluate the entire quality management system. This comprehensive audit ensures that the QMS is still suitable and effective for the organization's operations and objectives.
3. **Documentation Updates:** Keeping documentation up to date is critical in the maintenance of ISO 13485 certification. This includes updating the quality manual, policies, procedures, and records to reflect any changes in processes or organizational structure.
4. **Continuous Process Improvement:** Employing methodologies like Six Sigma, Lean Manufacturing, or Total Quality Management can help in making continuous improvements in processes, thereby enhancing the efficiency and effectiveness of the QMS.
5. **Technology and Innovation:** Integrating new technologies and innovations can improve the efficiency of processes and the quality of products. It's important to evaluate and incorporate such advancements regularly within the QMS framework.

Benefits of Continuous Improvement

- **Ensures Compliance:** Continuous improvement helps ensure that the organization remains in compliance with ISO 13485 standards and applicable regulatory requirements.
- **Enhances Product Quality:** Regular updates and improvements in processes contribute to enhanced product quality and reliability.
- **Increases Customer Satisfaction:** Improvements in the system often lead to better products and services, enhancing customer satisfaction and loyalty.
- **Fosters a Culture of Quality:** Continuous improvement instills a culture of quality throughout the organization, where every employee plays a part in maintaining high standards.

Continual improvement is not just a requirement for maintaining ISO 13485 certification; it is also a business strategy that drives the organization towards greater operational excellence, customer satisfaction, and regulatory compliance. This proactive approach ensures that a company not only maintains its ISO 13485 certification but also remains competitive and successful in the medical device industry.

3.4.1 Overview of Risk Management in the Medical Device Industry

Risk management is a crucial aspect of the medical device industry, serving as a systematic process to identify, evaluate, and mitigate risks associated with medical devices throughout their lifecycle. This process is essential not only for ensuring patient and user safety but also for complying with regulatory requirements and supporting the effectiveness and reliability of medical devices.

Importance of Risk Management

The primary goal of risk management in the medical device industry is to maximize the safety and efficacy of devices while minimizing adverse outcomes. This is achieved by identifying potential hazards associated with the use of the device, assessing the likelihood and potential severity of harm, and implementing appropriate control measures. Effective risk management ensures that:

- **Patient Safety:** By identifying and mitigating risks early in the device lifecycle, manufacturers can prevent harm to patients and users.
- **Regulatory Compliance:** Regulatory bodies worldwide require comprehensive risk management as part of the regulatory approval process for medical devices. Compliance with standards like ISO 14971 is often mandatory.
- **Product Quality:** Systematic risk management contributes to the overall quality of medical devices, ensuring that they perform as intended without causing undue risk to patients.
- **Brand Reputation:** Effective risk management helps maintain and enhance the manufacturer's reputation by demonstrating a commitment to safety and quality.

ISO 14971: The Standard for Risk Management

ISO 14971 is the international standard specifically designed for risk management in the medical device industry. It provides a thorough framework for manufacturers to identify risks, evaluate their impact, control them appropriately, and monitor the effectiveness of the controls. Key elements of ISO 14971 include:

1. **Risk Analysis:** During this phase, the manufacturer identifies hazards associated with the medical device, estimates and evaluates the associated risks, and considers the potential impact on patients and users.
2. **Risk Evaluation:** This process involves determining which risks are acceptable and which are not, based on the estimated risk and its comparison against the manufacturer's risk acceptability criteria.
3. **Risk Control:** Once risks have been identified and evaluated, appropriate measures are implemented to mitigate them. This might include changes in design, manufacturing processes, labeling, or the inclusion of safety features.
4. **Evaluation of Overall Residual Risk:** After risk control measures are applied, the overall residual risk is evaluated to determine if it is within acceptable limits.
5. **Risk Management Report:** This document is prepared to summarize the risk analysis, evaluation, and control processes, including a statement declaring the residual risk as acceptable.
6. **Production and Post-Production Information:** The manufacturer must monitor and review the safety of the medical device during its production and post-production phases to ensure continued safety and efficacy, and to identify any need for further risk control.

Integrating Risk Management Across the Device Lifecycle

For effective risk management, it's important that the process is not viewed as a one-time task but as a continuous activity throughout the entire lifecycle of the medical device. This includes:

- **Design and Development:** Integrating risk management early in the design process helps in identifying and mitigating risks before the device goes into production.
- **Manufacturing:** During manufacturing, continuous risk assessments can help in identifying new risks related to production processes or materials.
- **Post-Market Surveillance:** After the device is marketed, ongoing monitoring and reporting of any issues can help in identifying unexpected risks and taking corrective actions.

By adhering to ISO 14971 and integrating risk management throughout the lifecycle of a medical device, manufacturers can not only ensure compliance with global regulatory requirements but also significantly enhance the safety and efficacy of their products, ultimately benefiting both users and patients.

3.4.2 Principles and Framework of ISO 14971

ISO 14971 is the internationally recognized standard for risk management specifically tailored to medical devices. This standard outlines a comprehensive framework and principles for managing risks associated with medical device design, manufacture, and deployment, aiming to ensure the highest level of safety for users and patients. Understanding the principles and framework of ISO 14971 is crucial for manufacturers to effectively manage risks throughout a medical device's lifecycle.

Core Principles of ISO 14971

1. **Risk Management as an Ongoing Process:** Risk management is an integral part of the medical device lifecycle and should be conducted continuously from conception through post-market activities. It is not a one-time task but a dynamic process that evolves with the development of the medical device and its introduction to the market.
2. **Proactive Risk Identification:** Proactive risk identification involves anticipating potential risks before they manifest as actual problems. This proactive approach helps in implementing preventive measures early, significantly reducing the likelihood and impact of adverse events.
3. **Systematic Risk Analysis:** Risk analysis in ISO 14971 is systematic, structured, and comprehensive. It requires the identification and analysis of possible hazards associated with a medical device, the situations in which harm can occur, and the probable severity and probability of such harm.
4. **Risk Evaluation and Control:** Once risks are analyzed, they must be evaluated to determine their acceptability. Unacceptable risks must be mitigated through effective control measures. The principle of 'as low as reasonably practicable' (ALARP) is applied to minimize risks while considering technological options and economic considerations.
5. **Informed Decision-Making:** Decisions regarding risk acceptability and the suitability of risk control measures should be based on evidence and informed judgment. This involves balancing risk against the benefit of the medical device's intended use.

6. **Documentation and Record-Keeping:** Maintaining comprehensive documentation of all risk management activities is a fundamental requirement of ISO 14971. This documentation serves as a record of compliance and is crucial for ongoing risk assessment and regulatory scrutiny.

Framework of ISO 14971

The framework provided by ISO 14971 for risk management can be broken down into several key stages:

1. **Risk Management Plan:** Before starting the risk management process, a risk management plan must be established. This plan outlines the risk management activities, roles, responsibilities, and criteria for risk acceptability throughout the product lifecycle.
2. **Risk Assessment:** This includes:

- **Risk Analysis:** Identifying potential hazards and estimating the associated risks.
- **Risk Evaluation:** Determining whether the analyzed risks exceed acceptable levels.

1. **Risk Control:** Implementing measures to mitigate or eliminate risks. This includes selecting control options based on their ability to reduce risk and evaluating their effectiveness once implemented.
2. **Evaluation of Overall Residual Risk:** After applying risk control measures, an evaluation of the overall residual risk is conducted to ensure that it is within acceptable limits.
3. **Risk Management Report:** A comprehensive report documenting the risk analysis, evaluation, control measures, and overall residual risk assessment.
4. **Production and Post-Production Activities:** Monitoring the device during production and post-market phases to identify previously unrecognized risks or to confirm risk estimations.

The structured approach of ISO 14971 ensures that all potential risks are adequately managed and that the medical device is as safe as possible for its intended use. This framework not only aids manufacturers in achieving compliance with regulatory requirements but also supports the creation of safer medical devices, ultimately enhancing patient and user safety.

3.4.3 Risk Management Process: Risk Analysis, Evaluation, Control, and Monitoring

The risk management process outlined in ISO 14971 is a comprehensive approach designed to ensure the safety and efficacy of medical devices throughout their lifecycle. This process is structured into several key phases: risk analysis, risk evaluation, risk control, and risk monitoring. Each phase plays a crucial role in identifying, assessing, mitigating, and monitoring risks associated with medical devices.

Risk Analysis

Purpose: The primary objective of risk analysis is to identify potential sources of harm associated with the medical device and to estimate the associated risks.

Steps:

1. **Hazard Identification:** Identify any possible hazards that could result from the use of the medical device in its intended environment. Hazards could be biological, chemical, mechanical, electrical, or derived from software anomalies.
2. **Estimation of Risk:** For each identified hazard, estimate the potential severity of harm and the likelihood of its occurrence. This involves considering both the normal use and any foreseeable misuse of the device.

Risk Evaluation

Purpose: To assess the risks identified during the risk analysis phase and determine their acceptability based on predefined criteria.

Process:

1. **Compare Against Acceptability Criteria:** Each risk is compared against the risk acceptability criteria established in the risk management plan.
2. **Decision Making:** Decide if risk reduction is required based on the evaluation. Risks that exceed acceptable levels must be addressed through risk control measures.

Risk Control

Purpose: To implement measures that can eliminate or reduce unacceptable risks to an acceptable level.

Steps:

1. **Option Analysis:** Identify potential risk control options which could include design changes, protective measures in the medical device itself or in the manufacturing process, and information for safety in user instructions.
2. **Implementation of Controls:** Apply the most appropriate control measures. This might involve multiple layers of controls to address a single risk.
3. **Residual Risk Evaluation:** Assess the remaining risk after control measures have been implemented. If residual risk is still not acceptable, further measures may need to be considered.

Risk Monitoring

Purpose: Ongoing monitoring of the risk management process to ensure the effectiveness of the controls and to identify any new risks as medical devices are produced and used.

Activities:

1. **Post-Production Surveillance:** Continuously monitor the performance of the medical device after it reaches the market to gather data that could identify previously unrecognized risks or validate risk assumptions made during the development process.
2. **Feedback Mechanisms:** Implement mechanisms to receive feedback from all stakeholders, including patients, healthcare providers, and regulatory bodies. This feedback is crucial for detecting issues early and initiating corrective actions.
3. **Review and Update Risk Management:** Regularly review the risk management process and update it based on new findings or changes in standards or regulatory requirements. This review should consider whether existing risk control measures are still adequate and whether new risks have emerged.

The iterative nature of this process ensures that risk management is a dynamic part of the medical device lifecycle, adapting to new information and technologies. By systematically analyzing, evaluating, controlling, and monitoring risks, manufacturers can ensure that their products meet the highest safety standards and comply with regulatory requirements, thus safeguarding both the user and patient communities.

3.4.5 Risk Management Tools and Techniques

In the context of ISO 14971 and the broader field of medical device risk management, several tools and techniques are employed to effectively identify, analyze, and manage risks. These tools are essential for systematic risk assessment and for ensuring that medical devices are safe for their intended use. Here's an overview of some of the most commonly used risk management tools and techniques in the medical device industry.

1. Failure Mode and Effects Analysis (FMEA)

Description: FMEA is a systematic, step-by-step approach for identifying all possible failures in a design, a manufacturing or assembly process, or a product or service.

- **Purpose:** It's used to identify potential failure modes, determine their effect on the operation of the product, and identify actions to mitigate the failures.
- **Process:** Involves listing each component in a system, identifying failure modes for each component, determining their effects on the system, and classifying the severity and likelihood of each failure.

2. Fault Tree Analysis (FTA)

Description: FTA is a top-down, deductive failure analysis in which an undesired state of a system is analyzed using Boolean logic to combine a series of lower-level events.

- **Purpose:** This tool is particularly useful in understanding the logic leading to the top event and provides a method to quantify the probability of the occurrence.
- **Process:** Starts with a specific failure or event and works backwards to deduce the causes and interactions leading to the failure.

3. Hazard Analysis and Critical Control Points (HACCP)

Description: HACCP is a systematic preventive approach to food safety, but it has also been adapted for use in risk management of medical devices, particularly those that come into contact with biological systems.

- **Purpose:** To identify potential hazards and install critical control points at phases in the production or sterilization process where such hazards can be controlled or eliminated.

- **Process:** Involves identifying potential hazards, determining critical control points where controls can be applied, and monitoring these control points to ensure continued efficacy.

4. Risk Matrix

Description: A risk matrix is a matrix that is used during risk assessment to define the level of risk by considering the category of probability or likelihood against the category of consequence severity.

- **Purpose:** It's a quick and effective tool to prioritize the risk management efforts by highlighting which risks have the most severe impact and the highest likelihood of occurring.
- **Process:** Risks are plotted in the matrix, allowing for visualization of the severity and likelihood of risks, aiding in the decision-making process on which risks to manage first.

5. Root Cause Analysis (RCA)

Description: RCA is a method of problem solving aimed at identifying the root causes of faults or problems.

- **Purpose:** To dig into the underlying reasons for a defect or problem rather than just dealing with the immediate symptoms.
- **Process:** Involves identifying the initial problem, defining the problem in detail, identifying potential causes, analyzing the causes, and determining the root cause.

6. Clinical Risk Management (CRM)

Description: CRM specifically pertains to the identification, evaluation, and management of risks associated with the clinical use of medical devices.

- **Purpose:** To ensure that medical devices perform as intended in clinical environments without causing undue risk to patients.
- **Process:** Involves the application of standard risk management procedures but focused on the clinical interface, such as user handling, device interaction with other medical equipment, and variability in patient populations.

These tools and techniques, when used effectively, enable medical device manufacturers to fulfill their regulatory obligations under ISO 14971 and enhance the safety and effectiveness of their products. Each tool serves a specific purpose and, in many cases, is used in conjunction with others to provide a comprehensive approach to risk management.

3.4.6 Challenges and Best Practices in Implementing ISO 14971

Implementing ISO 14971, the standard for risk management in the medical device industry, involves numerous challenges. However, understanding and addressing these challenges effectively can significantly enhance the risk management process. Here are some common challenges faced by organizations and the best practices that can help overcome these obstacles.

Challenges in Implementing ISO 14971

1. **Complexity of Medical Devices:**
    - Medical devices can be highly complex, integrating advanced technologies and multiple functions, which can complicate the risk analysis process.
2. **Dynamic Regulatory Requirements:**
    - Regulations can vary significantly across different regions and are subject to change, making compliance an ongoing challenge.
3. **Identification of All Potential Risks:**
    - Given the variety of use cases and the diverse environments in which devices operate, identifying all potential risks can be daunting.
4. **Balancing Risk and Innovation:**
    - Innovating while ensuring that risks are minimized poses a significant challenge, especially with cutting-edge technologies.
5. **Integration with Quality Management Systems:**

- Fully integrating risk management processes into existing quality management systems can be complex and resource-intensive.

Best Practices for Effective Implementation of ISO 14971

1. **Thorough Training and Competence Building:**
   - Ensure that all team members involved in design, development, and quality assurance are thoroughly trained in risk management principles and ISO 14971 requirements.
   - Regular training sessions and updates can help keep everyone aware of their roles and responsibilities in managing risk.

2. **Comprehensive Risk Management Plan:**
   - Develop a comprehensive risk management plan that outlines specific processes, methodologies, and tools to be used for risk management activities.
   - Clearly define roles, responsibilities, and the timeline for risk management activities.

3. **Systematic and Iterative Risk Assessment:**
   - Use systematic tools such as FMEA, FTA, and risk matrices to identify and analyze risks comprehensively.
   - Treat risk management as an iterative process that evolves with the product development lifecycle.

4. **Stakeholder Engagement and Feedback:**
   - Engage with all stakeholders, including clinicians, patients, and regulatory bodies, to gain insights into potential risks from different perspectives.
   - Incorporate feedback mechanisms to capture real-world data on device performance and safety.

5. **Integration with Quality Management:**

- Integrate risk management processes with the organization's quality management system (QMS) to streamline activities and ensure consistency.
- Utilize common tools and documentation systems to facilitate integration and compliance tracking.

6. **Proactive Post-Market Surveillance:**

    - Implement robust post-market surveillance systems to monitor the safety and effectiveness of medical devices after they have been deployed.
    - Use real-world data to continuously update risk assessments and improve device design and function.

7. **Documentation and Traceability:**

    - Maintain detailed documentation of all risk management activities, including decisions made, the rationale for decisions, and actions taken.
    - Ensure traceability throughout the documentation to facilitate audits and regulatory reviews.

8. **Regular Reviews and Updates:**

    - Schedule regular reviews of the risk management process to ensure its effectiveness and compliance with ISO 14971.
    - Update risk management practices as new information becomes available or as technologies evolve.

By addressing these challenges through best practices, organizations can enhance the effectiveness of their risk management efforts, ensuring that medical devices are as safe as possible and compliant with both ISO 14971 and regulatory requirements. This proactive approach not only protects patients but also builds trust in the medical device market, ultimately contributing to the success and sustainability of medical device companies.

3.5.2 Types of Validation and Verification: Design, Process, and Software Validation

In the realm of medical device manufacturing, validation and verification are critical processes that ensure devices meet all specified requirements and are safe for intended use. These processes are categorized into design validation, process validation, and software validation. Each type has specific purposes and methodologies, which are crucial for compliance with regulatory standards and achieving functional and safety objectives.

Design Validation

Purpose: Design validation ensures that the device conforms to defined user needs and intended uses, and it is typically performed under actual or simulated use conditions.

Process:

- **Testing:** Conduct tests using actual or simulated use conditions to confirm that the design meets all user and product requirements.
- **Clinical Trials:** In some cases, clinical trials may be part of design validation to ensure the device performs safely and effectively in real-world scenarios.
- **User Feedback:** Collecting and incorporating feedback from actual device users (like healthcare professionals) can be a crucial part of this validation.

Outcome: Ensures the product meets the needs of the user and the intended performance in real-world settings.

Process Validation

Purpose: Process validation verifies that the manufacturing process consistently produces a product that meets its predetermined specifications and quality attributes.

Types:

1. **Installation Qualification (IQ):** Verifies that the equipment and ancillary systems are installed to the manufacturer's original specification.
2. **Operational Qualification (OQ):** Ensures that the equipment operates according to its operational specifications in the selected environment.
3. **Performance Qualification (PQ):** Confirms that the equipment consistently produces a product meeting its predetermined quality attributes and specifications under actual production conditions.

Process:

- **Validation Master Plan:** Create a plan that outlines the areas to be tested and the methodologies to be used.
- **Documentation:** Detailed documentation is crucial to validate that the process is performing within its determined parameters.
- **Statistical Methods:** Employ statistical methods to analyze process variation and ensure consistency.

Outcome: Guarantees that the device is manufactured in a reproducible manner that meets all design specifications and quality requirements.

Software Validation

Purpose: Software validation ensures that device software functions correctly and meets all specified requirements. This is critical for devices that depend on embedded software or are software-controlled.

Process:

- **Static Analysis:** Involves reviewing the software code without executing it to find vulnerabilities.
- **Dynamic Analysis:** Tests the software's functionality during execution, which can include unit testing, integration testing, and system testing.
- **Usability Testing:** Particularly important for user-interface-heavy software to ensure that the software can be used effectively and safely in its intended environment.

Outcome: Ensures that the software within a medical device functions safely, consistently, and as intended under all anticipated conditions of use.

Best Practices for Validation and Verification

- **Early Integration:** Integrate validation and verification processes early in the design phase to identify and address potential issues before they become more complex and costly to solve.
- **Comprehensive Documentation:** Maintain thorough documentation for all validation and verification activities to ensure traceability and regulatory compliance.
- **Regular Updates:** Regularly review and update validation and verification procedures to incorporate new regulatory requirements, technological advancements, or changes in user needs.

Implementing robust validation and verification processes not only fulfills regulatory requirements but also enhances product reliability and safety, ultimately contributing to greater customer satisfaction and trust in the medical device market.

3.5.3 Regulatory Requirements for Validation and Verification

Validation and verification (V&V) processes are critical components in the development and manufacturing of medical devices. These processes ensure that devices meet all specified requirements for performance, safety, and reliability. Regulatory bodies around the world have established specific requirements for V&V to ensure that medical devices are safe and effective for their intended uses. Understanding these regulatory requirements is essential for compliance and successful market entry.

Key Regulatory Bodies and Their Requirements

1. **U.S. Food and Drug Administration (FDA)**

    - **Guidance on Validation and Verification:** The FDA requires comprehensive V&V as part of the device premarket submission (510(k), PMA). Validation must demonstrate that the device conforms to defined user needs and intended uses, while verification confirms that it meets specified design requirements.
    - **Design Controls:** Under 21 CFR Part 820, the FDA outlines specific design controls that must include both validation and verification activities. Design validation must include clinical evaluations or simulated use where appropriate.

2. **European Union (MDD/MDR)**

    - **CE Marking Requirements:** The Medical Device Regulation (MDR) in the EU emphasizes the necessity of V&V in achieving CE marking. The processes must demonstrate that the device meets essential health and safety requirements.
    - **Technical Documentation:** Manufacturers need to prepare and maintain technical documentation that details V&V processes. This documentation must demonstrate that the design and production of the device comply with the requirements of the MDR.

3. **International Organization for Standardization (ISO)**

- **ISO 13485:** This standard specifies requirements for a quality management system where an organization needs to demonstrate its ability to provide medical devices and related services that consistently meet customer and applicable regulatory requirements. It includes specific clauses on validation, verification, and design transfer.

Specific Requirements for Validation and Verification

- **Design Validation:** Must be performed under actual or simulated use conditions. It must include software validation if applicable and risk analysis. Clinical evaluations are often required.
- **Process Validation:** This includes Installation Qualification (IQ), Operational Qualification (OQ), and Performance Qualification (PQ), especially for production processes that cannot be fully verified by subsequent inspection and testing of the product.
- **Software Verification and Validation:** For devices containing software, regulatory guidelines require specific V&V activities to ensure that software specifications meet user needs and intended uses. It includes static and dynamic testing, as well as environment and usability testing.

Best Practices for Meeting Regulatory Requirements

1. **Early Planning:** Integrate V&V planning early in the development process to align the design activities with regulatory expectations.
2. **Documentation:** Maintain rigorous documentation for all V&V activities. This includes detailed records of test results, methods used, and how the outcomes demonstrate compliance with user needs and regulatory requirements.
3. **Standards Compliance:** Adhere to relevant standards (e.g., ISO 13485, ISO 14971 for risk management) to streamline compliance with regulatory requirements.
4. **Continuous Updates:** Stay updated with changes in regulatory guidelines and standards in all target markets. Regular training and updates can help ensure compliance and prepare for regulatory inspections or audits.

Adhering to these regulatory requirements is not just about achieving market authorization; it's also about ensuring the safety and efficacy of medical devices throughout their lifecycle. Effective validation and verification are essential for manufacturers to gain the confidence of both regulators and users, ensuring successful deployment and sustained use of their medical devices.

3.5.4 Validation and Verification Protocols and Documentation

Validation and verification (V&V) are critical processes in the lifecycle of a medical device, ensuring that it meets the necessary safety, efficacy, and quality requirements. The development of thorough V&V protocols and the maintenance of comprehensive documentation are essential components of these processes. These documents not only support regulatory submissions but also serve as a reference throughout the product lifecycle for maintaining compliance and facilitating improvements.

Validation and Verification Protocols

Purpose of Protocols: Protocols are detailed plans that describe the objectives, methods, materials, and setups for conducting validation and verification activities. They are crucial for ensuring that V&V activities are executed consistently and that results are reproducible and reliable.

Key Elements of V&V Protocols:

1. **Objective:** Clearly define the purpose of the validation or verification. This includes detailing what is being tested and why.
2. **Scope:** Outline the extent of the activities, including the specific aspects of the device or process that will be tested.
3. **Responsibilities:** Assign roles and responsibilities to team members involved in the V&V processes.
4. **Methodology:** Describe the methods and procedures for conducting the tests. This includes the setup, the equipment to be used, how tests will be conducted, and how data will be collected.
5. **Acceptance Criteria:** Define clear, measurable criteria for what constitutes a pass or fail outcome for the tests.
6. **Documentation Requirements:** Specify the documentation needed to support the testing process, including data forms, data handling, and archiving procedures.
7. **Timeline:** Provide a timeline for completing the V&V activities, including milestones and key deliverables.

V&V Documentation

Purpose of Documentation: Documentation is essential for demonstrating compliance with regulatory requirements and for maintaining a traceable, auditable record of validation and verification activities.

Key Components of V&V Documentation:

1. **V&V Plan:** This document outlines the overall strategy for validation and verification, including phases, timelines, and responsibilities. It provides a roadmap for the V&V activities to be undertaken.
2. **Test Reports:** Detailed reports should be generated for each test conducted as part of the V&V processes. These reports should include the methodology used, the results obtained, and an analysis of whether the device or process meets the defined acceptance criteria.
3. **Traceability Matrix:** A traceability matrix links requirements, specifications, and design documents to the corresponding V&V activities and results. This ensures that all requirements are addressed and tested.
4. **Risk Assessment Documentation:** Document any risk assessments conducted as part of the V&V processes. This should link to the risk management file, demonstrating how identified risks have been mitigated or controlled.
5. **Change Control Records:** Document any changes made to the device or process during the V&V activities, including the justification for changes and their impact on the overall validation and verification.
6. **Summary Reports:** Upon completion of all V&V activities, summary reports should be prepared to provide an overview of the outcomes, demonstrating that the device or process meets all predefined criteria and regulatory requirements.

Best Practices for V&V Protocols and Documentation

1. **Standardization:** Use standardized templates and language for protocols and documentation to ensure consistency and completeness.
2. **Review and Approval:** Protocols and documentation should be reviewed and approved by designated personnel before and after V&V activities to ensure compliance and accuracy.
3. **Training:** Ensure all personnel involved in V&V activities are trained on the protocols and understand the documentation requirements.

4. **Audits:** Regularly audit V&V documentation and processes to ensure ongoing compliance and to identify areas for improvement.

Effective management of V&V protocols and documentation not only supports regulatory compliance but also enhances the quality and reliability of medical devices, contributing to their success in the market and the safety of end-users.

3.5.4 Validation and Verification Protocols and Documentation

Validation and verification (V&V) are crucial steps in the development and manufacturing of medical devices, ensuring that devices meet all required specifications and regulatory standards for safety and efficacy. Effective V&V relies heavily on rigorous protocols and comprehensive documentation to ensure consistency, compliance, and traceability. Here's a closer look at how to establish and maintain effective V&V protocols and documentation.

Validation and Verification Protocols

Purpose of Protocols: Protocols serve as detailed plans that describe how validation and verification activities will be conducted. They are designed to ensure that every aspect of V&V is carried out systematically and that results are reproducible and reliable.

Key Elements of V&V Protocols:

1. **Objective:** Clearly state the purpose of the validation or verification, detailing the specific aspects of the device or process to be tested.
2. **Scope:** Define the extent of the testing and identify the specific features or functionalities that will be examined.
3. **Responsibilities:** Assign clear roles and responsibilities to all team members involved in the V&V processes.
4. **Methodology:** Describe the methods and procedures for testing, including equipment setup, test conditions, and the procedures for executing tests.
5. **Acceptance Criteria:** Establish criteria for what constitutes acceptable results, detailing how decisions on pass or fail outcomes will be determined.
6. **Documentation Requirements:** Outline all documentation needed to support the V&V activities, including how data will be recorded and stored.

7. **Timeline:** Provide a detailed schedule for the V&V activities, including key milestones and deadlines.

V&V Documentation

Purpose of Documentation: Documentation is critical for demonstrating compliance with regulatory standards, facilitating audits, and maintaining a traceable record of all V&V activities. It serves as proof that the device was properly tested and meets all necessary criteria.

Key Components of V&V Documentation:

1. **V&V Plan:** This overarching document outlines the strategy for V&V, including phases, timelines, and specific responsibilities. It acts as a roadmap for all subsequent V&V activities.
2. **Test Protocols:** Each test conducted should have a corresponding protocol, which was previously outlined, and a detailed report documenting the test results, methodologies used, and an analysis of outcomes relative to the acceptance criteria.
3. **Traceability Matrix:** This document links each requirement for the device to the corresponding test performed and results obtained, ensuring that all requirements have been verified.
4. **Risk Assessment:** Include documentation of any risk assessments performed as part of the V&V process, linking these assessments to mitigation strategies documented in the risk management file.
5. **Change Control Documentation:** Record any changes made to the device or testing procedures during the V&V process, including rationale for the changes and their impact on the overall process and product.
6. **Summary Reports:** At the conclusion of V&V activities, compile summary reports that provide a comprehensive review of all testing, results, and conclusions, confirming that the device meets all requirements.

Best Practices for V&V Protocols and Documentation

1. **Standardization:** Utilize standardized templates and forms for all V&V documentation to ensure consistency across different teams and projects.
2. **Regular Reviews:** Protocols and documentation should undergo regular reviews and updates to ensure they remain current with regulatory

standards and technological advancements.

3. **Detailed Record-Keeping:** Maintain meticulous records of all V&V activities to support regulatory submissions and audits.
4. **Training:** Ensure that all personnel involved in V&V processes are properly trained on the protocols, documentation requirements, and regulatory standards.

By adhering to these guidelines for V&V protocols and documentation, medical device manufacturers can ensure that their products are both compliant with regulatory requirements and meet the highest standards of safety and efficacy. This approach not only supports successful product approvals but also builds a foundation for ongoing quality assurance throughout the product lifecycle.

3.5.5 Common Challenges and Pitfalls in Validation and Verification

Validation and verification (V&V) are critical phases in the development and production of medical devices, ensuring that products meet all necessary safety, efficacy, and regulatory requirements. Despite their importance, several common challenges and pitfalls can hinder the effectiveness of these processes. Understanding these challenges can help organizations anticipate potential issues and implement strategies to mitigate them effectively.

Common Challenges in Validation and Verification

1. **Inadequate Planning:**

   - **Issue:** Failure to adequately plan the V&V processes can lead to incomplete testing, scope creep, or missing critical performance criteria.
   - **Impact:** This often results in delays, increased costs, and potential regulatory non-compliance.

2. **Undefined Acceptance Criteria:**

   - **Issue:** Not clearly defining what constitutes a pass or fail outcome for each test can lead to ambiguity in interpreting test results.
   - **Impact:** Ambiguous results can complicate regulatory submissions and may require additional rounds of testing.

3. **Insufficient Resources:**
    - **Issue:** Lack of sufficient skilled personnel, time, or equipment can restrict the thoroughness of V&V activities.
    - **Impact:** This can compromise the quality of the validation and verification, leading to potential failures or non-compliance.
4. **Complex Software Integration:**
    - **Issue:** Devices with integrated software may face challenges in verifying and validating software functionality and interaction with hardware.
    - **Impact:** Software-related issues can lead to device malfunctions, which compromise user safety and device efficacy.
5. **Changing Regulatory Requirements:**
    - **Issue:** Regulatory requirements can evolve, and failing to stay updated with these changes can lead to non-compliance.
    - **Impact:** Non-compliance with current regulations can delay product approvals and lead to significant financial losses.
6. **Poor Documentation Practices:**
    - **Issue:** Inadequate documentation of the V&V processes can lead to difficulties during regulatory reviews and quality audits.
    - **Impact:** This can result in regulatory actions, product recalls, or a failure to receive market approval.

Pitfalls to Avoid in Validation and Verification

1. **Overlooking Early Stage V&V:**
    - Avoid postponing V&V activities until the later stages of product development. Early stage testing can identify potential issues when they are easier and less costly to address.
2. **Underestimating the Importance of Software V&V:**

- Given the increasing role of software in medical devices, it's crucial not to underestimate the complexity and importance of software validation and verification.

3. **Neglecting User-Centered Design and Testing:**

    - Failing to consider the end-user's needs and environments in V&V activities can result in products that are difficult to use or fail in real-world applications.

4. **Relying Solely on Internal Assessments:**

    - External audits and third-party testing can provide unbiased insights and help identify issues that internal teams might overlook.

Best Practices for Overcoming Challenges

1. **Robust V&V Planning:**

    - Develop a comprehensive V&V plan at the outset of the project that includes detailed timelines, resources, and specific deliverables.

2. **Clear Acceptance Criteria:**

    - Define and document clear, objective acceptance criteria for all tests to ensure consistency and objectivity in results interpretation.

3. **Regular Regulatory Updates:**

    - Stay informed about changes in regulatory requirements and integrate these changes into the V&V process in a timely manner.

4. **Thorough Documentation:**

    - Maintain meticulous records of all V&V activities, including protocols, results, and decisions, to ensure transparency and traceability.

5. **Engage Stakeholders:**

   - Regularly engage with stakeholders, including end-users and regulatory consultants, to ensure that all requirements and perspectives are considered in the V&V processes.

By addressing these challenges and avoiding common pitfalls, organizations can enhance the effectiveness of their validation and verification efforts, leading to safer and more effective medical devices that meet all necessary regulatory requirements.

3.5.6 Strategies for Effective Validation and Verification Processes

Validation and verification (V&V) are crucial methodologies in the development of medical devices, ensuring that products meet all design specifications, regulatory requirements, and user needs. Effective V&V processes not only support regulatory compliance but also enhance product quality and safety. Implementing robust strategies for V&V can help organizations achieve these goals efficiently and effectively.

Strategies for Effective V&V Processes

1. **Integrated Planning and Early Involvement:**

   - **Strategy:** Integrate V&V activities early in the development process. This allows for the identification and mitigation of potential issues before they become costly or critical.
   - **Benefits:** Early detection of design flaws, reduced development time, and cost savings.

2. **Develop Comprehensive V&V Protocols:**

   - **Strategy:** Establish detailed V&V protocols that include clear objectives, scope, methodologies, responsibilities, and acceptance criteria.
   - **Benefits:** Ensures consistency, repeatability, and reliability of V&V activities. Provides a clear roadmap that guides the entire V&V process.

3. **Employ Risk-Based Approaches:**

- **Strategy:** Utilize a risk-based approach to prioritize V&V activities based on the potential impact on patient safety and device performance.
- **Benefits:** Focuses resources on high-risk areas, enhances safety, and ensures regulatory compliance.

4. **Leverage Technology and Automation:**

- **Strategy:** Implement technological solutions and automation in the V&V process where appropriate, such as automated testing tools for software validation.
- **Benefits:** Increases efficiency, reduces human error, and provides more consistent and reliable results.

5. **Regular Training and Competency Development:**

- **Strategy:** Conduct regular training sessions for all team members involved in V&V activities to ensure they are knowledgeable about the latest V&V techniques, technologies, and regulatory requirements.
- **Benefits:** Enhances the quality of V&V activities and ensures adherence to industry standards and regulations.

6. **Stakeholder Engagement and Feedback Integration:**

- **Strategy:** Actively engage with all stakeholders, including end-users, during the V&V process to gather feedback and incorporate it into the product development.
- **Benefits:** Ensures the product meets real-world needs and user expectations, improving usability and satisfaction.

7. **Iterative Testing and Feedback Loops:**

- **Strategy:** Apply iterative testing and feedback loops throughout the development process to continually refine and improve the product.
- **Benefits:** Allows for continuous improvement, ensures the final product is well-polished, and reduces the likelihood of post-market issues.

8. **Thorough Documentation and Traceability:**

    - **Strategy:** Maintain comprehensive documentation of all V&V activities, including detailed records of tests, results, and decisions made.
    - **Benefits:** Provides evidence of compliance for regulatory review, facilitates audits, and supports post-market surveillance.

9. **External Audits and Third-Party Testing:**

    - **Strategy:** Utilize external audits and third-party testing to validate and verify product quality and compliance.
    - **Benefits:** Offers an unbiased assessment of the V&V process, and can help identify potential oversights or areas for improvement.

CHAPTER FOUR

REGULATORY APPROVAL PROCESSES IN THE USA

4.1 Introduction to Regulatory Approval Processes

4.1.1 Overview of FDA's Role in Medical Device Approval

The Food and Drug Administration (FDA) serves as the primary regulatory body for medical device approval in the United States. Its mandate includes ensuring the safety and efficacy of medical devices before they are marketed. The FDA categorizes devices into three classes based on the level of risk they pose: Class I, II, and III. Class I devices are deemed to have the lowest risk and are subject to the least regulatory control. Class II devices require greater regulatory oversight due to higher risk, and Class III devices, which include life-supporting or life-sustaining equipment, undergo the most stringent regulatory scrutiny.

The approval process varies significantly depending on the device classification. For Class I devices, manufacturers are mostly required to adhere to general controls, which include compliance with basic manufacturing and labeling standards. A significant proportion of Class I devices are exempt from the premarket notification, commonly known as 510(k). In contrast, Class II devices generally require a 510(k) submission, which involves demonstrating that the new device is substantially equivalent to an already legally marketed device. Class III devices require a Pre-Market Approval (PMA), the most rigorous type of device marketing application required by the FDA. The PMA process involves a thorough examination of clinical trial data and other evidence to assure the device is safe and effective.

The FDA's role extends beyond initial approvals through the lifecycle of the device with continuous post-market surveillance to monitor adverse events and ensure ongoing compliance with health and safety standards. The intricate balance maintained by the FDA in regulating these devices seeks to foster innovation while safeguarding public health, ensuring that medical advancements provide benefits without imposing undue risk to users.

4.1.2 Significance of Regulatory Compliance for Market Access

Regulatory compliance is critical for gaining market access in the medical device industry in the United States. The adherence to FDA regulations serves as a fundamental gateway for companies aspiring to introduce new medical technologies to the market. This compliance is not merely a legal obligation but also a significant market differentiator that enhances trust and reliability among healthcare providers and patients.

The process of meeting FDA standards ensures that a device is safe for use and performs as intended. This not only protects public health but also shields manufacturers from potential legal and financial repercussions associated with the distribution of non-compliant devices. For instance, failure to comply with regulatory requirements can lead to severe consequences such as product recalls, legal sanctions, and damage to a company's reputation, which in turn can have long-lasting financial impacts.

Furthermore, regulatory compliance facilitates smoother market entry and scalability. Devices that receive FDA clearance or approval can be marketed more effectively and are more likely to be adopted quickly by healthcare systems. For medical device companies, achieving compliance means navigating a complex landscape of testing, quality assurance, and meticulous documentation. This includes everything from pre-market submissions, such as 510(k) notifications for Class II devices and PMAs for Class III, to maintaining rigorous quality systems under 21 CFR Part 820.

4.1.3 Comparative Overview with Other Regulatory Systems

The regulatory landscape for medical devices in the United States, primarily governed by the FDA, presents notable contrasts when compared with other global regulatory systems, such as the European Union's (EU) Medical Device Regulation (MDR) and China's National Medical Products Administration (NMPA).

European Union: The EU's regulatory framework underwent a significant overhaul with the introduction of the Medical Device Regulation (MDR) in 2017, which replaced the previous Medical Device Directive

(MDD). The MDR aims to enhance transparency, increase traceability, and strengthen safety measures. It requires more rigorous clinical evidence for classifying and approving devices, aligning more closely with the FDA's emphasis on safety and efficacy but with different procedural mandates. For example, the EU system relies more heavily on Notified Bodies—third-party organizations designated by EU countries to assess device compliance. This approach differs from the FDA's direct oversight model.

China: The regulatory system overseen by the NMPA also emphasizes the safety and efficacy of medical devices but operates within a different administrative structure. The approval process in China has traditionally been slower compared to the U.S., with a more centralized control. However, recent reforms aim to streamline procedures and accelerate market entry for innovative devices. Like the FDA, the NMPA classifies devices based on risk, but the criteria and categorization can vary, affecting the approval pathway.

Japan: Japan's Pharmaceuticals and Medical Devices Agency (PMDA) also requires rigorous review processes, similar to the FDA. Japan uses a system that can be particularly stringent for high-risk devices, involving multiple layers of approval that demand comprehensive clinical data. However, Japan has been working towards harmonizing its standards with international guidelines to facilitate quicker approvals and greater foreign device market entry.

In essence, while the foundational goal of ensuring device safety and effectiveness is a common thread across these systems, the methods and processes for achieving these goals vary. The FDA's direct involvement in the evaluation process contrasts with the EU's reliance on Notified Bodies and China's central regulatory oversight. These differences can affect not just the speed of market access but also the strategic planning necessary for global medical device companies. Understanding these variances is crucial for manufacturers aiming for international distribution, requiring them to navigate multiple regulatory environments adeptly.

4.2 Classification of Medical Devices

4.2.1 Criteria for Classification (Class I, II, III)

The classification of medical devices in the United States by the FDA is a critical first step in determining the regulatory pathways that a device must follow before reaching the market. This classification is primarily based on the intended use of the device and the risks associated with its use. Devices are categorized into three main classes: Class I, II, and III, with increasing levels of regulatory control corresponding to higher potential risks to patients and users.

Class I Devices: These are the simplest devices in terms of design and have the lowest risk to the user. Examples include non-sterile bandages, examination gloves, and basic dental floss. Most Class I devices are exempt from premarket notification requirements (510(k)) and are subject to general controls which include compliance with basic manufacturing processes, proper labeling, and registration of the device and manufacturing facilities with the FDA.

Class II Devices: Class II devices involve higher risk compared to Class I and require more regulatory controls to provide assurance of their safety and effectiveness. These devices typically require premarket notification, also known as 510(k) clearance. This process involves demonstrating that the device is substantially equivalent to another legally marketed device. Examples of Class II devices include powered wheelchairs, infusion pumps, and surgical drapes. Special controls, such as special labeling requirements, mandatory performance standards, and postmarket surveillance, may also be applicable to these devices.

Class III Devices: These are the highest risk devices and therefore require the most stringent regulatory oversight. Class III devices support or sustain human life, are critically important to prevent impairment of human health, or present a potential, unreasonable risk of illness or injury. Examples include implantable pacemakers and heart valves. These devices must typically receive premarket approval (PMA) from the FDA, which involves a thorough review of clinical trial data and other evidence to ensure the device's safety and effectiveness.

The FDA's classification system thus serves to appropriately scale the regulatory scrutiny to the level of risk presented by the device, ensuring that all medical devices marketed in the U.S. provide a reasonable assurance of safety and effectiveness. Understanding this classification system is crucial for manufacturers as it directly influences the complexity and duration of the regulatory process they must navigate to bring their devices to market.

4.2.3 Case Studies of Device Classifications

The classification of medical devices can be elucidated through specific case studies, each demonstrating how different products are classified under the FDA's regulatory framework based on their intended use and associated risks. These examples highlight the practical application of classification criteria for Class I, II, and III devices.

Class I Example: Dental Floss Dental floss is a common example of a Class I device. It is designed for cleaning between the teeth to prevent plaque buildup and does not pose a significant risk to health if used as intended. Because it presents minimal risk, dental floss is subject to general controls such as proper labeling and good manufacturing practices but does not require premarket notification (510(k)). This classification facilitates easier and quicker market entry for such low-risk devices.

Class II Example: Infusion Pumps Infusion pumps, which deliver fluids, including nutrients and medications, into a patient's body in controlled amounts, are categorized as Class II devices. The risks associated with these devices, including over-infusion or under-infusion, infection, and operational failure, necessitate more stringent regulatory controls. Consequently, manufacturers must obtain 510(k) clearance, demonstrating that their new infusion pump is substantially equivalent to an already existing, legally marketed infusion pump. This process often requires detailed technical documentation and sometimes clinical data, ensuring that the pumps meet safety and efficacy standards.

Class III Example: Heart Valves Heart valves are classified as Class III devices due to their critical role in sustaining human life and the high risk associated with their implantation. These devices require a Pre-Market Approval (PMA), the most stringent type of marketing application required by the FDA. The PMA process for heart valves involves extensive clinical trials to provide valid scientific evidence that the devices are safe and effective. Approval can be costly and time-consuming, reflecting the high level of scrutiny required to ensure the safety of devices that can significantly impact health outcomes.

These case studies demonstrate how the FDA's device classification system impacts the regulatory pathway for medical devices, from the relatively straightforward requirements for Class I devices to the complex and rigorous demands for Class III devices. Each classification level is designed to balance the need to protect public health with the goal of facilitating technological innovation and availability of medical devices.

4.3 510(k) Premarket Notification

4.3.1 Definition and Purpose of 510(k) Notification

The 510(k) premarket notification is a regulatory process used by the FDA to evaluate the safety and effectiveness of medical devices that are not exempt from premarket submission requirements. Named after Section 510(k) of the Federal Food, Drug, and Cosmetic Act, this process requires manufacturers to demonstrate that a proposed device is "substantially equivalent" to a device already legally on the market (known as a predicate device). Substantial equivalence means that the new device must be as safe and effective as the predicate and either has the same intended use or the same technological characteristics, or, if it has different technological characteristics, that the information submitted to the FDA demonstrates that the device is safe and effective.

The primary purpose of the 510(k) notification is to ensure that new devices, which are not subject to the more rigorous pre-market approval (PMA) process, still meet necessary safety and efficacy standards before they are marketed. The 510(k) process allows for a relatively quicker and less expensive route to market than the PMA route, primarily because it typically does not require clinical trial data. Instead, the focus is on comparison testing and analyses between the new device and one or more predicate devices.

This notification process is critical for manufacturers as it balances the need for innovation with the necessity for safety. It provides a pathway for newer, potentially more effective devices to enter the market more swiftly, provided they can be appropriately benchmarked against existing products. The 510(k) process thus plays a vital role in the continual advancement of medical technologies, ensuring that newer developments can be made available to healthcare providers and patients without undue delay.

4.3 510(k) Premarket Notification

4.3.2 Process and Requirements for Submission

The 510(k) submission process is a critical step for medical device manufacturers seeking FDA clearance for their Class II devices, and sometimes Class I or III devices. The process involves several key requirements and steps that must be meticulously followed to demonstrate substantial equivalence to a predicate device.

Step 1: Determine if a 510(k) is Required Before initiating a 510(k) submission, manufacturers must first determine if their device indeed requires this type of notification. This involves verifying whether the device falls under a category that is not exempt from premarket notification requirements.

Step 2: Identify a Predicate Device Manufacturers must identify an appropriate predicate device—already legally marketed in the United States—that is similar in terms of intended use and technological characteristics. The chosen predicate is crucial as it sets the benchmark for demonstrating substantial equivalence.

Step 3: Prepare Supporting Documentation The submission must include detailed information that supports the claim of substantial equivalence. This documentation generally includes:

- **Device Description:** Detailed description of the device and its components, including specifications, materials, and principles of operation.
- **Comparative Analysis:** Side-by-side comparison with the predicate device showing similarities and differences in design, materials, and performance.
- **Performance Data:** Non-clinical laboratory studies and, if necessary, clinical data demonstrating that the device is at least as safe and effective as the predicate.
- **Proposed Labeling:** Draft labels, labeling, and advertisements that describe the device, its intended use, and directions for use.

Step 4: Quality System Regulation Manufacturers must also ensure that their device is developed under the Quality System Regulation (21 CFR Part 820) which includes requirements for quality management systems, ensuring that devices consistently meet applicable requirements and specifications.

Step 5: Submit the 510(k) Notification The prepared 510(k) notification is submitted electronically to the FDA. The submission includes a user fee which varies each fiscal year.

Step 6: FDA Review Upon receiving the submission, the FDA has 90 calendar days to review the provided materials and determine whether the device is substantially equivalent to the predicate device. During this review, the FDA may request additional information, which can extend the review process.

Step 7: FDA Decision If the FDA determines that the device is substantially equivalent to the predicate, it will issue a letter of substantial equivalence, allowing the device to be marketed in the U.S. If not, the FDA will issue a not substantially equivalent (NSE) letter, and the device may require a Pre-Market Approval (PMA) or another regulatory pathway.

Understanding and navigating the 510(k) process is essential for manufacturers to ensure compliance and successful market entry for their medical devices. This process underscores the FDA's commitment to ensuring that new medical devices on the market provide patient safety and effective treatment or diagnostic options.

4.3 510(k) Premarket Notification

4.3.3 Review Process and Timeline

The review process and timeline for a 510(k) premarket notification are designed to ensure that new medical devices meet safety and effectiveness standards before they are allowed to enter the U.S. market. Here is an outline of how the FDA handles this process:

Initial Review Upon submission, the FDA conducts an initial review to ensure that the 510(k) notification is administratively complete. This involves checking whether all necessary sections are filled out and whether the required information is included. If the submission is incomplete, the FDA will issue a Refuse to Accept (RTA) notice, specifying the deficiencies. The manufacturer must address these deficiencies before the review process can continue.

Substantive Review Once the submission is accepted, it enters the substantive review phase. During this period, the FDA reviewers evaluate the detailed information provided, including device descriptions, comparative analyses, and supporting performance data. The primary goal is to assess whether the device is substantially equivalent to the predicate device in terms of safety and effectiveness. The FDA may request additional information from the manufacturer, known as an Additional Information (AI) request, which pauses the review clock until the requested information is provided.

Interactive Review Throughout the review process, the FDA may engage in an interactive review with the manufacturer, involving communication through phone calls, emails, or meetings to clarify specific issues or expedite the review process. This helps in resolving minor issues quickly without formal requests for additional information.

FDA Decision The FDA aims to make a decision within 90 calendar days of the 510(k) submission date. However, this timeline can be extended if the FDA issues an AI request. The decision will typically be one of the following:

- **Substantial Equivalence (SE) Determination**: If the FDA finds that the device is substantially equivalent to the predicate, a clearance letter is issued, allowing the device to be marketed in the U.S.

- **Not Substantial Equivalence (NSE) Determination**: If the device is not found to be substantially equivalent, an NSE letter is issued. The manufacturer then may need to consider other regulatory pathways, such as a Pre-Market Approval (PMA), or modify the device and/or its intended use and submit a new 510(k).

Post-Decision Requirements After receiving SE clearance, manufacturers are not required to submit further premarket submissions unless they intend to make changes affecting the safety or effectiveness of the device. However, they must comply with other regulatory obligations, such as registration and listing, medical device reporting, quality system regulations, and post-market surveillance requirements.

Understanding the 510(k) review process and timeline is crucial for manufacturers to plan their product development and market launch strategies effectively. This knowledge helps in anticipating potential delays and preparing comprehensive submissions to facilitate a smoother review process.

4.4 Pre-Market Approval (PMA)

4.4.1 Comparison with 510(k) Notification

The Pre-Market Approval (PMA) is the FDA's process of scientific and regulatory review to evaluate the safety and effectiveness of Class III medical devices. Unlike the 510(k) notification, which is used primarily for Class I and II devices that are substantially equivalent to devices already on the market, the PMA is required for devices that represent a significant risk to patients or that do not have a comparable predicate device.

Nature of the Process:

- **510(k) Notification:** This process requires manufacturers to demonstrate that their device is substantially equivalent to another device that is already legally marketed in the United States. The main focus is on comparing the new device to the predicate device, without necessarily proving safety and effectiveness independently.
- **PMA:** This process requires manufacturers to provide substantial evidence of the safety and effectiveness of their device for its intended use. The evidence usually must include data from clinical trials, laboratory tests, and sometimes animal studies.

Data Requirements:

- **510(k) Notification:** Generally does not require clinical trial data unless the device differs significantly in design or function from the predicate. The submission focuses more on technical comparisons and may include bench testing and biocompatibility studies.
- **PMA:** Always requires clinical trial data, along with extensive laboratory and animal testing data. This data must convincingly demonstrate safety and effectiveness.

Review Time:

- **510(k) Notification:** The FDA aims to complete the review process within 90 days of submission, though this can be extended if additional information is requested.
- **PMA:** The review process is more extensive and can take significantly longer, typically around 180 days as a target, but often extending up to a year or more due to the complexity and necessity for additional information or data analysis.

Regulatory Scrutiny:

- **510(k) Notification:** The scrutiny is relatively less as the device is compared to one that is already on the market; however, substantial equivalence must still be thoroughly demonstrated.
- **PMA:** Involves a high level of scrutiny, with the FDA reviewing every aspect of the manufacturing process, labeling, and marketing of the device. The review also includes a public advisory committee meeting where independent experts may weigh in on the device's safety and effectiveness.

Cost and Resource Intensity:

- **510(k) Notification:** Less expensive and resource-intensive than PMA, as it often does not require clinical data and involves fewer complexities in the submission.
- **PMA:** Significantly more costly due to the need for clinical trials and extensive data collection and analysis. This process also requires more substantial human, financial, and time resources.

4.4 Pre-Market Approval (PMA)

4.4.2 Detailed Steps in the PMA Process

The Pre-Market Approval (PMA) process is the most stringent of the FDA's device review processes, intended for high-risk medical devices. Here are the detailed steps involved in navigating through the PMA process:

Step 1: Pre-Submission Meeting Before submitting a PMA, manufacturers often request a pre-submission meeting with the FDA. This meeting provides an opportunity to discuss and clarify the regulatory pathway, data requirements, and potential issues that could arise during the review process. It helps align the manufacturer's plans with FDA expectations, ensuring a smoother submission process.

Step 2: Submission of the PMA Application The PMA application must include comprehensive information about the device, such as its design, manufacturing processes, and intended use. It should also contain all data from preclinical studies and clinical trials, demonstrating the safety and effectiveness of the device. Detailed labeling and marketing information must also be included.

Step 3: Acceptance Review Once submitted, the FDA conducts an acceptance review to determine if the PMA application is sufficiently complete to permit a substantive review. If the application lacks necessary elements, the FDA can refuse to accept it and request additional information.

Step 4: Filing Review Following acceptance, the FDA performs a filing review to decide if the application contains all the necessary information to continue with a full scientific review. This step assesses the quality and completeness of the submitted data and proposed labeling.

Step 5: Substantive Review The substantive review is a thorough examination of all scientific data provided in the PMA. The FDA evaluates the data to ensure that the device is safe and effective for its intended use. This phase may involve multiple interactions between the FDA and the applicant, with requests for additional information or clarification.

Step 6: Advisory Committee Review (Optional) For some PMAs, particularly those involving novel technologies or where there is significant scientific uncertainty, the FDA may seek input from an advisory committee. This committee, composed of external experts, provides an independent assessment of the application's safety and effectiveness.

Step 7: FDA Decision After the substantive review and any necessary advisory committee consultations, the FDA makes its decision. If the FDA determines that the evidence adequately supports the safety and effectiveness of the device, it will issue an approval order. If not, the FDA will issue a not approvable letter detailing the deficiencies and, often, what is needed to make the application approvable.

Step 8: Post-Approval Requirements Once a device is approved, the manufacturer must comply with specific post-approval requirements. These can include post-market studies to monitor long-term effects and compliance with special controls. The manufacturer must also report any adverse effects found post-marketing and may need to comply with restrictions or surveillance measures.

Step 9: Facility Inspection The FDA may also inspect the manufacturing facilities to ensure compliance with Good Manufacturing Practices (GMP) before or after the PMA approval.

Navigating the PMA process requires a substantial commitment of resources, including time, expertise, and financial investment, due to its comprehensive and rigorous nature. This process ensures that high-risk medical devices meet the highest standards of safety and efficacy before they can be marketed.

4.5 Investigational Device Exemption (IDE)

4.5.1 Purpose and Criteria for IDE

The Investigational Device Exemption (IDE) allows investigational devices to be used in clinical studies to collect safety and effectiveness data required to support a Pre-Market Approval (PMA) application or a 510(k) notification to the FDA. The IDE process is crucial for the development and eventual approval of new medical devices, as it enables researchers to test devices in human subjects under controlled conditions.

Purpose of the IDE: The primary purpose of the IDE is to ensure that patients participating in clinical trials are protected and that the studies are scientifically sound. It allows a medical device that has not yet been proven safe and effective to be used in the context of a clinical study to gather necessary data. This data plays a critical role in determining whether the device will be approved for marketing.

Criteria for IDE Approval:

1. **Risk Assessment:** The FDA classifies investigational devices as either significant risk (SR) or non-significant risk (NSR) devices. Significant risk devices are those that present a potential for serious risk to the health, safety, or welfare of a subject and are usually subject to a full

IDE application. Non-significant risk devices are those that do not pose a serious risk and are subject to less regulatory burden.

2. **Scientific Validity:** The clinical study must be scientifically sound and provide a practical method to collect data necessary to establish the safety and effectiveness of the device. The study must have a clear statement of the research objectives and a justification for the belief that the device as used will meet those objectives.
3. **Clinical Protocol:** The application must include a detailed clinical protocol describing the study methodology, including how many subjects will be involved, what the control group will be, the methods of data collection, and the mechanisms in place to protect the participants.
4. **Institutional Review Board (IRB) Approval:** Before an IDE application can be approved, it must be reviewed and approved by an Institutional Review Board (IRB). The IRB ensures that the clinical trial is ethical and that the rights and welfare of the participants are fully protected.
5. **Informed Consent:** All clinical studies under an IDE must ensure that informed consent is obtained from all participants. This involves providing detailed information about the study, including its purpose, duration, required procedures, and key contacts, as well as the risks and potential benefits of participation.
6. **Labeling Requirements:** The investigational device must be properly labeled to ensure that it is used only within the confines of the clinical study. The labeling must state that the device is for investigational use only and must also include the name and place of business of the manufacturer or distributor.
7. **Monitoring:** The study must be appropriately monitored to ensure that the rights, safety, and well-being of the trial subjects are protected and that the data generated will be accurate and reliable.

The IDE process is a critical pathway for the advancement of medical technology, facilitating the development and testing of new devices in a way that prioritizes patient safety and robust, scientifically sound data collection.

4.5 Investigational Device Exemption (IDE)

4.5.2 Application Process and Regulatory Requirements

The application process for an Investigational Device Exemption (IDE) involves several steps and regulatory requirements to ensure the safety and scientific validity of clinical studies involving investigational medical devices.

Step 1: Preparing the IDE Application

Before submitting an IDE application to the FDA, the sponsor or investigator must compile all necessary documentation and ensure that the proposed clinical study meets regulatory requirements. This includes developing a detailed clinical protocol outlining the study objectives, methodology, participant selection criteria, and data collection methods. The protocol must be scientifically rigorous and ethically sound.

Step 2: Submission to the FDA

Once the IDE application is prepared, it is submitted to the FDA for review. The application typically includes:

- **Cover Letter:** Provides an overview of the application and identifies the device, study sponsor, and principal investigator.
- **Investigator's Brochure:** Provides detailed information about the device, including its design, intended use, manufacturing process, and preclinical data.
- **Clinical Protocol:** Describes the study objectives, design, participant eligibility criteria, study procedures, and safety monitoring plan.
- **Informed Consent Documents:** Outline the risks and benefits of participation in the study and ensure that participants provide voluntary informed consent.
- **Device Labeling:** Ensures that the device is properly labeled for investigational use only and includes necessary warnings and precautions.
- **IRB Approval:** Documentation of approval from an Institutional Review Board (IRB) confirming that the study protocol is ethical and complies with regulatory requirements.

Step 3: FDA Review Process

Upon receiving the IDE application, the FDA conducts a thorough review to evaluate the scientific and ethical aspects of the proposed clinical study. The review process includes assessing the device's safety and effectiveness, the adequacy of the study protocol, the protection of human subjects, and compliance with regulatory requirements.

Step 4: Approval or Disapproval

After completing the review, the FDA issues a decision on the IDE application. If approved, the sponsor or investigator receives an IDE approval letter, allowing them to proceed with the clinical study as outlined in the protocol. If disapproved, the FDA provides a written explanation of the reasons for the decision, and the sponsor or investigator may have the opportunity to address any deficiencies and resubmit the application.

Regulatory Requirements During the Study:

- **Monitoring:** The sponsor or investigator must monitor the study to ensure participant safety, data quality, and compliance with the protocol.
- **Reporting:** Adverse events, protocol deviations, and other significant study findings must be reported to the FDA and the IRB as required.
- **Device Modifications:** Any changes to the investigational device or study protocol must be reported to the FDA and the IRB for review and approval.

Navigating the IDE application process and meeting regulatory requirements is essential for conducting clinical studies involving investigational medical devices. Compliance with FDA regulations ensures the ethical conduct of research and the generation of reliable data to support device safety and effectiveness.

4.5 Investigational Device Exemption (IDE)

4.5.3 Monitoring and Compliance during Clinical Trials

Monitoring and compliance during clinical trials conducted under an Investigational Device Exemption (IDE) are essential to ensure the safety of participants, the integrity of the study data, and compliance with regulatory requirements. Here are the key aspects of monitoring and compliance:

Monitoring Procedures:

1. **Site Visits:** Monitors, typically representatives of the sponsor or Contract Research Organizations (CROs), conduct regular visits to clinical trial sites to review study documentation, assess participant safety, and ensure adherence to the protocol.
2. **Source Data Verification (SDV):** Monitors compare the data recorded in the clinical trial documents (source documents) with the data entered into the study database (case report forms) to ensure accuracy and completeness.
3. **Adverse Event Monitoring:** Monitors review adverse event reports submitted by investigators to ensure they are properly documented, reported in a timely manner, and managed appropriately.

4. **Protocol Compliance:** Monitors verify that study procedures are conducted according to the approved protocol and that deviations are appropriately documented and reported.
5. **Informed Consent:** Monitors ensure that informed consent is obtained from all study participants and that the consent process complies with regulatory requirements.
6. **Device Accountability:** Monitors track the distribution, use, and return of investigational devices to ensure proper handling and prevent unauthorized use.

Compliance Requirements:

1. **Good Clinical Practice (GCP):** Clinical trials conducted under an IDE must adhere to Good Clinical Practice guidelines, which provide standards for the design, conduct, monitoring, and reporting of clinical studies.
2. **IRB Oversight:** The study protocol and any modifications must receive approval from an Institutional Review Board (IRB) before implementation. The IRB ensures that the rights and welfare of study participants are protected.
3. **Adverse Event Reporting:** Investigators are required to promptly report all adverse events and unanticipated problems to the sponsor, IRB, and FDA, as specified in the study protocol and regulatory requirements.
4. **Data Integrity:** Study data must be accurate, complete, and verifiable. Investigators and sponsors are responsible for maintaining the integrity of the data and ensuring that it is properly recorded and reported.
5. **Regulatory Reporting:** Sponsors are responsible for submitting regular progress reports to the FDA, including updates on study enrollment, adverse events, and study progress.
6. **Training and Qualifications:** Investigators, study coordinators, and other study personnel must be appropriately trained and qualified to conduct the study procedures and comply with regulatory requirements.

Monitoring and compliance activities are critical components of clinical trials conducted under an IDE. By ensuring that study procedures are conducted in accordance with regulatory requirements and ethical standards, these activities help to protect the rights and safety of study participants and support the validity of the study data.

4.6 Quality System Requirements (21 CFR Part 820)

4.6.1 Key Elements of Quality System Regulations

The Quality System Regulations (QSR) outlined in 21 CFR Part 820 establish the minimum requirements for the design, manufacture, packaging, labeling, storage, installation, and servicing of medical devices intended for commercial distribution in the United States. These regulations are essential for ensuring that medical devices are safe, effective, and meet established quality standards throughout their lifecycle. Here are the key elements of the Quality System Regulations:

1. **Management Responsibility:** Management must establish and maintain a quality system that meets regulatory requirements. This includes assigning responsibilities for quality-related activities, providing adequate resources, and establishing quality objectives and policies.
2. **Quality Policy:** Manufacturers must establish a quality policy that defines their commitment to quality and compliance with regulatory requirements. This policy must be communicated and understood at all levels of the organization.
3. **Quality System Procedures:** Written procedures must be established and maintained for all aspects of the quality system, including design controls, document controls, purchasing controls, production and process controls, and corrective and preventive actions.
4. **Design Controls:** Manufacturers must establish and maintain procedures to ensure that medical devices are designed in accordance with specified requirements. This includes planning, input, output, verification, validation, review, and transfer activities.
5. **Document Controls:** Procedures must be in place to control the creation, review, approval, distribution, and maintenance of documents, including specifications, drawings, procedures, and records.
6. **Purchasing Controls:** Manufacturers must ensure that purchased or otherwise received products and services conform to specified requirements. This includes evaluating suppliers, establishing purchasing controls, and maintaining records of supplier evaluations and performance.
7. **Production and Process Controls:** Procedures must be established and maintained to ensure that medical devices are produced and controlled in accordance with specified requirements. This includes establishing process validation, monitoring, and control procedures.

8. **Corrective and Preventive Actions:** Manufacturers must establish procedures for investigating and addressing nonconformities and implementing corrective and preventive actions to prevent recurrence.
9. **Handling, Storage, Distribution, and Installation:** Procedures must be in place to ensure that medical devices are properly handled, stored, distributed, and installed to prevent damage or deterioration that could affect their performance or safety.
10. **Records and Recordkeeping:** Manufacturers must establish and maintain records documenting the implementation and effectiveness of the quality system. These records must be readily retrievable and maintained in a manner that ensures their integrity and confidentiality.
11. **Servicing:** Manufacturers must establish procedures for servicing medical devices to ensure that they remain safe and effective throughout their intended lifecycle. This includes procedures for maintenance, repair, and refurbishment.

Adherence to the Quality System Regulations is essential for ensuring the safety, effectiveness, and quality of medical devices throughout their lifecycle. By establishing and maintaining robust quality management systems, manufacturers can demonstrate their commitment to meeting regulatory requirements and producing high-quality products that meet the needs of patients and healthcare providers.

4.6 Quality System Requirements (21 CFR Part 820)

4.6.2 Importance of Quality Systems in Device Manufacturing

Quality systems play a pivotal role in medical device manufacturing, ensuring that products meet stringent safety and efficacy standards while maintaining consistency and reliability throughout their lifecycle. The importance of quality systems in device manufacturing can be elucidated through several key aspects:

1. **Ensuring Patient Safety:** Quality systems are paramount in safeguarding patient safety by ensuring that medical devices meet rigorous standards for performance, reliability, and effectiveness. Adherence to quality system regulations helps minimize the risk of device-related adverse events, ensuring that patients receive safe and reliable medical care.
2. **Compliance with Regulatory Requirements:** Regulatory bodies, such as the FDA in the United States, require manufacturers to adhere to quality system regulations (QSR) to ensure that medical devices meet

established standards for safety, efficacy, and quality. Compliance with QSR, such as 21 CFR Part 820, is essential for obtaining regulatory approval and commercial distribution of medical devices.

3. **Facilitating Product Development and Innovation:** Quality systems provide a framework for systematic product development, ensuring that devices are designed, manufactured, and tested in accordance with established protocols and procedures. By adhering to quality system requirements, manufacturers can streamline the product development process, accelerate time-to-market, and facilitate innovation in medical device technology.
4. **Enhancing Product Quality and Reliability:** Quality systems promote the adoption of robust manufacturing processes and quality assurance measures to maintain consistent product quality and reliability. By implementing rigorous quality control procedures, manufacturers can identify and address potential defects or deviations early in the manufacturing process, minimizing the risk of product failures and recalls.
5. **Supporting Continuous Improvement:** Quality systems emphasize a culture of continuous improvement, encouraging manufacturers to monitor and evaluate their processes, identify areas for optimization, and implement corrective and preventive actions to enhance product quality and efficiency. Through ongoing monitoring, analysis, and feedback, manufacturers can refine their processes and drive continuous improvement across the organization.
6. **Building Customer Confidence and Trust:** Adherence to quality systems demonstrates a manufacturer's commitment to producing safe, effective, and high-quality medical devices. By consistently delivering products that meet or exceed customer expectations, manufacturers can build trust and confidence among healthcare providers, patients, regulatory authorities, and other stakeholders, strengthening their reputation and market position.
7. **Mitigating Risk and Liability:** Quality systems help mitigate the risk of product defects, recalls, and liability issues by ensuring that devices are designed, manufactured, and distributed in accordance with established standards and regulations. By proactively addressing quality-related risks and implementing robust quality assurance measures, manufacturers can minimize legal and financial exposure associated with product failures or adverse events.

4.6 Quality System Requirements (21 CFR Part 820)

4.6.3 Compliance Assessment and Common Pitfalls

Compliance assessment with quality system requirements (QSR), such as those outlined in 21 CFR Part 820, is critical for medical device manufacturers to ensure that their products meet regulatory standards and are safe and effective for patient use. However, navigating the complexities of compliance can present challenges and pitfalls. Here's an overview of compliance assessment and common pitfalls:

Compliance Assessment:

1. **Internal Audits:** Conducting regular internal audits is essential to assess compliance with quality system requirements. These audits evaluate the effectiveness of quality management systems, identify areas of non-compliance or improvement, and ensure that corrective actions are implemented promptly.
2. **Document Reviews:** Reviewing documentation, including standard operating procedures (SOPs), work instructions, and quality records, helps ensure that processes are documented and followed in accordance with regulatory requirements.
3. **Training and Competency Assessments:** Ensuring that personnel are adequately trained and competent in their roles is essential for maintaining compliance with quality system regulations. Regular competency assessments help identify training needs and ensure that personnel understand and adhere to quality procedures.
4. **Supplier Audits:** Assessing the compliance of suppliers and contractors with quality system requirements is crucial for ensuring the quality and reliability of components and services used in device manufacturing. Supplier audits help identify and mitigate risks associated with external suppliers.
5. **Management Reviews:** Regular management reviews of quality system performance provide oversight and ensure that quality objectives are being met. These reviews also help identify areas for improvement and allocate resources effectively.

Common Pitfalls:

1. **Lack of Document Control:** Inadequate document control processes, such as incomplete or outdated procedures, can lead to non-compliance

with quality system requirements. Proper document control is essential to ensure that accurate and up-to-date documentation is available to personnel.

2. **Insufficient Training:** Inadequate training of personnel can result in errors, deviations from procedures, and non-compliance with quality system requirements. Ensuring that personnel are adequately trained and competent in their roles is critical for maintaining compliance.
3. **Failure to Address Non-Conformities:** Failure to address non-conformities identified during internal audits or inspections can lead to recurring compliance issues and regulatory action. It is essential to promptly investigate non-conformities, implement corrective actions, and verify their effectiveness.
4. **Inadequate Supplier Management:** Poor oversight of suppliers and contractors can result in the use of substandard components or services, leading to product defects or failures. Effective supplier management processes, including supplier audits and performance monitoring, are essential for ensuring the quality and reliability of supplied materials and services.
5. **Lack of Management Support:** Without strong management support and commitment to quality, compliance with quality system requirements may be compromised. Management involvement in quality system oversight and decision-making is essential for fostering a culture of quality and ensuring organizational compliance.

By proactively assessing compliance with quality system requirements and addressing common pitfalls, medical device manufacturers can ensure the safety, effectiveness, and quality of their products while maintaining regulatory compliance. Effective compliance management is essential for sustaining business success and upholding the trust of stakeholders, including regulatory authorities, healthcare providers, and patients.

4.7 Labeling Requirements (21 CFR Part 801)

4.7.1 Overview of Labeling Requirements for Medical Devices

Labeling requirements for medical devices, as outlined in 21 CFR Part 801, are essential for ensuring the safe and effective use of devices by healthcare professionals and patients. These requirements encompass various aspects of device labeling, including content, format, and presentation. Here's an overview of the key elements of labeling requirements for medical devices:

1. Labeling Content:

- **Device Identification:** Labels must include clear and accurate identification of the device, including its name, intended use, and any specific model or version information.
- **Manufacturer Information:** Labels must prominently display the name and address of the manufacturer, packer, or distributor responsible for the device.
- **Instructions for Use:** Labels must provide clear and comprehensive instructions for the safe and effective use of the device, including proper handling, storage, assembly, and operation instructions.
- **Warnings and Precautions:** Labels must include appropriate warnings, precautions, contraindications, and adverse reactions associated with device use to alert users to potential risks and ensure safe usage.
- **Indications for Use:** Labels must specify the intended use of the device and any limitations or restrictions on its use, helping healthcare professionals and patients understand its appropriate clinical application.
- **Performance Characteristics:** Labels may include information on device performance characteristics, specifications, and clinical performance data to assist users in assessing device suitability for specific applications.

2. Labeling Format:

- **Readability and Clarity:** Labels must be legible, clear, and easy to read to ensure that users can understand the information provided.
- **Language and Translation:** Labels must be provided in the language(s) understood by the intended user population. For devices distributed internationally, labeling may need to be translated into multiple languages.
- **Font Size and Style:** Labels must use appropriate font size, style, and formatting to enhance readability and ensure that essential information is easily discernible.

3. Labeling Presentation:

- **Placement and Positioning:** Labels must be affixed to the device or its packaging in a prominent and easily visible location to ensure that users can access important information without difficulty.
- **Color and Contrast:** Labels must use colors and contrasts that enhance visibility and readability, particularly for critical information such as warnings and precautions.
- **Durability and Longevity:** Labels must be durable and resistant to wear, tear, and environmental conditions to maintain legibility throughout the device's lifecycle.

Compliance with labeling requirements is essential for medical device manufacturers to ensure the safe and effective use of their products and regulatory compliance. By providing clear, accurate, and comprehensive labeling, manufacturers can support healthcare professionals and patients in making informed decisions about device usage and promote patient safety and quality of care.

4.7 Labeling Requirements (21 CFR Part 801)

4.7.2 Specific Labeling Requirements for Different Device Classes

Labeling requirements for medical devices vary depending on the device class and its intended use. The FDA classifies medical devices into three main classes (I, II, and III) based on the level of risk they pose to patients and users. Here's an overview of the specific labeling requirements for different device classes:

1. Class I Devices:

- **General Controls:** Class I devices are subject to general controls, which include labeling requirements outlined in 21 CFR Part 801. These requirements focus on providing essential information to users to ensure the safe and effective use of the device.
- **Labeling Content:** Labels for Class I devices must include device identification, manufacturer information, instructions for use, warnings, precautions, and indications for use. The content must be clear, accurate, and comprehensive to facilitate proper device usage.

2. Class II Devices:

- **Special Controls:** In addition to general controls, Class II devices may be subject to special controls, such as performance standards, post-market surveillance, patient registries, and FDA guidance documents. These special controls may impose additional labeling requirements specific to the device type or intended use.

- **Labeling Content:** Labels for Class II devices must meet the same basic requirements as Class I devices, but may also include additional information specified by special controls. This may include specific warnings, precautions, or performance characteristics relevant to the device's classification.

3. Class III Devices:

- **Premarket Approval (PMA):** Class III devices are subject to the most stringent regulatory oversight and may require premarket approval (PMA) by the FDA. PMA applications must include comprehensive labeling that provides detailed information on device safety, effectiveness, and performance.
- **Labeling Content:** Labels for Class III devices must meet the same basic requirements as Class I and II devices but are often more extensive and detailed. They may include data from clinical studies, performance testing, and risk assessments to support the device's safety and efficacy.

Additional Considerations:

- **Unique Device Identification (UDI):** All medical devices, regardless of class, must bear a Unique Device Identifier (UDI) in accordance with FDA regulations. The UDI system helps facilitate device identification, traceability, and post-market surveillance.
- **Combination Products:** Devices that are combined with drugs, biologics, or other components may have unique labeling requirements determined by the FDA's Center for Drug Evaluation and Research (CDER) or Center for Biologics Evaluation and Research (CBER).

Compliance with specific labeling requirements for different device classes is essential for manufacturers to obtain regulatory approval and market their products legally. By ensuring that labels provide accurate, clear, and comprehensive information, manufacturers can support safe and effective device usage and regulatory compliance.

4.7.3 Case Studies on Labeling Non-compliance Issues

Examining real-world case studies can provide valuable insights into the consequences of labeling non-compliance and highlight the importance of adhering to regulatory requirements. Here are two illustrative case studies:

Case Study 1: Inadequate Warnings and Precautions

A manufacturer of Class II medical devices failed to include adequate warnings and precautions on the labeling of their product, a surgical implant used in orthopedic procedures. Although the device had undergone thorough testing and was deemed safe for use, the labeling failed to adequately warn surgeons about the potential risks associated with implantation in patients with specific medical conditions, such as osteoporosis or compromised bone density.

Consequently, several adverse events were reported, including device migration, fracture, and bone resorption, in patients with underlying bone health issues. Upon investigation, the FDA determined that the labeling did not adequately communicate the risks associated with the device, leading to inappropriate use and patient harm.

The manufacturer received a Warning Letter from the FDA, citing violations of labeling requirements under 21 CFR Part 801. They were required to revise the labeling to include clear and comprehensive warnings and precautions regarding patient selection criteria, potential risks, and contraindications. Failure to address the labeling deficiencies could result in further regulatory action, including product recalls or market withdrawal.

Case Study 2: Misleading Marketing Claims

A manufacturer of Class III implantable medical devices marketed their product with misleading claims on the labeling and promotional materials. The device, indicated for the treatment of a specific medical condition, was promoted as offering superior efficacy and patient outcomes compared to alternative treatments, without sufficient clinical evidence to support such claims.

Healthcare providers and patients were misled by the exaggerated marketing claims, leading to widespread adoption of the device in clinical practice. However, post-market surveillance data revealed higher-than-expected rates of adverse events and device failures, undermining the device's purported benefits.

The FDA conducted a review of the device's labeling and promotional materials and identified multiple instances of misleading or unsubstantiated claims. The manufacturer was issued a Notice of Violation, and corrective actions were mandated to revise the labeling and promotional materials to accurately reflect the device's safety and efficacy profile.

These case studies underscore the importance of adhering to labeling requirements and avoiding misleading or inaccurate information in medical device labeling and marketing materials. Non-compliance with labeling regulations can lead to serious consequences, including patient harm, regulatory sanctions, and damage to the manufacturer's reputation. By prioritizing regulatory compliance and transparency in labeling practices, manufacturers can mitigate risks and ensure the safe and effective use of their products.

4.8 Post-Market Surveillance

4.8.1 Objectives of Post-Market Surveillance

Post-market surveillance (PMS) is a critical aspect of the medical device lifecycle management process, encompassing activities aimed at monitoring the safety, performance, and effectiveness of devices once they are commercially available. The objectives of post-market surveillance include:

1. **Detecting Adverse Events:** One of the primary objectives of post-market surveillance is to promptly detect and investigate adverse events or safety concerns associated with medical devices. This includes identifying unexpected or rare adverse events that may not have been observed during pre-market clinical trials.
2. **Assessing Device Performance:** Post-market surveillance allows manufacturers to monitor the performance of their devices in real-world clinical settings and identify any issues related to device functionality, durability, or reliability. This information helps manufacturers make informed decisions about product improvements or modifications.
3. **Evaluating Long-Term Safety and Efficacy:** Post-market surveillance provides valuable data on the long-term safety and efficacy of medical devices, as well as their performance over extended periods of use. By collecting and analyzing real-world clinical data, manufacturers can assess the durability of device materials, the occurrence of late complications, and the effectiveness of long-term treatment outcomes.
4. **Monitoring Device Utilization:** Post-market surveillance activities also involve monitoring the patterns and trends of device utilization, including the types of patients receiving the device, the clinical indications for use, and the frequency of device-related procedures. This information helps identify potential misuse or off-label use of devices and inform targeted educational interventions.

5. **Compliance with Regulatory Requirements:** Regulatory authorities, such as the FDA in the United States, require manufacturers to establish post-market surveillance systems to comply with regulatory requirements and ensure ongoing monitoring of device safety and performance. Compliance with post-market surveillance regulations is essential for maintaining regulatory approval and market access for medical devices.
6. **Facilitating Risk Management:** Post-market surveillance plays a crucial role in risk management by identifying and mitigating potential risks associated with medical devices. Manufacturers can use post-market surveillance data to assess the severity and likelihood of identified risks, implement risk mitigation strategies, and communicate risk information to healthcare providers and patients.
7. **Supporting Continuous Improvement:** By collecting and analyzing post-market surveillance data, manufacturers can identify opportunities for product enhancements, design modifications, or manufacturing process improvements. This continuous feedback loop enables manufacturers to iteratively improve device safety, quality, and performance over time..

4.8 Post-Market Surveillance

4.8.1 Objectives of Post-Market Surveillance

Post-market surveillance (PMS) is a crucial aspect of ensuring the ongoing safety, efficacy, and quality of medical devices once they are available on the market. The objectives of post-market surveillance include:

1. **Detecting Adverse Events:** One of the primary goals of post-market surveillance is to promptly identify and investigate adverse events or safety concerns associated with medical devices. This includes monitoring for unexpected adverse events, device malfunctions, or other issues that may arise during real-world use.
2. **Assessing Device Performance:** Post-market surveillance allows manufacturers to monitor the performance of their devices in clinical practice. By collecting data on device functionality, reliability, and durability, manufacturers can identify any issues that may affect device performance and take appropriate corrective actions.
3. **Evaluating Long-Term Safety and Efficacy:** Post-market surveillance provides valuable insights into the long-term safety and efficacy of

medical devices. By monitoring device performance over extended periods, manufacturers can assess the durability of device materials, the occurrence of late complications, and the effectiveness of long-term treatment outcomes.

4. **Monitoring Device Utilization:** Post-market surveillance activities involve tracking the utilization of medical devices in clinical practice. This includes monitoring the types of patients receiving the device, the clinical indications for use, and the frequency of device-related procedures. Monitoring device utilization helps identify potential patterns of misuse or off-label use and inform appropriate interventions.
5. **Compliance with Regulatory Requirements:** Regulatory authorities require manufacturers to establish post-market surveillance systems to comply with regulatory requirements and ensure ongoing monitoring of device safety and performance. Compliance with post-market surveillance regulations is essential for maintaining regulatory approval and market access for medical devices.
6. **Facilitating Risk Management:** Post-market surveillance plays a vital role in risk management by identifying and mitigating potential risks associated with medical devices. By analyzing post-market surveillance data, manufacturers can assess the severity and likelihood of identified risks, implement risk mitigation strategies, and communicate risk information to healthcare providers and patients.
7. **Supporting Continuous Improvement:** Post-market surveillance data can provide valuable feedback for continuous improvement efforts. By analyzing trends and patterns in device performance, manufacturers can identify opportunities for product enhancements, design modifications, or manufacturing process improvements to optimize device safety and performance over time.

4.8.2 Tools and Methods Used in Surveillance

Post-market surveillance (PMS) relies on various tools and methods to effectively monitor the safety, performance, and utilization of medical devices in real-world clinical settings. These tools and methods enable manufacturers, regulatory authorities, and healthcare professionals to collect, analyze, and interpret data to identify potential safety concerns and make informed decisions. Here are some common tools and methods used in post-market surveillance:

1. **Adverse Event Reporting Systems:** Adverse event reporting systems allow healthcare professionals, patients, and manufacturers to report adverse events or device-related problems encountered during clinical practice. These systems serve as a valuable source of real-world data on device safety and performance.
2. **Medical Device Registries:** Medical device registries collect and maintain data on device implants or procedures performed in specific patient populations or clinical settings. Registries provide longitudinal data on device utilization, outcomes, and adverse events, allowing for comprehensive post-market surveillance.
3. **Electronic Health Records (EHRs):** Electronic health records capture detailed information about patient demographics, medical history, treatments, and outcomes. Analyzing EHR data can provide insights into device utilization, clinical outcomes, and adverse event rates across different patient populations.
4. **Surveillance Studies:** Surveillance studies involve systematic data collection and analysis to monitor device safety, performance, and utilization in specific patient populations or clinical settings. These studies may use prospective or retrospective study designs to assess device-related outcomes and identify potential safety concerns.
5. **Post-Approval Studies (PAS):** Post-approval studies are conducted after regulatory approval to further evaluate device safety and effectiveness in real-world clinical practice. These studies may be required by regulatory authorities as a condition of approval for certain medical devices and provide additional data for post-market surveillance.
6. **Signal Detection Methods:** Signal detection methods involve statistical and analytical techniques to identify potential safety signals or trends from large datasets of adverse event reports, registries, or other surveillance sources. These methods help prioritize further investigation and risk assessment of potential safety concerns.
7. **Data Mining and Analytics:** Data mining and analytics techniques are used to analyze large datasets of surveillance data, including adverse event reports, registries, and electronic health records. These techniques can help identify patterns, trends, and associations related to device safety, performance, and utilization.
8. **Literature Reviews and Meta-Analyses:** Literature reviews and meta-analyses systematically evaluate published studies and clinical reports to assess the safety and effectiveness of medical devices. These methods

help synthesize existing evidence and identify gaps or inconsistencies in the literature for further investigation.

By employing these tools and methods, stakeholders involved in post-market surveillance can systematically monitor and evaluate the safety, performance, and utilization of medical devices, identify potential safety concerns, and take appropriate corrective actions to protect patient safety and enhance public health.

4.8.3 Role of Surveillance in Ensuring Device Safety

Post-market surveillance (PMS) plays a pivotal role in safeguarding the safety of medical devices throughout their lifecycle. By monitoring device performance, detecting adverse events, and assessing real-world utilization, surveillance activities contribute to ongoing risk management and regulatory compliance. Here's how surveillance ensures device safety:

1. **Early Detection of Adverse Events:** Surveillance systems allow for the timely detection and reporting of adverse events associated with medical devices. By collecting and analyzing data from various sources, including adverse event reports, registries, and electronic health records, surveillance helps identify potential safety concerns as soon as they arise.
2. **Monitoring Device Performance:** Surveillance activities enable continuous monitoring of device performance in real-world clinical settings. By tracking device outcomes, including effectiveness, reliability, and durability, surveillance helps identify performance issues or deviations from expected results that may indicate safety risks or quality concerns.
3. **Assessment of Long-Term Safety:** Surveillance facilitates the evaluation of long-term safety outcomes associated with medical devices. By collecting longitudinal data on device utilization and patient outcomes, surveillance helps assess the persistence of device-related adverse events and identify any delayed or latent safety risks that may emerge over time.
4. **Identification of Emerging Risks:** Surveillance systems are instrumental in identifying emerging safety risks or trends associated with medical devices. By analyzing data from multiple sources and employing signal detection methods, surveillance helps detect patterns, clusters, or changes in adverse event reporting that may indicate new or previously

unrecognized safety concerns.

5. **Risk Stratification and Prioritization:** Surveillance activities support risk stratification and prioritization efforts by distinguishing between different levels of safety concerns based on their severity, frequency, and potential impact on patient health. By prioritizing high-risk events for further investigation and risk mitigation, surveillance helps allocate resources effectively to address the most pressing safety issues.
6. **Support for Regulatory Decision-Making:** Surveillance data inform regulatory decision-making processes by providing evidence-based insights into device safety and performance. Regulatory authorities use surveillance data to evaluate the overall benefit-risk profile of medical devices, make informed regulatory decisions, and take appropriate enforcement actions to protect public health.
7. **Continuous Improvement:** Surveillance fosters a culture of continuous improvement by providing feedback on device safety and performance to manufacturers, healthcare providers, and regulatory authorities. By identifying areas for enhancement or optimization, surveillance drives iterative improvements in device design, manufacturing processes, and clinical practices to enhance overall safety and quality of care.

Overall, the role of surveillance in ensuring device safety is multifaceted and essential for maintaining public confidence in the safety and effectiveness of medical devices. By proactively monitoring device performance, detecting adverse events, and assessing real-world outcomes, surveillance contributes to ongoing risk management efforts and promotes patient safety across the healthcare continuum.

4.9 Unique Device Identification (UDI)

4.9.1 Concept and Implementation of UDI

Unique Device Identification (UDI) is a system for uniquely identifying and tracking medical devices throughout their distribution and use. The concept and implementation of UDI involve several key components and considerations:

1. **Concept of UDI:**

    - UDI is based on the principle of assigning a unique identifier to each medical device, allowing for unambiguous identification and traceability throughout its lifecycle.

- The UDI comprises a standardized set of alphanumeric or numeric characters that encode specific information about the device, such as its manufacturer, model, version, and production lot.

1. **Objectives of UDI:**

- Enhancing Patient Safety: UDI facilitates the rapid and accurate identification of medical devices, enabling timely retrieval of device-related information and supporting effective adverse event reporting and product recalls.
- Improving Supply Chain Efficiency: UDI streamlines inventory management, distribution processes, and product tracking across the healthcare supply chain, reducing errors, minimizing waste, and optimizing resource utilization.
- Supporting Regulatory Oversight: UDI enables regulatory authorities to monitor device safety and effectiveness more effectively, track device performance in real-world clinical settings, and facilitate post-market surveillance activities.

3. **Implementation of UDI:**

- Regulatory Requirements: Regulatory bodies, such as the FDA in the United States and the European Commission, have mandated the implementation of UDI for certain classes of medical devices. Manufacturers are required to comply with specific UDI regulations and standards to ensure regulatory approval and market access.
- UDI Components: The UDI consists of two main components: the Device Identifier (DI), which identifies the specific device model and manufacturer, and the Production Identifier (PI), which provides additional information such as the device's lot or serial number and expiration date.
- Data Capture and Encoding: Manufacturers encode the UDI into machine-readable formats, such as barcodes or data matrices, which are affixed to the device label or packaging. Healthcare facilities and stakeholders use scanning devices or software systems to capture and decode the UDI for documentation and tracking purposes.

4. **Benefits of UDI:**

- Enhanced Patient Safety: UDI enables healthcare providers to accurately identify and trace medical devices used in patient care, reducing the risk of device-related errors, adverse events, and patient harm.
- Improved Supply Chain Management: UDI streamlines inventory management, facilitates product recalls, and enhances traceability throughout the supply chain, leading to greater efficiency, transparency, and cost-effectiveness.
- Regulatory Compliance: Compliance with UDI regulations ensures that manufacturers meet regulatory requirements for device identification, labeling, and traceability, supporting market access and regulatory compliance.

5. **Challenges and Considerations:**

- Implementation Costs: Implementing UDI systems may require significant investments in infrastructure, technology, and staff training, particularly for small manufacturers or healthcare facilities.
- Data Standardization: Ensuring consistent data standards and interoperability across different UDI systems and stakeholders is essential for maximizing the benefits of UDI and enabling seamless data exchange.
- Global Harmonization: Harmonizing UDI requirements and standards across different regulatory jurisdictions and international markets is critical for facilitating global trade, interoperability, and regulatory compliance.

In summary, UDI represents a fundamental shift in the identification and traceability of medical devices, with far-reaching implications for patient safety, supply chain management, and regulatory oversight. By adopting standardized UDI systems and processes, stakeholders can harness the full potential of UDI to improve healthcare quality, efficiency, and transparency across the continuum of care.

4.9.2 Benefits of UDI in Device Tracking and Recall

Unique Device Identification (UDI) offers several significant benefits in tracking medical devices and facilitating product recalls. These benefits contribute to enhancing patient safety, streamlining supply chain management, and supporting regulatory compliance. Here's an overview of the key advantages of UDI in device tracking and recall:

1. **Improved Traceability:** UDI enables accurate and efficient tracking of medical devices throughout their lifecycle, from manufacturing to patient use and beyond. Each device is assigned a unique identifier that contains essential information about its manufacturer, model, version, and production lot, allowing stakeholders to trace its origin and movement within the supply chain.
2. **Enhanced Product Visibility:** By encoding UDIs into machine-readable formats, such as barcodes or data matrices, medical devices become easily identifiable and scannable. Healthcare facilities, distributors, and regulatory authorities can use scanning devices or software systems to capture and decode UDIs, facilitating real-time visibility into device inventory, utilization, and location.
3. **Rapid Identification of Devices:** In the event of a product recall or safety alert, UDI enables rapid identification and retrieval of affected devices. Healthcare providers can scan device labels or packaging to access critical information, such as lot numbers, expiration dates, and recall status, allowing for prompt removal of recalled products from inventory and patient care settings.
4. **Targeted Communication:** UDI supports targeted communication and notification of affected stakeholders during a recall or safety advisory. Manufacturers can use UDI data to generate accurate lists of affected devices and notify healthcare providers, distributors, and patients directly, minimizing the risk of confusion or oversight in recall communications.
5. **Efficient Recall Execution:** UDI streamlines the execution of product recalls by automating and standardizing recall processes. Manufacturers can leverage UDI data to generate recall notices, track the disposition of recalled products, and monitor the effectiveness of recall actions in real time, ensuring timely and comprehensive resolution of safety issues.
6. **Comprehensive Post-Market Surveillance:** UDI facilitates post-market surveillance activities by providing a standardized mechanism for tracking device performance and safety outcomes. Regulatory authorities can use UDI data to monitor adverse event reports, track device utilization trends, and identify emerging safety concerns, enabling proactive regulatory action to protect public health.

7. **Regulatory Compliance:** Compliance with UDI regulations ensures that manufacturers meet regulatory requirements for device identification, labeling, and traceability. By implementing UDI systems and processes, manufacturers demonstrate their commitment to patient safety, regulatory compliance, and quality assurance, supporting market access and regulatory approval for their products.

4.9.3 Integration of UDI with Global Regulatory Practices

The integration of Unique Device Identification (UDI) with global regulatory practices is crucial for harmonizing standards, promoting interoperability, and facilitating international trade in medical devices. Here's how UDI is being integrated with global regulatory practices:

1. **Alignment with International Standards:** Regulatory authorities worldwide are aligning UDI requirements with international standards to promote consistency and interoperability. Organizations such as the International Medical Device Regulators Forum (IMDRF) work to harmonize UDI policies and practices across different regulatory jurisdictions, reducing barriers to market access and fostering global cooperation.
2. **Mutual Recognition Agreements:** Some countries and regions participate in mutual recognition agreements (MRAs) to recognize each other's regulatory requirements and assessments. By harmonizing UDI regulations and practices, MRAs facilitate the acceptance of UDI-compliant devices across participating jurisdictions, streamlining market access and reducing regulatory burdens for manufacturers.
3. **UDI Database Sharing:** Many countries have established UDI databases or repositories to centralize UDI data and facilitate information sharing among regulatory authorities, manufacturers, and other stakeholders. These databases serve as valuable resources for tracking medical devices, monitoring safety outcomes, and coordinating regulatory activities on a global scale.
4. **Collaborative Initiatives:** Regulatory authorities collaborate through initiatives such as the World Health Organization's Global Medical Device Nomenclature (GMDN) to develop standardized coding systems and terminology for medical devices. By adopting common identifiers and nomenclature, regulators can enhance data exchange, promote transparency, and improve the accuracy and reliability of UDI data.

5. **Adoption of International Guidelines:** Regulatory authorities incorporate international guidelines and best practices into their UDI frameworks to ensure alignment with global standards. Guidelines such as those developed by the International Organization for Standardization (ISO) provide recommendations for UDI implementation, data formatting, and labeling requirements, facilitating interoperability and regulatory compliance across borders.
6. **Cross-Border Collaboration:** Regulatory authorities engage in cross-border collaboration and information sharing to address common challenges and promote regulatory convergence. Initiatives such as the IMDRF facilitate dialogue and cooperation among regulators, industry stakeholders, and other interested parties to develop consensus-based approaches to UDI implementation and regulation.
7. **Capacity Building and Training:** Regulatory authorities invest in capacity building and training programs to enhance regulatory expertise and promote UDI compliance among manufacturers and stakeholders. By providing guidance, resources, and training opportunities, regulators empower stakeholders to understand and implement UDI requirements effectively, fostering compliance and promoting patient safety.
8. **Periodic Review and Update:** Regulatory authorities periodically review and update UDI regulations and guidance documents to reflect evolving technologies, market trends, and international standards. By staying abreast of developments in the field and engaging with stakeholders, regulators ensure that UDI frameworks remain relevant, effective, and aligned with global regulatory practices.

4.10 Summary and Future Directions

4.10.1 Key Takeaways from Current Practices

As we reflect on the current practices surrounding regulatory approval processes, Unique Device Identification (UDI), and post-market surveillance in the medical device industry, several key takeaways emerge:

1. **Regulatory Approval Processes:** The regulatory approval processes in the USA, including 510(k) Premarket Notification and Pre-Market Approval (PMA), are essential for ensuring the safety, efficacy, and quality of medical devices. Manufacturers must navigate complex regulatory requirements and demonstrate compliance with rigorous standards to obtain market approval.

2. **UDI Implementation:** The implementation of Unique Device Identification (UDI) offers significant benefits in device tracking, recall management, and post-market surveillance. By assigning unique identifiers to medical devices and integrating them into global regulatory practices, stakeholders can enhance patient safety, streamline supply chain management, and facilitate international trade.
3. **Post-Market Surveillance:** Post-market surveillance plays a critical role in monitoring the safety, performance, and effectiveness of medical devices in real-world clinical settings. Surveillance activities enable the early detection of adverse events, support targeted recalls, and provide valuable data for regulatory decision-making and continuous improvement efforts.
4. **Global Harmonization:** Harmonizing UDI requirements and regulatory practices on a global scale is essential for promoting interoperability, reducing trade barriers, and enhancing patient safety. Regulatory authorities collaborate through international initiatives to align standards, share UDI data, and develop consensus-based approaches to UDI implementation and regulation.

Looking ahead, several future directions and opportunities emerge for advancing regulatory practices and improving patient outcomes in the medical device industry:

1. **Enhanced Data Analytics:** Leveraging advanced data analytics and artificial intelligence (AI) technologies can enhance the effectiveness of post-market surveillance and signal detection efforts. By analyzing large datasets of UDI and adverse event reports, regulators can identify emerging safety trends, prioritize interventions, and proactively mitigate risks.
2. **Real-World Evidence (RWE):** Incorporating real-world evidence into regulatory decision-making processes can provide valuable insights into device safety and effectiveness in diverse patient populations and clinical settings. Regulators are exploring ways to leverage RWE from electronic health records, medical registries, and other sources to complement traditional clinical trial data and support regulatory approvals.
3. **Digital Health Technologies:** The rise of digital health technologies, such as wearable devices, remote monitoring systems, and mobile health

apps, presents new opportunities and challenges for regulatory oversight. Regulators must adapt existing frameworks to accommodate innovative technologies while ensuring patient safety, data privacy, and cybersecurity.

4. **International Collaboration:** Strengthening international collaboration and information sharing among regulatory authorities, industry stakeholders, and healthcare providers is crucial for addressing global challenges and promoting regulatory convergence. Initiatives such as the IMDRF and WHO Global Benchmarking Tool facilitate dialogue, cooperation, and capacity building in regulatory practices.

In conclusion, regulatory approval processes, UDI implementation, and post-market surveillance are integral components of ensuring the safety, efficacy, and quality of medical devices. By embracing innovative approaches, fostering global collaboration, and prioritizing patient-centricity, stakeholders can navigate evolving regulatory landscapes, drive technological advancements, and ultimately improve patient outcomes in the medical device industry.

4.10.2 Emerging Trends and Innovations in Regulatory Approaches

The landscape of regulatory approaches in the medical device industry is evolving rapidly, driven by technological advancements, changing healthcare needs, and emerging global challenges. Several emerging trends and innovations are shaping the future of regulatory practices:

1. **Advanced Digital Health Technologies:** The proliferation of digital health technologies, including wearable devices, telemedicine platforms, and artificial intelligence (AI) applications, is revolutionizing healthcare delivery and patient monitoring. Regulators are exploring new regulatory frameworks to ensure the safety, effectiveness, and cybersecurity of digital health products while promoting innovation and market access.
2. **Real-World Evidence (RWE):** There is growing recognition of the value of real-world evidence (RWE) in supplementing traditional clinical trial data and informing regulatory decision-making. Regulators are exploring ways to incorporate RWE from electronic health records, medical registries, and patient-generated data into pre-market evaluations, post-market surveillance, and regulatory approvals.

3. **Regulatory Science and Predictive Modeling:** Regulatory science initiatives are harnessing cutting-edge technologies and predictive modeling techniques to enhance regulatory decision-making and risk assessment. By leveraging data analytics, computational modeling, and simulation studies, regulators can predict device performance, assess safety risks, and expedite regulatory reviews while maintaining high standards of safety and efficacy.
4. **Patient-Centric Regulatory Approaches:** There is a growing emphasis on patient-centricity in regulatory practices, with regulators increasingly involving patients in decision-making processes, soliciting patient input on device design and development, and considering patient preferences and priorities in regulatory assessments. Patient engagement initiatives aim to improve transparency, trust, and accountability in regulatory decision-making and promote patient-centered innovation.
5. **Global Harmonization and Collaboration:** Regulatory authorities are prioritizing global harmonization and collaboration to streamline regulatory processes, reduce duplication of efforts, and facilitate international trade in medical devices. Initiatives such as the International Medical Device Regulators Forum (IMDRF) and mutual recognition agreements (MRAs) promote regulatory convergence, information sharing, and capacity building among regulators worldwide.
6. **Agile Regulatory Pathways:** Regulators are exploring agile regulatory pathways and innovative approval mechanisms to accelerate access to breakthrough technologies and address unmet medical needs. Expedited review programs, adaptive pathways, and conditional approvals enable faster market entry for innovative devices while ensuring appropriate safeguards for patient safety and public health.
7. **Regulatory Transparency and Communication:** Regulators are enhancing transparency and communication with stakeholders by providing clearer guidance, more accessible information, and increased opportunities for public consultation and feedback. Open dialogue, stakeholder engagement, and proactive communication foster trust, collaboration, and accountability in regulatory decision-making processes.

4.10.3 Anticipated Challenges and Strategies for Future Compliance

As the medical device industry continues to evolve, stakeholders face anticipated challenges in maintaining compliance with regulatory requirements while navigating dynamic market trends and technological advancements. Strategies for future compliance must address these challenges proactively to ensure patient safety, promote innovation, and maintain regulatory alignment. Key challenges and corresponding strategies include:

1. **Rapid Technological Advancements:** The pace of technological innovation presents challenges in ensuring that regulatory frameworks keep pace with evolving product designs and functionalities. Strategies include:

    - Engaging in ongoing dialogue with regulators to anticipate emerging technologies and update regulatory guidance accordingly.
    - Adopting agile regulatory pathways that accommodate iterative development cycles and rapid product iterations.
    - Investing in regulatory science initiatives to develop novel evaluation methods for innovative technologies.

2. **Data Privacy and Security Concerns:** The increasing use of digital health technologies raises concerns about data privacy, security, and cybersecurity vulnerabilities. Strategies include:

    - Implementing robust data protection measures, encryption protocols, and access controls to safeguard patient information.
    - Conducting comprehensive risk assessments and vulnerability testing to identify and mitigate cybersecurity threats.
    - Collaborating with regulatory authorities, industry partners, and cybersecurity experts to develop standards and best practices for securing digital health products.

3. **Global Regulatory Divergence:** Variations in regulatory requirements and standards across different jurisdictions create challenges for manufacturers seeking to access international markets. Strategies include:

    - Participating in global harmonization initiatives and mutual recognition agreements to promote regulatory convergence and streamline market access.

- Establishing regulatory intelligence functions to monitor and track regulatory changes in key markets and adapt compliance strategies accordingly.
- Leveraging regulatory consultancy services and industry associations to navigate complex regulatory landscapes and obtain expert guidance on compliance requirements.

4. **Resource Constraints and Capacity Challenges:** Limited resources, expertise, and infrastructure may impede compliance efforts, particularly for small and medium-sized enterprises (SMEs) and manufacturers in emerging markets. Strategies include:

    - Investing in workforce training, professional development, and talent acquisition to build regulatory expertise and capacity internally.
    - Collaborating with industry consortia, trade associations, and regulatory agencies to pool resources, share best practices, and address common compliance challenges collectively.
    - Exploring outsourcing options, such as contract regulatory services and third-party consulting firms, to augment internal capabilities and access specialized expertise on an as-needed basis.

5. **Complex Supply Chains and Outsourcing Practices:** Globalized supply chains and outsourcing practices introduce complexities in ensuring compliance with regulatory requirements across multiple stakeholders and geographies. Strategies include:

    - Implementing robust supplier management processes, risk assessments, and quality agreements to ensure compliance throughout the supply chain.
    - Conducting regular audits, inspections, and quality control checks to verify supplier compliance with regulatory standards and contractual obligations.
    - Leveraging digital tools, such as supply chain management software and blockchain technology, to enhance transparency, traceability, and accountability in supply chain operations.

CHAPTER FIVE

REGULATORY APPROVAL PROCESSES IN THE EUROPEAN UNION

5.1 Overview of EU Directives

5.1.1 Introduction to EU Medical Device Directives

The European Union (EU) regulatory framework for medical devices is governed by a set of directives that outline the requirements for placing medical devices on the market and ensuring their safety, efficacy, and quality. These directives include the Medical Device Directive (MDD), the Active Implantable Medical Device Directive (AIMDD), and the In Vitro Diagnostics Directive (IVDD). Each directive addresses specific categories of medical devices and establishes regulatory requirements tailored to their characteristics and intended use. The directives aim to harmonize regulations across EU member states, facilitating the free movement of medical devices within the European Economic Area (EEA) while safeguarding public health and ensuring patient safety. Compliance with EU directives is mandatory for manufacturers seeking to market medical devices in the EU, and non-compliance may result in sanctions or market withdrawal of the device. Thus, understanding the scope and requirements of EU medical device directives is essential for manufacturers to navigate regulatory approval processes effectively and access the EU market.

5.1.2 Scope and Objectives of the Medical Device Directive (MDD)

The Medical Device Directive (MDD) is a cornerstone of the EU regulatory framework for medical devices, providing comprehensive guidelines for the evaluation, approval, and post-market surveillance of medical devices. The scope of the MDD encompasses a wide range of medical devices, including instruments, apparatus, appliances, software, and materials used for diagnosis, prevention, monitoring, treatment, or alleviation of disease or injury in humans. The MDD aims to ensure the safety, performance, and quality of medical devices by establishing essential requirements related to design, manufacturing, labeling, and clinical evaluation. These requirements encompass aspects such as risk management, biocompatibility, sterility, and usability, with the overarching goal of protecting public health and ensuring the safety and efficacy of medical devices marketed within the EU. The MDD also defines the responsibilities of manufacturers, authorized representatives, notified bodies, and competent authorities in the regulatory process, outlining their roles and obligations to comply with regulatory requirements and ensure continuous monitoring of device safety and performance throughout their lifecycle. By harmonizing regulatory standards and procedures across EU member states, the MDD facilitates the free movement of medical devices within the EU market while upholding rigorous standards of patient safety and product quality. Compliance with the MDD is a prerequisite for obtaining CE marking, which signifies conformity with EU regulatory requirements and allows manufacturers to market their devices within the EU and the EEA. Thus, understanding the scope and objectives of the MDD is essential for manufacturers seeking regulatory approval for their medical devices in the EU market.

5.1.3 Overview of the Active Implantable Medical Device Directive (AIMDD)

The Active Implantable Medical Device Directive (AIMDD) is a key component of the EU regulatory framework for medical devices, specifically focusing on devices intended to be implanted into the human body and powered by an internal source of energy. These devices, such as pacemakers, implantable cardioverter-defibrillators (ICDs), and neurostimulators, play a critical role in the diagnosis, treatment, and management of various medical conditions. The AIMDD establishes specific requirements and conformity assessment procedures tailored to the unique characteristics and risks associated with active implantable medical devices. These requirements address aspects such as biocompatibility, electrical safety, software validation, and long-term device performance, aiming to ensure the safety, reliability, and effectiveness of these devices in clinical practice. The AIMDD also delineates the roles and responsibilities of manufacturers, notified bodies, competent authorities, and other stakeholders in the regulatory process, outlining requirements for device documentation, labeling, and post-market surveillance. Compliance with the AIMDD is mandatory for manufacturers seeking to market active implantable medical devices in the EU, and CE marking is required to demonstrate conformity with regulatory requirements and enable market access within the EU and the EEA. By setting stringent standards for the evaluation and approval of active implantable medical devices, the AIMDD aims to protect patient safety, enhance device performance, and promote innovation in this critical area of medical technology. Understanding the overview and requirements of the AIMDD is essential for manufacturers to navigate regulatory approval processes effectively and ensure compliance with EU regulations for active implantable medical devices.

5.1.4 Introduction to the In Vitro Diagnostics Directive (IVDD)

The In Vitro Diagnostics Directive (IVDD) is a fundamental component of the European Union's regulatory framework for medical devices, specifically addressing in vitro diagnostic medical devices (IVDs). These devices are intended for the examination of specimens derived from the human body, such as blood, tissue, or urine, to provide information for medical purposes. The IVDD sets out regulatory requirements and conformity assessment procedures tailored to the unique characteristics and intended use of IVDs, aiming to ensure their safety, reliability, and performance. The directive covers a broad spectrum of IVDs, including reagents, instruments, and software used for diagnostic testing, disease screening, and patient management. Key aspects addressed by the IVDD include analytical performance, clinical validation, quality management systems, and labeling requirements for IVD products. The IVDD also defines the roles and responsibilities of manufacturers, notified bodies, competent authorities, and other stakeholders in the regulatory process, outlining requirements for device documentation, technical documentation, and post-market surveillance. Compliance with the IVDD is mandatory for manufacturers seeking to market IVDs in the European Union, and CE marking is required to demonstrate conformity with regulatory requirements and enable market access within the EU and the European Economic Area (EEA). By establishing clear standards and procedures for the evaluation and approval of IVDs, the IVDD aims to protect patient safety, enhance diagnostic accuracy, and facilitate access to innovative diagnostic technologies. Understanding the introduction and requirements of the IVDD is essential for manufacturers to navigate regulatory approval processes effectively and ensure compliance with EU regulations for in vitro diagnostic medical devices.

5.2 Medical Device Directive (MDD)

5.2.1 Regulatory Framework and Classification Criteria

The Medical Device Directive (MDD) establishes a comprehensive regulatory framework for medical devices within the European Union (EU), outlining requirements for their evaluation, approval, and post-market surveillance. Central to the MDD is the classification of medical devices into different risk categories based on their intended use, duration of contact with the human body, and potential risks to patients and users. The classification criteria, outlined in Annex IX of the directive, classify devices into four classes: Class I, IIa, IIb, and III, with increasing levels of regulatory scrutiny and conformity assessment requirements. Class I devices are considered low risk and may be subject to self-certification by the manufacturer, while Class IIa, IIb, and III devices require involvement of notified bodies for conformity assessment procedures. The regulatory framework established by the MDD encompasses essential requirements related to design, manufacturing, labeling, and clinical evaluation of medical devices, ensuring their safety, performance, and quality throughout their lifecycle. Compliance with the MDD is mandatory for manufacturers seeking to market medical devices in the EU, and CE marking is required to demonstrate conformity with regulatory requirements and enable market access within the EU and the European Economic Area (EEA). By providing clear guidelines for device classification and regulatory requirements, the MDD facilitates the free movement of medical devices within the EU market while upholding rigorous standards of patient safety and product quality. Understanding the regulatory framework and classification criteria outlined in the MDD is essential for manufacturers to navigate compliance requirements effectively and ensure regulatory approval for their medical devices in the EU market.

5.2.2 Essential Requirements and Conformity Assessment Procedures

The Medical Device Directive (MDD) lays down essential requirements that medical devices must meet to ensure their safety and performance. These requirements, detailed in Annex I of the directive, cover various aspects such as design, manufacture, packaging, labeling, and instructions for use. They address essential criteria such as biocompatibility, sterility, risk management, and clinical evaluation, ensuring that medical devices are safe, effective, and suitable for their intended purpose.

Compliance with these essential requirements is demonstrated through conformity assessment procedures, which vary depending on the classification of the device. For Class I devices, manufacturers can self-certify compliance with the essential requirements based on their own assessment. However, for higher-risk devices (Classes IIa, IIb, and III), conformity assessment involves the intervention of notified bodies, independent organizations designated by EU member states to assess the compliance of medical devices with regulatory requirements.

Conformity assessment procedures may include a combination of conformity assessment modules, such as examination of the manufacturer's quality management system, type examination of the device, assessment of the technical documentation, and ongoing surveillance of the manufacturing process. The specific modules required depend on the classification of the device and its associated risks.

Once conformity assessment is successfully completed, manufacturers affix the CE marking to their devices, indicating compliance with the MDD and enabling market access within the EU and the European Economic Area (EEA). However, compliance with the essential requirements does not end with the initial certification. Manufacturers are required to maintain compliance throughout the lifecycle of the device through post-market surveillance, vigilance reporting, and ongoing quality management practices.

Understanding the essential requirements and conformity assessment procedures outlined in the MDD is essential for manufacturers to ensure compliance with EU regulatory requirements and obtain regulatory approval for their medical devices in the EU market. By adhering to these requirements and procedures, manufacturers can demonstrate the safety, efficacy, and quality of their medical devices and contribute to the protection of patient health and safety within the EU.

5.2.3 Notified Bodies and Their Role in Certification

Notified Bodies play a crucial role in the certification process for medical devices under the Medical Device Directive (MDD). These independent organizations are designated by EU member states and authorized by competent authorities to assess the conformity of medical devices with regulatory requirements. Notified Bodies evaluate the technical documentation, quality management systems, and manufacturing processes of medical device manufacturers to ensure compliance with the essential requirements outlined in the MDD.

The designation of Notified Bodies is based on their competence, expertise, and ability to perform conformity assessment activities effectively. Notified Bodies must demonstrate their technical competence and impartiality through accreditation by national accreditation bodies, ensuring that they have the necessary expertise and resources to carry out their duties objectively and reliably.

The role of Notified Bodies in the certification process varies depending on the classification of the medical device. For higher-risk devices (Classes IIa, IIb, and III), Notified Bodies are directly involved in the conformity assessment process and may conduct on-site audits, inspections, and testing to verify compliance with regulatory requirements. They assess the technical documentation submitted by manufacturers, review the results of conformity assessment activities, and issue certificates of conformity if all requirements are met.

Notified Bodies also play a crucial role in post-market surveillance and vigilance reporting, monitoring the performance of medical devices on the market and investigating complaints, incidents, and adverse events. They collaborate with competent authorities and manufacturers to address issues related to device safety and performance, taking appropriate corrective and preventive actions when necessary.

The involvement of Notified Bodies in the certification process adds an additional layer of assurance for patients, healthcare providers, and regulatory authorities, helping to ensure the safety, efficacy, and quality of medical devices marketed within the EU. By working with accredited Notified Bodies and demonstrating compliance with regulatory requirements, manufacturers can obtain CE marking for their medical devices and gain access to the EU market, contributing to the protection of public health and safety. Understanding the role of Notified Bodies and their responsibilities in the certification process is essential for manufacturers seeking regulatory approval for their medical devices in the EU.

5.3 Active Implantable Medical Device Directive (AIMDD)

5.3.1 Scope and Specific Requirements for Active Implantable Devices

The Active Implantable Medical Device Directive (AIMDD) is a regulatory framework specific to active implantable medical devices intended to be implanted into the human body. These devices, such as pacemakers, implantable cardioverter-defibrillators (ICDs), and neurostimulators, are powered by an internal source of energy and play a critical role in the diagnosis, treatment, and management of various medical conditions.

The scope of the AIMDD covers a wide range of active implantable devices, including those intended for cardiac rhythm management, neuromodulation, drug delivery, and monitoring of physiological parameters. Specific requirements for these devices are outlined in the directive, addressing aspects such as biocompatibility, electrical safety, software validation, and long-term device performance.

Compliance with the AIMDD is mandatory for manufacturers seeking to market active implantable devices within the European Union (EU) and the European Economic Area (EEA). The directive establishes conformity assessment procedures tailored to the unique characteristics and risks associated with these devices, ensuring their safety, reliability, and effectiveness in clinical practice.

Notified Bodies, independent organizations designated by EU member states, play a key role in the conformity assessment process for active implantable devices under the AIMDD. They assess the technical documentation, quality management systems, and manufacturing processes of manufacturers to verify compliance with regulatory requirements.

The AIMDD also sets requirements for post-market surveillance and vigilance reporting to monitor the performance of active implantable devices on the market and address issues related to device safety and performance. Manufacturers are required to establish post-market surveillance systems, conduct periodic reviews of device performance, and report adverse events and incidents to competent authorities and Notified Bodies.

Overall, the AIMDD aims to ensure the safety, efficacy, and quality of active implantable medical devices marketed within the EU, protecting patient health and safety while facilitating innovation in this critical area of medical technology. Understanding the scope and specific requirements of the AIMDD is essential for manufacturers to navigate regulatory approval processes effectively and ensure compliance with EU regulations for active implantable devices.

5.3.2 Clinical Evaluation and Post-Market Surveillance Requirements

Clinical evaluation and post-market surveillance are essential components of the regulatory process for active implantable medical devices under the Active Implantable Medical Device Directive (AIMDD). These processes ensure ongoing assessment of device safety, performance, and effectiveness throughout its lifecycle, from pre-market development to post-market distribution and use.

Clinical evaluation involves the systematic assessment of clinical data pertaining to the safety and performance of the active implantable device. Manufacturers are required to conduct clinical investigations or gather clinical data from existing sources to demonstrate compliance with regulatory requirements. The aim is to provide robust evidence supporting the safety, performance, and intended use of the device in clinical practice. Clinical evaluation must consider factors such as patient population, intended use, risk-benefit analysis, and comparison with alternative treatments or devices.

Post-market surveillance entails continuous monitoring of the device's performance and safety once it is placed on the market. Manufacturers are obligated to establish post-market surveillance systems to collect, analyze, and report data on device performance, adverse events, and other relevant information. This includes monitoring feedback from healthcare professionals, patients, and other stakeholders, as well as conducting periodic reviews of clinical data and conducting trend analysis to detect potential safety issues or emerging risks.

Manufacturers are required to report adverse events, incidents, and other relevant information to competent authorities and Notified Bodies in a timely manner. This enables regulatory authorities to take appropriate actions to mitigate risks and ensure patient safety. Manufacturers must also implement corrective and preventive actions as necessary to address identified issues and improve device safety and performance.

Compliance with clinical evaluation and post-market surveillance requirements is critical for manufacturers seeking regulatory approval for active implantable medical devices under the AIMDD. By conducting rigorous clinical evaluations, establishing robust post-market surveillance systems, and promptly reporting adverse events, manufacturers can demonstrate the safety, performance, and effectiveness of their devices and contribute to the protection of patient health and safety within the European Union (EU) and the European Economic Area (EEA). Understanding and adhering to these requirements is essential for manufacturers to navigate the regulatory process effectively and ensure compliance with EU regulations for active implantable devices.

5.3.3 Unique Considerations for Implantable Device Certification

Certification of implantable medical devices under the Active Implantable Medical Device Directive (AIMDD) entails unique considerations due to the nature of these devices and their intended use within the human body. Several factors distinguish the certification process for implantable devices from that of other medical devices:

1. **Biocompatibility:** Implantable devices come into direct contact with bodily tissues and fluids, necessitating rigorous assessment of biocompatibility to ensure they do not cause adverse reactions or tissue responses. Manufacturers must demonstrate compliance with biocompatibility standards, including testing for cytotoxicity, sensitization, and irritation, to mitigate the risk of adverse biological reactions.
2. **Long-term Performance:** Implantable devices are intended for long-term use within the body, requiring assurance of their durability, reliability, and performance over extended periods. Manufacturers must conduct comprehensive testing and validation to assess device longevity, functionality, and resistance to physiological stresses encountered within the body environment.
3. **Surgical Implantation Procedures:** Implantable devices often require surgical implantation procedures, necessitating consideration of surgical techniques, implantation site, and compatibility with surgical instruments and techniques. Manufacturers may need to provide instructions for use, surgical training materials, and support services to ensure safe and effective implantation of the device by healthcare professionals.
4. **Monitoring and Remote Management:** Some implantable devices, such as cardiac pacemakers and neurostimulators, may feature remote monitoring and management capabilities. Certification of these devices may involve additional considerations related to data security, wireless communication, and interoperability with external monitoring systems.
5. **Risk Management:** Implantable devices pose unique risks related to implantation surgery, device malfunction, and long-term performance issues. Manufacturers must implement robust risk management processes to identify, assess, and mitigate potential risks throughout the device lifecycle, from design and development to post-market surveillance.

6. **Regulatory Oversight:** Due to the higher risks associated with implantable devices, regulatory oversight and scrutiny during certification are more stringent compared to other medical devices. Notified Bodies play a critical role in assessing the conformity of implantable devices with regulatory requirements and ensuring their safety, efficacy, and quality.

By addressing these unique considerations, manufacturers can navigate the certification process for implantable medical devices under the AIMDD effectively. Ensuring compliance with regulatory requirements, conducting thorough testing and validation, and prioritizing patient safety are paramount to achieving certification and gaining access to the European Union (EU) market for implantable devices.

5.4 In Vitro Diagnostics Directive (IVDD)

5.4.1 Regulatory Framework for In Vitro Diagnostic Devices (IVDs)

The In Vitro Diagnostics Directive (IVDD) establishes a regulatory framework for in vitro diagnostic devices (IVDs) within the European Union (EU) and the European Economic Area (EEA). IVDs are medical devices used to perform diagnostic tests on specimens derived from the human body, such as blood, urine, or tissue, outside the body in a laboratory setting.

The regulatory framework outlined in the IVDD aims to ensure the safety, performance, and quality of IVDs marketed within the EU and EEA. It covers a broad range of IVDs, including reagents, instruments, software, and systems used for diagnostic testing, disease screening, and patient management.

Under the IVDD, IVDs are classified into different risk categories based on their intended use, characteristics, and potential risks to patients and users. The classification determines the level of regulatory scrutiny and conformity assessment procedures required for each device. IVDs are categorized into four classes: Class A, Class B, Class C, and Class D, with increasing levels of risk and regulatory requirements.

Manufacturers of IVDs must comply with essential requirements outlined in Annex I of the IVDD, which cover various aspects such as design, manufacturing, performance, and labeling of IVDs. These requirements aim to ensure the safety, effectiveness, and reliability of IVDs for their intended use.

Conformity assessment procedures are conducted to assess the compliance of IVDs with regulatory requirements and determine their suitability for market placement. The procedures vary depending on the classification of the device and may involve self-assessment by the manufacturer for lower-risk devices or involvement of Notified Bodies for higher-risk devices.

Once conformity assessment is successfully completed, manufacturers affix the CE marking to their IVDs, indicating compliance with regulatory requirements and enabling market access within the EU and EEA. However, compliance with the IVDD does not end with the initial certification. Manufacturers are required to establish post-market surveillance systems to monitor the performance of IVDs on the market and report adverse events or incidents to competent authorities.

Overall, the regulatory framework established by the IVDD ensures that IVDs marketed within the EU and EEA meet rigorous standards of safety, performance, and quality, contributing to the protection of patient health and safety. Understanding the regulatory framework for IVDs outlined in the IVDD is essential for manufacturers to navigate the certification process effectively and ensure compliance with EU regulations for in vitro diagnostic devices.

5.4.2 Performance Evaluation and Clinical Evidence Requirements

Performance evaluation and the provision of clinical evidence are fundamental components of the regulatory process for in vitro diagnostic devices (IVDs) under the In Vitro Diagnostics Directive (IVDD). These processes are essential for demonstrating the safety, performance, and effectiveness of IVDs in diagnosing diseases or conditions and guiding patient management decisions.

Performance evaluation involves the systematic assessment of the analytical and clinical performance characteristics of the IVD. Manufacturers must conduct studies and tests to evaluate parameters such as accuracy, precision, analytical sensitivity, analytical specificity, and clinical sensitivity/clinical specificity. These studies aim to demonstrate that the IVD reliably detects and measures the analyte or target of interest in clinical samples and produces accurate and reproducible results.

Clinical evidence refers to data derived from clinical studies or real-world use of the IVD in clinical practice, demonstrating its clinical utility, effectiveness, and impact on patient outcomes. Clinical evidence may include clinical validation studies, comparative studies, clinical utility studies, and real-world evidence from post-market surveillance. Manufacturers must gather sufficient clinical evidence to support the intended use claims of the IVD and demonstrate its clinical performance in relevant patient populations and clinical settings.

The level of performance evaluation and clinical evidence required depends on the classification of the IVD and its intended use. Higher-risk devices or those with novel technologies or intended uses may require more extensive performance evaluation and clinical evidence to demonstrate safety and effectiveness. Manufacturers must also consider factors such as the intended patient population, clinical context, intended use claims, and regulatory requirements when designing and conducting performance evaluation and clinical studies.

Compliance with performance evaluation and clinical evidence requirements is critical for obtaining regulatory approval and CE marking for IVDs under the IVDD. Manufacturers must design and conduct robust performance evaluation studies and clinical investigations, adhere to good clinical practice (GCP) guidelines, and ensure the integrity, reliability, and validity of thc data collected. By providing comprehensive performance evaluation and clinical evidence, manufacturers can demonstrate the safety and effectiveness of their IVDs and contribute to the improvement of patient care and public health. Understanding and fulfilling these requirements are essential for manufacturers seeking regulatory approval for IVDs within the European Union (EU) and the European Economic Area (EEA).

5.4.3 Conformity Assessment Routes for IVDs

Conformity assessment is a crucial step in the regulatory process for in vitro diagnostic devices (IVDs) under the In Vitro Diagnostics Directive (IVDD). It involves the evaluation of the IVD's compliance with regulatory requirements to ensure its safety, performance, and quality before it can be placed on the market within the European Union (EU) and the European Economic Area (EEA). The IVDD outlines several conformity assessment routes that manufacturers can follow based on the classification of the IVD and its associated risks:

1. **Self-Assessment (Declaration of Conformity):** Lower-risk IVDs, typically classified as Class A or Class B under the IVDD, may undergo self-assessment by the manufacturer. In this route, the manufacturer compiles technical documentation demonstrating compliance with

essential requirements and declares conformity with the directive. However, this route may still involve involvement of a Notified Body depending on certain criteria.

2. **Involvement of a Notified Body:** Higher-risk IVDs, classified as Class C or Class D under the IVDD, require the involvement of a Notified Body in the conformity assessment process. Notified Bodies are independent organizations designated by EU member states to assess the conformity of medical devices with regulatory requirements. Depending on the classification and characteristics of the IVD, manufacturers may choose from various conformity assessment modules involving Notified Bodies. These modules may include:

   - **Type Examination:** The Notified Body assesses the design, manufacturing processes, and documentation of the IVD to verify compliance with essential requirements. This module is typically used for higher-risk IVDs with complex technologies or novel features.
   - **Full Quality Assurance:** The Notified Body audits the manufacturer's quality management system to ensure ongoing compliance with regulatory requirements. This module is suitable for manufacturers with established quality systems and a range of IVD products.
   - **Product Verification:** The Notified Body verifies the conformity of individual IVD units or batches with specified requirements. This module is used for IVDs where full quality assurance is not required, but periodic verification of product quality is necessary.

1. **Mutual Recognition of Conformity Assessment:** Manufacturers may also benefit from mutual recognition agreements between EU member states and non-EU countries, allowing the recognition of conformity assessment results conducted by designated bodies in those countries. This streamlines the regulatory process for manufacturers seeking market access in both EU and non-EU markets.

By selecting the appropriate conformity assessment route and working closely with Notified Bodies when necessary, manufacturers can ensure compliance with regulatory requirements and obtain CE marking for their IVDs, enabling market access within the EU and EEA. Understanding the various conformity assessment routes and their implications is essential for manufacturers seeking regulatory approval for IVDs under the IVDD.

5.5 CE Certification Process

5.5.1 Introduction to CE Marking and Its Significance

CE marking is a mandatory requirement for medical devices, including in vitro diagnostic devices (IVDs), placed on the market within the European Union (EU) and the European Economic Area (EEA). It indicates that the device complies with essential health and safety requirements and conforms to relevant EU legislation, including the In Vitro Diagnostic Devices Directive (IVDD).

The CE marking serves as a passport for medical devices to access the EU market, demonstrating that they meet rigorous standards of safety, performance, and quality. It signifies that the manufacturer has conducted conformity assessment procedures to assess compliance with regulatory requirements and has fulfilled obligations related to product safety and performance.

The CE certification process involves several key steps:

1. **Identification of Applicable Directives:** Manufacturers must determine which EU directives apply to their medical devices, including the IVDD for in vitro diagnostic devices. They must understand the regulatory requirements and essential health and safety requirements outlined in the directives.
2. **Conformity Assessment:** Manufacturers conduct conformity assessment procedures to demonstrate compliance with regulatory requirements. This may involve self-assessment for lower-risk devices or involvement of a Notified Body for higher-risk devices. Conformity assessment includes evaluation of design, manufacturing processes, quality management systems, and clinical evidence.
3. **Compilation of Technical Documentation:** Manufacturers prepare technical documentation containing essential information about the device, including design specifications, risk management processes, results of performance evaluation studies, clinical evidence, and instructions for use. This documentation serves as evidence of compliance with regulatory requirements.
4. **Declaration of Conformity:** Based on the results of conformity assessment and technical documentation, the manufacturer issues a declaration of conformity, declaring that the device meets the essential requirements of the relevant directives and is eligible for CE marking.

5. **Affixing the CE Mark:** Upon successful completion of the certification process, the manufacturer affixes the CE marking to the device and its packaging. The CE marking must be visible, legible, and indelible, and it indicates compliance with EU regulatory requirements.
6. **Post-Market Surveillance:** After obtaining CE marking, manufacturers must establish post-market surveillance systems to monitor the performance of their devices on the market, report adverse events or incidents, and take appropriate corrective and preventive actions to ensure ongoing compliance with regulatory requirements.

Overall, CE marking signifies that the medical device meets EU regulatory standards and can be marketed within the EU and EEA. Understanding the CE certification process and fulfilling regulatory requirements are essential for manufacturers seeking to obtain CE marking for their medical devices and ensure market access within the EU.

5.5.2 Steps Involved in CE Certification Process

The process of obtaining CE certification for medical devices, including in vitro diagnostic devices (IVDs), involves several key steps to demonstrate compliance with European Union (EU) regulatory requirements and ensure market access within the EU and the European Economic Area (EEA). The steps involved in the CE certification process typically include:

1. **Identification of Applicable Directives:** Manufacturers identify the EU directives that apply to their medical devices, such as the In Vitro Diagnostic Devices Directive (IVDD) for IVDs. They carefully review the regulatory requirements and essential health and safety requirements outlined in the directives to understand their obligations.
2. **Conformity Assessment:** Depending on the classification of the device and associated risks, manufacturers conduct conformity assessment procedures to assess compliance with regulatory requirements. This may involve self-assessment for lower-risk devices or involvement of a Notified Body for higher-risk devices. Conformity assessment includes evaluation of design, manufacturing processes, quality management systems, and clinical evidence.
3. **Compilation of Technical Documentation:** Manufacturers compile technical documentation containing essential information about the device, including design specifications, risk management processes,

results of performance evaluation studies, clinical evidence, and instructions for use. The technical documentation serves as evidence of compliance with regulatory requirements and is submitted to regulatory authorities or Notified Bodies during the certification process.

4. **Declaration of Conformity:** Based on the results of conformity assessment and technical documentation, the manufacturer issues a declaration of conformity. This declaration declares that the device meets the essential requirements of the relevant EU directives, such as the IVDD, and is eligible for CE marking.
5. **Affixing the CE Mark:** Upon successful completion of the certification process, the manufacturer affixes the CE marking to the device and its packaging. The CE marking must be visible, legible, and indelible, and it indicates compliance with EU regulatory requirements.
6. **Post-Market Surveillance:** After obtaining CE marking, manufacturers establish post-market surveillance systems to monitor the performance of their devices on the market. They collect and analyze data on device safety, performance, and adverse events, and report any incidents or issues to regulatory authorities. Manufacturers also implement corrective and preventive actions as necessary to ensure ongoing compliance with regulatory requirements.

By following these steps and fulfilling regulatory requirements, manufacturers can obtain CE certification for their medical devices and gain access to the EU market. Compliance with CE certification demonstrates that the device meets rigorous standards of safety, performance, and quality, contributing to the protection of patient health and safety within the EU and EEA. Understanding and adhering to the CE certification process are essential for manufacturers seeking regulatory approval for their medical devices within the EU regulatory framework.

5.5.3 Post-Market Surveillance Requirements for CE Marked Devices

Post-market surveillance (PMS) is a crucial aspect of maintaining regulatory compliance and ensuring ongoing safety and performance of medical devices, including those with CE marking, within the European Union (EU) and the European Economic Area (EEA). CE marked devices are subject to specific PMS requirements outlined by EU regulations, including the Medical Devices Regulation (MDR) and the In Vitro Diagnostic Devices Regulation (IVDR). The key steps and requirements for post-market surveillance of CE marked devices include:

1. **Establishment of Post-Market Surveillance System:** Manufacturers must establish and maintain a post-market surveillance system to systematically collect, review, and analyze information on the safety and performance of their devices once they are placed on the market. This system includes procedures for monitoring, investigating, and reporting adverse events, incidents, and other relevant information related to device performance and safety.
2. **Collection and Analysis of Post-Market Data:** Manufacturers collect data from various sources, including feedback from healthcare professionals, patients, and users, as well as complaints, adverse event reports, clinical studies, scientific literature, and market surveillance activities. They analyze this data to identify trends, patterns, and potential safety issues associated with their devices.
3. **Risk Management and Risk Assessment:** Manufacturers conduct ongoing risk management activities to assess and mitigate risks associated with their devices throughout the product lifecycle. They evaluate the severity and probability of identified risks, prioritize them based on potential impact on patient safety, and implement appropriate risk control measures to minimize or eliminate risks.
4. **Reporting of Adverse Events and Incidents:** Manufacturers are required to report adverse events, incidents, and other relevant information to competent authorities and Notified Bodies in accordance with regulatory requirements. They must submit timely and accurate reports, including details of the event, its potential impact on patient safety, and any actions taken or planned to address the issue.
5. **Documentation and Record-Keeping:** Manufacturers maintain comprehensive documentation and records of their post-market surveillance activities, including data collection, analysis, risk assessments, and reporting. They ensure that records are accurate, up-to-date, and accessible for review by regulatory authorities during inspections or audits.
6. **Communication and Transparency:** Manufacturers communicate openly and transparently with regulatory authorities, healthcare professionals, patients, and other stakeholders regarding the safety and performance of their devices. They provide timely updates on any significant findings, safety issues, or corrective actions taken to address concerns related to device performance or safety.

By fulfilling post-market surveillance requirements, manufacturers demonstrate their commitment to ongoing monitoring of device safety and performance, prompt identification of potential risks or issues, and implementation of appropriate corrective and preventive actions to protect patient health and safety. Compliance with PMS requirements is essential for maintaining CE marking and market access for medical devices within the EU and EEA, contributing to the overall effectiveness of the regulatory system and the protection of public health.

CHAPTER SIX

REGULATORY APPROVALS IN ASEAN,CHINA,AND JAPAN

6.1 Introduction to Regulatory Approvals in Asia

Regulatory approvals play a pivotal role in ensuring the safety, efficacy, and quality of medical products entering the market. In the context of Asia, encompassing ASEAN, China, and Japan, regulatory approvals are not only crucial for market access but also for fostering public trust and confidence in healthcare products. These approvals serve as a gatekeeper, allowing only those products that meet stringent regulatory standards to be available to consumers. Moreover, regulatory frameworks in Asia are evolving rapidly in response to advancements in technology, globalization of markets, and increasing demand for healthcare products. Therefore, understanding the nuances of regulatory approvals in these regions is imperative for stakeholders involved in the development, manufacturing, and distribution of medical products.

6.1.1 Importance of Regulatory Approvals for Market Access

The significance of regulatory approvals for market access cannot be overstated. These approvals serve as a regulatory stamp of approval, indicating that a product has undergone rigorous evaluation and meets the necessary safety, efficacy, and quality standards. For manufacturers, obtaining regulatory approval is not only a legal requirement but also a strategic imperative to gain entry into lucrative markets. Without proper approvals, products may face barriers to entry, leading to delays in commercialization and loss of market share. Furthermore, regulatory compliance is essential for maintaining public health and safety, as it ensures that only safe and effective products reach the hands of consumers. In the context of Asia, where diverse regulatory frameworks exist across countries, navigating the regulatory landscape requires careful planning, coordination, and compliance with local regulations. Therefore, understanding the importance of regulatory approvals and their implications for market access is essential for companies operating in the healthcare sector.

6.1.2 Overview of Regulatory Bodies in ASEAN, China, and Japan

In ASEAN countries, regulatory oversight of medical products is typically conducted by national regulatory authorities (NRAs) of individual member states, such as the Thai Food and Drug Administration (FDA) or the Malaysian National Pharmaceutical Regulatory Agency (NPRA). However, efforts have been made to harmonize regulations through initiatives like the ASEAN Medical Device Directive (AMDD) and the ASEAN Common Technical Dossier (ACTD), aiming to facilitate market access within the region. China, on the other hand, has a centralized regulatory authority known as the National Medical Products Administration (NMPA), formerly the China Food and Drug Administration (CFDA), responsible for regulating drugs, medical devices, and cosmetics. NMPA oversees product registration, clinical trials, and quality control, and it has implemented reforms to streamline regulatory processes and improve transparency. In Japan, the Pharmaceuticals and Medical Devices Agency (PMDA) serves as the regulatory authority for pharmaceuticals and medical devices. PMDA evaluates the safety, efficacy, and quality of medical products based on scientific evidence and ensures compliance with Japan's Pharmaceutical Affairs Law (PAL). Despite differences in organizational structure and regulatory processes, these regulatory bodies share a common goal of safeguarding public health and promoting access to safe and effective medical products. Understanding the roles and responsibilities of these regulatory bodies is essential for navigating the complex regulatory landscape in Asia and ensuring compliance with local regulations.

6.1.3 Regulatory Harmonization Efforts in the Region

Regulatory harmonization efforts in the Asia-Pacific region aim to streamline regulatory processes, enhance transparency, and facilitate access to healthcare products across borders. One significant initiative is the Association of Southeast Asian Nations (ASEAN) cooperation in harmonizing regulatory requirements for pharmaceuticals and medical devices. Through the ASEAN Consultative Committee on Standards and

Quality (ACCSQ) and the ASEAN Medical Device Product Working Group (MDPWG), member states collaborate to align regulatory standards and procedures. The adoption of the ASEAN Common Technical Requirements (ACTR) and the ASEAN Common Technical Dossier (ACTD) for pharmaceuticals reflects these harmonization efforts, simplifying registration processes and promoting mutual recognition of regulatory approvals. Similarly, the International Medical Device Regulators Forum (IMDRF) facilitates collaboration among regulatory authorities from Asia and other regions to develop common principles and standards for medical device regulation. Furthermore, bilateral agreements and mutual recognition arrangements (MRAs) between regulatory authorities, such as the ASEAN MRA on Good Manufacturing Practice (GMP), contribute to regulatory convergence and facilitate market access for healthcare products. While regulatory harmonization efforts in the region have made significant progress, challenges remain, including disparities in regulatory capacity, divergent regulatory requirements, and varying levels of economic development among member states. Nonetheless, continued collaboration and dialogue among regulatory authorities, industry stakeholders, and other relevant parties are crucial for advancing regulatory harmonization efforts and promoting public health in the Asia-Pacific region.

6.2 Registration Procedures

Navigating registration procedures is a critical aspect of gaining market approval for medical products in the Asia-Pacific region. Understanding the intricacies of registration requirements in individual countries is essential for manufacturers seeking market access.

6.2.1 Registration Requirements in ASEAN Countries

Registration requirements for medical products vary across ASEAN countries due to differences in regulatory frameworks and healthcare systems. However, there are overarching principles outlined in the ASEAN Common Technical Requirements (ACTR) and the ASEAN Common Technical Dossier (ACTD) that aim to harmonize registration processes within the region. Generally, registration applications must include comprehensive data on product safety, efficacy, and quality, including but not limited to, clinical trial data, manufacturing processes, labeling, and post-market surveillance plans. Each ASEAN member state has its own national regulatory authority (NRA), such as the Thai Food and Drug Administration (FDA) or the Indonesian National Agency of Drug and Food Control (BPOM), responsible for reviewing registration applications and granting market approval. Manufacturers must adhere to specific submission requirements and timelines specified by the respective NRAs, which may vary depending on the classification of the product (e.g., pharmaceuticals, medical devices, or biologics) and its intended use. Additionally, manufacturers may need to appoint a local representative or distributor in each ASEAN country to facilitate communication with regulatory authorities and ensure compliance with local regulations. Despite efforts to harmonize registration procedures, differences in interpretation and implementation of regulations among ASEAN member states can pose challenges for manufacturers seeking market approval across multiple jurisdictions. Therefore, engaging with regulatory consultants or leveraging regional regulatory expertise can be beneficial in navigating the complexities of registration requirements in ASEAN countries and optimizing the registration process for medical products.

6.2.2 Registration Procedures in China

China's regulatory landscape for medical product registration is characterized by a centralized approval system overseen by the National Medical Products Administration (NMPA). The registration process in China is rigorous and involves multiple stages, each with specific requirements and timelines. Manufacturers seeking market approval for pharmaceuticals, medical devices, or other healthcare products must submit a comprehensive registration dossier to the NMPA, which includes detailed data on product safety, efficacy, quality, and manufacturing processes.

The registration dossier typically includes preclinical and clinical trial data, evidence of compliance with Good Manufacturing Practice (GMP) standards, product specifications, labeling information, and post-market surveillance plans. For pharmaceuticals, clinical trial data demonstrating the product's safety and efficacy in Chinese patients may be required, along with bioequivalence studies if the product is a generic drug. Similarly, medical device registration requires evidence of product safety and performance through clinical evaluation and testing, as well as conformity assessment documentation.

Upon submission of the registration dossier, the NMPA conducts a comprehensive review to assess the quality, safety, and efficacy of the product. This review process may involve expert panels, technical evaluations, and site inspections to verify compliance with regulatory requirements. The timelines for registration review vary depending on the product category and complexity, with expedited pathways available for certain priority products, such as innovative drugs or medical devices addressing unmet medical needs.

Once the NMPA completes the review process and determines that the product meets regulatory standards, it issues a registration certificate, granting market approval for commercialization in China. Manufacturers are then required to comply with post-market surveillance obligations, including adverse event reporting, product quality monitoring, and compliance with pharmacovigilance requirements.

Navigating the registration process in China requires a thorough understanding of regulatory requirements, local market dynamics, and cultural nuances. Manufacturers often engage with regulatory consultants or local agents with expertise in Chinese regulations to facilitate the registration process and ensure compliance with applicable standards. Despite the challenges posed by China's complex regulatory environment, the country's rapidly expanding healthcare market offers significant opportunities for manufacturers who successfully navigate the registration process and bring innovative medical products to market.

6.2.3 Registration Process in Japan

In Japan, the Pharmaceuticals and Medical Devices Agency (PMDA) oversees the registration process for pharmaceuticals and medical devices, ensuring compliance with the country's strict regulatory standards. The registration process in Japan is thorough and involves several key steps, each aimed at evaluating the safety, efficacy, and quality of medical products before they can be marketed and distributed.

To initiate the registration process, manufacturers must prepare a comprehensive registration dossier containing detailed data on the product's safety, efficacy, quality, and manufacturing processes. This dossier typically includes preclinical and clinical trial data, evidence of compliance with Good Manufacturing Practice (GMP) standards, product specifications, labeling information, and post-market surveillance plans.

Once the registration dossier is submitted to the PMDA, it undergoes a rigorous review process by expert reviewers and regulatory assessors. The PMDA evaluates the scientific evidence provided in the dossier to assess the product's safety, efficacy, and quality, ensuring that it meets Japan's regulatory standards. This review process may involve consultations with external experts, as well as on-site inspections of manufacturing facilities to verify compliance with GMP requirements.

The timelines for registration review vary depending on the product category and complexity, with expedited pathways available for certain priority products, such as innovative drugs or medical devices addressing unmet medical needs. Throughout the review process, manufacturers are expected to respond promptly to any requests for additional information or clarifications from the PMDA to facilitate timely review and approval.

Upon successful completion of the review process, the PMDA issues a marketing approval, granting permission for the product to be commercialized and distributed in Japan. Manufacturers are then required to comply with post-market surveillance obligations, including pharmacovigilance activities, adverse event reporting, and product quality monitoring, to ensure ongoing safety and efficacy.

Navigating the registration process in Japan requires careful planning, attention to detail, and a thorough understanding of regulatory requirements. Manufacturers often work closely with regulatory consultants or local representatives with expertise in Japanese regulations to facilitate the registration process and ensure compliance with applicable standards. Despite the stringent regulatory requirements, Japan's well-established healthcare market offers significant opportunities for manufacturers who successfully navigate the registration process and bring innovative medical products to market.

6.2.4 Comparison of Registration Processes Across Countries

Comparing the registration processes for medical products across ASEAN countries, China, and Japan reveals both similarities and distinct differences influenced by each region's regulatory frameworks, healthcare systems, and cultural factors.

In ASEAN countries, the registration process is characterized by a decentralized approach, with individual member states having their own regulatory authorities responsible for reviewing registration applications. While efforts have been made to harmonize regulations through initiatives like the ASEAN Common Technical Requirements (ACTR) and the ASEAN Common Technical Dossier (ACTD), there are still variations in requirements and timelines across countries. Manufacturers must navigate these differences and submit separate applications to each ASEAN member state where they seek market approval.

Conversely, China employs a centralized approval system overseen by the National Medical Products Administration (NMPA), formerly the China Food and Drug Administration (CFDA). The registration process in China is rigorous and involves multiple stages, including submission of a comprehensive registration dossier, review by the NMPA, and issuance of a registration certificate upon successful evaluation. Manufacturers must adhere to strict regulatory requirements and timelines set by the NMPA, which may include clinical trial data specific to the Chinese population for pharmaceuticals.

In Japan, the Pharmaceuticals and Medical Devices Agency (PMDA) regulates the registration process for pharmaceuticals and medical devices. Similar to China, the registration process in Japan is thorough and involves submission of a detailed registration dossier, review by the PMDA, and issuance of marketing approval upon successful evaluation. However, Japan's regulatory standards may differ from those of other countries, requiring manufacturers to tailor their submissions accordingly.

While registration processes across countries share common objectives of ensuring product safety, efficacy, and quality, differences in regulatory requirements, review timelines, and documentation may present challenges for manufacturers seeking market approval in multiple jurisdictions. Manufacturers must carefully assess these differences and develop tailored strategies to navigate the registration process effectively, leveraging regional regulatory expertise and resources to optimize their regulatory submissions and expedite market access for their medical products.

6.3 Quality System Requirements

Ensuring adherence to quality system requirements is paramount for maintaining the safety, efficacy, and reliability of medical products throughout their lifecycle. Understanding the specific quality system standards applicable in different regions, such as ASEAN countries, is essential for manufacturers to meet regulatory expectations and achieve compliance.

6.3.1 Quality System Standards in ASEAN Countries

In ASEAN countries, quality system standards for medical products are influenced by international guidelines and harmonization efforts aimed at facilitating trade and ensuring patient safety. While ASEAN member states may have their own specific regulations and requirements, many align with globally recognized standards such as ISO 13485:2016, which sets out requirements

6.3.2 GMP Requirements in China

Good Manufacturing Practice (GMP) requirements in China are fundamental to ensuring the quality, safety, and efficacy of medical products manufactured within the country. The regulatory framework for GMP in China is overseen by the National Medical Products Administration (NMPA), formerly known as the China Food and Drug Administration (CFDA). GMP regulations in China are governed by various guidelines and standards, including the "Good Manufacturing Practice for Pharmaceutical Products" (referred to as Chinese GMP or cGMP) and relevant annexes, such as those specific to pharmaceuticals, biological products, and traditional Chinese medicines.

Compliance with GMP requirements in China is mandatory for manufacturers of pharmaceuticals, medical devices, and other healthcare products. These requirements encompass various aspects of manufacturing, including facility design and construction, equipment validation, personnel training, documentation practices, quality control, and product testing. Manufacturers must establish and maintain comprehensive quality management systems (QMS) to ensure that their manufacturing processes consistently meet GMP standards and produce products of consistent quality.

The NMPA conducts regular inspections of manufacturing facilities to assess compliance with GMP requirements and verify the quality and integrity of medical products. Inspections may be conducted both pre- and post-market approval to ensure ongoing compliance with regulatory standards. Non-compliance with GMP requirements can result in regulatory sanctions, including product recalls, manufacturing suspensions, or revocation of manufacturing licenses.

Manufacturers operating in China's healthcare market must therefore prioritize compliance with GMP requirements to ensure the safety, efficacy, and quality of their products. This involves establishing robust quality management systems, implementing stringent manufacturing practices, and maintaining ongoing vigilance to identify and address any deviations from GMP standards. By adhering to GMP requirements, manufacturers can build trust with regulators, healthcare professionals, and patients, and contribute to the overall integrity and reliability of China's healthcare system.

6.3.3 Quality Management System in Japan

In Japan, the establishment and maintenance of a robust Quality Management System (QMS) are crucial for ensuring the safety, efficacy, and quality of medical products. The Pharmaceuticals and Medical Devices Agency (PMDA) oversees the regulation of QMS for pharmaceuticals and medical devices, ensuring compliance with Japan's stringent regulatory standards.

The foundation of the QMS in Japan is based on internationally recognized standards such as ISO 13485:2016, which specifies requirements for a comprehensive QMS for medical devices. Additionally, Japan's regulatory framework incorporates specific guidelines and regulations tailored to the unique characteristics of the healthcare industry in the country.

Key components of the QMS in Japan include quality policy and objectives, organizational structure and responsibilities, documentation and record-keeping procedures, process controls, risk management, and continual improvement initiatives. Manufacturers are required to establish and maintain documented procedures and processes that govern all aspects of product design, development, manufacturing, distribution, and post-market surveillance.

The PMDA conducts inspections and audits of manufacturing facilities to assess compliance with QMS requirements and verify the quality and integrity of medical products. These inspections may occur both pre- and post-market approval to ensure ongoing compliance with regulatory standards. Non-compliance with QMS requirements can result in regulatory sanctions, including product recalls, manufacturing suspensions, or revocation of manufacturing licenses.

Manufacturers operating in Japan's healthcare market must therefore prioritize the establishment and maintenance of an effective QMS to ensure the safety, efficacy, and quality of their products. This involves implementing robust quality management practices, investing in employee training and development, and fostering a culture of quality and continuous improvement throughout the organization. By adhering to QMS requirements, manufacturers can demonstrate their commitment to product quality and patient safety, contributing to the overall integrity and reliability of Japan's healthcare system.

6.3.4 Challenges in Harmonizing Quality Standards

Harmonizing quality standards across different regulatory jurisdictions poses significant challenges due to variations in regulatory frameworks, cultural differences, and divergent interpretations of international guidelines. While the ultimate goal of harmonization is to streamline regulatory processes and facilitate global market access for medical products, several factors hinder the achievement of this objective.

One of the primary challenges in harmonizing quality standards is the lack of uniformity in regulatory requirements and expectations among different regions. Each regulatory authority may have its own set of guidelines, standards, and interpretations of international regulations, leading to discrepancies in expectations for manufacturers. These differences can create confusion and increase compliance burdens for companies seeking to market their products globally.

Cultural differences and varying levels of regulatory expertise among different regions also contribute to challenges in harmonizing quality standards. Cultural nuances and historical regulatory practices may influence the interpretation and implementation of international guidelines, leading to inconsistencies in regulatory enforcement and oversight. Additionally, disparities in regulatory capacity and resources among countries can impact their ability to effectively implement and enforce harmonized quality standards.

Furthermore, divergent interpretations of international guidelines and standards by regulatory authorities can result in conflicting requirements for manufacturers. For example, differences in the interpretation of data requirements for product registration or variations in GMP inspection practices can create barriers to market access and increase regulatory complexity for manufacturers operating in multiple jurisdictions.

Addressing these challenges requires collaborative efforts among regulatory authorities, industry stakeholders, and international organizations to promote mutual recognition of regulatory approvals and harmonization of quality standards. Initiatives such as the International Council for Harmonisation of Technical Requirements for Pharmaceuticals for Human Use (ICH) and the Medical Device Single Audit Program (MDSAP) aim to foster convergence of regulatory requirements and promote regulatory harmonization globally.

Despite these challenges, ongoing efforts to harmonize quality standards are essential for facilitating global market access, reducing regulatory burden, and ensuring the safety, efficacy, and quality of medical products worldwide. By addressing the root causes of regulatory divergence and promoting collaboration among stakeholders, regulatory harmonization initiatives can help streamline regulatory processes and enhance patient access to innovative healthcare products.

6.4 Clinical Evaluation and Investigation

Ensuring the safety and efficacy of medical products through rigorous clinical evaluation and investigation is paramount in the regulatory approval process. Understanding the specific clinical trial requirements in different regions, such as ASEAN countries, is essential for manufacturers to navigate the complex landscape of clinical research and regulatory approval.

6.4.1 Clinical Trial Requirements in ASEAN Countries

Clinical trial requirements in ASEAN countries vary depending on the regulatory frameworks and healthcare systems of individual member states. While efforts have been made to harmonize clinical trial regulations through initiatives such as the ASEAN Common Technical Requirements (ACTR), there are still differences in requirements and processes across countries.

Generally, clinical trial requirements in ASEAN countries encompass several key aspects, including study protocol development, ethics committee approval, patient recruitment, data collection and analysis, and reporting of adverse events. Manufacturers conducting clinical trials in ASEAN countries must adhere to specific guidelines and regulations set forth by national regulatory authorities (NRAs) and ethics committees in each country where trials are conducted.

Manufacturers are typically required to submit a comprehensive clinical trial protocol outlining the objectives, study design, patient population, endpoints, and statistical analysis plan to the relevant NRAs and ethics committees for review and approval. Ethics committee approval is essential to ensure that clinical trials are conducted ethically and in accordance with internationally recognized ethical principles, such as those outlined in the Declaration of Helsinki.

Patient recruitment and informed consent procedures are also critical aspects of clinical trial conduct in ASEAN countries. Manufacturers must obtain informed consent from all study participants and ensure that patient rights and privacy are protected throughout the trial. Additionally, manufacturers are required to collect and analyze clinical trial data in accordance with Good Clinical Practice (GCP) guidelines to ensure the reliability and integrity of study results.

Reporting of adverse events and safety data is another important requirement in clinical trials conducted in ASEAN countries. Manufacturers must promptly report any adverse events or serious adverse events that occur during the trial to the relevant NRAs and ethics committees and take appropriate measures to mitigate risks to patient safety.

Navigating the clinical trial requirements in ASEAN countries requires careful planning, coordination, and compliance with local regulations and ethical standards. Manufacturers often engage with clinical research organizations (CROs) or regulatory consultants with expertise in the region to facilitate the design, conduct, and oversight of clinical trials and ensure compliance with applicable requirements. By adhering to clinical trial requirements and conducting high-quality research, manufacturers can generate robust clinical evidence to support regulatory approval and market access for their medical products in ASEAN countries.

6.4.2 Clinical Investigation Regulations in China

China's regulatory framework for clinical investigations plays a pivotal role in ensuring the safety, efficacy, and quality of medical products intended for the Chinese market. The regulatory oversight of clinical investigations is primarily governed by the National Medical Products Administration (NMPA), formerly known as the China Food and Drug Administration (CFDA), in accordance with the "Regulations for the Administration of Drug Clinical Trials" and other relevant guidelines.

Clinical investigation regulations in China outline the requirements and procedures for conducting clinical trials, including pre-market clinical trials for new drugs, biological products, and medical devices, as well as post-market clinical studies for product registration, safety monitoring, and efficacy evaluation.

Manufacturers seeking to conduct clinical investigations in China must obtain approval from the NMPA and ethics committee(s) before initiating any clinical trial activities. The approval process involves the submission of a comprehensive clinical trial application dossier, including detailed study protocols, investigator brochures, informed consent forms, and safety monitoring plans, among other required documents.

Clinical investigations in China are subject to stringent regulatory oversight to ensure patient safety and data integrity. The NMPA and ethics committee(s) review the proposed clinical trial protocol, study design, patient recruitment strategies, and data management plans to assess compliance with regulatory requirements and ethical standards.

In addition to regulatory approval, manufacturers are required to comply with Good Clinical Practice (GCP) guidelines throughout the conduct of clinical investigations in China. GCP principles outline the ethical and scientific standards for designing, conducting, recording, and reporting clinical trials to ensure the credibility and reliability of clinical trial data.

During the clinical investigation process, manufacturers are responsible for monitoring and managing the safety of study participants, collecting and analyzing clinical trial data, and reporting adverse events or serious adverse events to the NMPA and ethics committee(s) in a timely manner.

Non-compliance with clinical investigation regulations in China can result in regulatory sanctions, including suspension or termination of clinical trials, fines, or other administrative penalties. Therefore, manufacturers must diligently adhere to regulatory requirements and maintain ongoing communication with regulatory authorities and ethics committee(s) to ensure compliance throughout the clinical investigation process.

Navigating the clinical investigation regulations in China requires a thorough understanding of the regulatory requirements, cultural nuances, and language barriers. Manufacturers often seek the expertise of regulatory consultants or local agents with experience in China's regulatory landscape to facilitate the approval process and ensure compliance with applicable regulations and standards. By adhering to clinical investigation regulations and conducting high-quality clinical trials, manufacturers can generate robust clinical evidence to support regulatory approval and market access for their medical products in China.

6.4.3 Clinical Study Requirements in Japan

Japan's regulatory framework for clinical studies is governed by the Pharmaceuticals and Medical Devices Agency (PMDA) and is designed to ensure the safety, efficacy, and quality of medical products intended for the Japanese market. Clinical study requirements in Japan encompass a range of regulations and guidelines that govern the conduct of clinical trials, post-market surveillance studies, and other clinical investigations.

To initiate a clinical study in Japan, manufacturers must obtain approval from the PMDA and ethics committees, as outlined in the "Ministerial Ordinance on Good Clinical Practice for Drugs" and other relevant regulations. The approval process involves the submission of a comprehensive clinical study protocol, investigator's brochure, informed consent forms, and other essential documents detailing the study design, objectives, patient eligibility criteria, endpoints, and data analysis plan.

Clinical studies in Japan are subject to rigorous oversight to ensure patient safety and data integrity. The PMDA and ethics committees review the proposed study protocol, patient recruitment strategies, data management plans, and safety monitoring procedures to assess compliance with regulatory requirements and ethical standards. Additionally, manufacturers are required to adhere to Good Clinical Practice (GCP) guidelines throughout the conduct of clinical studies to maintain the credibility and reliability of study data.

During the clinical study process, manufacturers are responsible for monitoring and managing the safety of study participants, collecting and analyzing clinical study data, and reporting adverse events or serious adverse events to the PMDA and ethics committees in a timely manner. Post-market surveillance studies may also be required to evaluate the long-term safety and efficacy of medical products after they have been approved for marketing in Japan.

Non-compliance with clinical study requirements in Japan can result in regulatory sanctions, including suspension or termination of clinical studies, fines, or other administrative penalties. Therefore, manufacturers must diligently adhere to regulatory requirements and maintain ongoing communication with regulatory authorities and ethics committees to ensure compliance throughout the clinical study process.

Navigating the clinical study requirements in Japan requires a comprehensive understanding of the regulatory landscape, language, and cultural nuances. Manufacturers often engage with regulatory consultants or local representatives with experience in Japan's regulatory environment to facilitate the approval process and ensure compliance with applicable regulations and standards. By adhering to clinical study requirements and conducting high-quality clinical studies, manufacturers can generate robust clinical evidence to support regulatory approval and market access for their medical products in Japan.

6.4.4 Ethical Considerations in Clinical Trials Across Regions

Ethical considerations play a crucial role in the conduct of clinical trials across regions, ensuring the protection of human subjects' rights, welfare, and dignity. While international guidelines such as the Declaration of Helsinki provide overarching ethical principles for clinical research, variations in cultural norms, regulatory requirements, and healthcare systems necessitate careful consideration of ethical issues specific to each region.

One of the primary ethical considerations in clinical trials is obtaining informed consent from study participants. Informed consent ensures that participants have been adequately informed about the purpose, risks, benefits, and alternatives of participating in the trial, enabling them to make voluntary and autonomous decisions regarding their participation. However, cultural differences in attitudes towards consent, decision-making processes, and perceptions of research may influence the consent process and require tailored approaches to ensure meaningful and culturally sensitive communication.

Another ethical consideration is ensuring equitable access to clinical trials and minimizing disparities in research participation. Vulnerable populations, such as minorities, children, elderly individuals, and socioeconomically disadvantaged groups, may be disproportionately underrepresented in clinical research, raising concerns about fairness, justice, and inclusivity. Efforts to address these disparities may include targeted outreach and recruitment strategies, culturally competent research practices, and community engagement initiatives to enhance diversity and representation in clinical trials.

Additionally, ethical considerations extend to the design and conduct of clinical trials, including the selection of study endpoints, control groups, and study populations. Ethical principles such as beneficence, non-maleficence, and scientific validity guide decisions regarding study design, ensuring that trials are conducted ethically, rigorously, and with minimal risk to participants.

Furthermore, ethical considerations in clinical trials encompass the protection of privacy and confidentiality, respect for autonomy, and the fair and transparent dissemination of research findings. Regulatory oversight and institutional review processes play a critical role in safeguarding ethical standards and ensuring compliance with ethical guidelines and regulations.

Navigating ethical considerations in clinical trials across regions requires sensitivity to cultural differences, regulatory requirements, and ethical principles. Collaborative efforts among researchers, sponsors, regulatory authorities, ethics committees, and community stakeholders are essential for promoting ethical conduct, protecting human subjects' rights, and upholding the integrity of clinical research globally. By prioritizing ethical considerations and fostering a culture of ethical conduct, stakeholders can enhance public trust in clinical research and contribute to the advancement of scientific knowledge and patient care.

6.5 Overview of IMDRF Study Groups and Guidance Documents

The International Medical Device Regulators Forum (IMDRF) serves as a platform for regulatory authorities from around the world to collaborate and harmonize medical device regulations. Through its study groups and guidance documents, the IMDRF plays a critical role in promoting global regulatory convergence and enhancing patient access to safe and effective medical devices.

6.5.1 Introduction to IMDRF and Its Role in Regulatory Harmonization

The IMDRF was established in 2011 with the goal of facilitating international cooperation and convergence in medical device regulation. Comprising regulatory authorities from regions including the United States, European Union, Japan, Canada, Australia, and China, the IMDRF aims to develop consensus-based approaches to regulatory issues and promote the alignment of regulatory requirements and practices across jurisdictions.

At the core of the IMDRF's activities are its study groups, which focus on specific regulatory topics and collaborate to develop guidance documents and recommendations for regulatory harmonization. These study groups cover a wide range of areas, including clinical evaluation, quality management systems, adverse event reporting, and medical device nomenclature, among others.

The IMDRF's guidance documents provide regulatory authorities, industry stakeholders, and other interested parties with clear and transparent guidance on best practices for medical device regulation. These documents are developed through a collaborative process involving input from regulatory authorities, industry representatives, healthcare professionals, and patient advocates, ensuring that diverse perspectives are considered in the development of regulatory guidance.

By harmonizing regulatory requirements and practices, the IMDRF's guidance documents help streamline the regulatory process for medical device manufacturers, reduce duplication of efforts, and facilitate the global market access of medical devices. Additionally, regulatory convergence driven by the IMDRF enhances patient safety by ensuring consistent standards for the evaluation and oversight of medical devices across jurisdictions.

6.5.2 Key Study Groups and Their Focus Areas

The International Medical Device Regulators Forum (IMDRF) operates through various study groups, each dedicated to addressing specific regulatory challenges and promoting harmonization in medical device regulation. These study groups play a crucial role in developing consensus-based approaches and guidance documents to facilitate global regulatory convergence. Below are some of the key study groups and their focus areas:

1. **Clinical Evaluation Study Group:** This study group focuses on developing guidance on clinical evaluation requirements for medical devices. It addresses issues related to clinical trial design, data collection, analysis, and interpretation to ensure the safety and effectiveness of medical devices.
2. **Quality Management Systems (QMS) Working Group:** The QMS Working Group is responsible for developing guidance documents related to quality management systems for medical device manufacturers. It covers topics such as ISO 13485 compliance, risk management, post-market surveillance, and corrective and preventive actions (CAPA).
3. **Adverse Event Terminology Working Group:** This study group focuses on standardizing the terminology used for reporting adverse events related to medical devices. By harmonizing adverse event terminology, this group aims to improve the consistency and comparability of adverse event data across jurisdictions.
4. **Unique Device Identification (UDI) Working Group:** The UDI Working Group develops guidance on the implementation of unique device identification systems for medical devices. It addresses issues such as UDI labeling requirements, data standards, and database management to enhance the traceability and post-market surveillance of medical devices.
5. **Regulatory Nomenclature Working Group:** This study group focuses on developing standardized nomenclature and classification systems for medical devices. It aims to improve the clarity and consistency of regulatory terminology used by regulatory authorities and industry stakeholders worldwide.
6. **Software as a Medical Device (SaMD) Working Group:** The SaMD Working Group addresses regulatory challenges related to software-based medical devices. It develops guidance on software validation, risk management, and post-market surveillance for SaMD products, ensuring their safety and effectiveness.

These study groups collaborate to develop guidance documents, recommendations, and best practices that contribute to regulatory harmonization and facilitate global market access for medical devices. By addressing key regulatory challenges and promoting consensus-based approaches, these study groups play a critical role in advancing the IMDRF's mission of promoting patient access to safe and effective medical devices worldwide.

6.5.3 Impact of IMDRF Guidance on Regulatory Practices in Asia

The guidance documents and recommendations developed by the International Medical Device Regulators Forum (IMDRF) have had a significant impact on regulatory practices in Asia, contributing to greater harmonization, efficiency, and transparency in medical device regulation across the region. The IMDRF's efforts have facilitated regulatory convergence and alignment with international standards, benefiting both regulatory authorities and industry stakeholders in Asia in several ways:

1. **Harmonization of Regulatory Requirements:** IMDRF guidance documents serve as valuable references for regulatory authorities in Asia when developing or updating their own regulations and guidelines. By adopting internationally recognized standards and best practices, regulatory authorities can align their regulatory requirements with those of other jurisdictions, reducing regulatory barriers and facilitating the global market access of medical devices.
2. **Streamlining Regulatory Processes:** The adoption of IMDRF guidance documents helps streamline regulatory processes in Asia by providing clear and consistent guidance on regulatory requirements, submission procedures, and evaluation criteria. This streamlining of processes accelerates the review and approval of medical devices, reducing time-to-market for manufacturers and enhancing patient access to innovative healthcare technologies.
3. **Enhancing Regulatory Capacity and Expertise:** IMDRF guidance documents provide regulatory authorities in Asia with access to global expertise and best practices in medical device regulation. By implementing IMDRF-recommended approaches, regulatory authorities can enhance their regulatory capacity and expertise, improving their ability to evaluate the safety, efficacy, and quality of medical devices effectively.
4. **Facilitating International Collaboration:** The IMDRF serves as a platform for regulatory authorities in Asia to collaborate with counterparts from other regions and share experiences, insights, and best practices in medical device regulation. This collaboration promotes mutual learning, fosters exchange of information, and strengthens relationships among regulatory authorities, facilitating international

cooperation and alignment in regulatory practices.

5. **Promoting Innovation and Market Access:** IMDRF guidance documents provide manufacturers in Asia with clear and transparent guidance on regulatory requirements, facilitating compliance and reducing regulatory uncertainty. This clarity and predictability in regulatory expectations encourage investment in research and development, spur innovation, and promote market access for medical devices, ultimately benefiting patients by expanding access to safe and effective healthcare technologies.

6.5.4 Future Directions in IMDRF Collaboration and Guidance Development

As the landscape of medical device regulation continues to evolve, the International Medical Device Regulators Forum (IMDRF) remains committed to fostering collaboration and advancing regulatory harmonization worldwide. Looking ahead, several key areas are poised to shape the future direction of IMDRF collaboration and guidance development:

1. **Expansion of Membership and Participation:** The IMDRF may seek to expand its membership to include additional regulatory authorities from regions with emerging medical device markets, such as Latin America, Africa, and the Middle East. By broadening participation, the IMDRF can enhance its global reach and promote regulatory convergence on a wider scale.
2. **Focus on Emerging Technologies:** With the rapid advancement of technologies such as artificial intelligence, digital health, and personalized medicine, the IMDRF may prioritize the development of guidance documents to address regulatory challenges associated with these emerging technologies. This includes considerations related to software as a medical device (SaMD), cybersecurity, data privacy, and interoperability.
3. **Enhanced Post-Market Surveillance:** The IMDRF may place greater emphasis on post-market surveillance and vigilance activities to monitor the safety and performance of medical devices throughout their lifecycle. This includes the development of guidance documents on adverse event reporting, post-market studies, real-world evidence generation, and signal detection to ensure timely identification and

mitigation of potential risks.

4. **Promotion of Global Access and Equity:** The IMDRF may work towards promoting equitable access to safe and effective medical devices globally, particularly in underserved regions and resource-limited settings. This could involve the development of guidance documents on regulatory pathways for low-cost medical devices, streamlined review processes for humanitarian use devices, and capacity-building initiatives to strengthen regulatory systems in developing countries.
5. **Integration of Patient Perspectives:** Recognizing the importance of patient-centered healthcare, the IMDRF may seek to integrate patient perspectives into its guidance development processes. This includes engaging patient representatives in study groups, soliciting feedback from patient advocacy organizations, and ensuring that patient preferences and priorities are considered in regulatory decision-making.
6. **Adaptation to Technological Advances:** The IMDRF may adapt its collaboration and guidance development processes to leverage technological advances such as artificial intelligence, machine learning, and data analytics. This could involve the use of advanced analytical tools to assess real-world data, predict safety issues, and identify emerging trends in medical device regulation.

6.6 Challenges and Opportunities in Regulatory Approvals

Navigating regulatory approvals for medical products presents both challenges and opportunities for manufacturers seeking to bring their products to market. Understanding the complexities and addressing the hurdles while leveraging opportunities is essential for successful regulatory approval processes. One significant challenge lies in achieving cross-border market access, which involves overcoming regulatory hurdles across multiple jurisdictions.

6.6.1 Regulatory Hurdles for Cross-Border Market Access

One of the primary challenges in obtaining cross-border market access is the divergence in regulatory requirements among different jurisdictions. Each country or region may have its own set of regulations, standards, and review processes for evaluating the safety, efficacy, and quality of medical products. These variations in regulatory requirements can pose significant hurdles for manufacturers seeking to market their products globally, as they must navigate multiple regulatory frameworks and comply with diverse sets of requirements.

Additionally, differences in regulatory timelines, submission processes, and documentation requirements further complicate the cross-border market access process. Manufacturers may encounter delays and inefficiencies in obtaining regulatory approvals due to the need to tailor submissions to each jurisdiction, respond to specific regulatory queries, and address variations in review timelines.

Moreover, language barriers, cultural differences, and logistical challenges may impact communication and coordination with regulatory authorities in different regions, further exacerbating the complexities of cross-border market access. Manufacturers must invest resources in building regulatory expertise, establishing effective communication channels, and navigating cultural nuances to effectively engage with regulatory authorities and expedite the approval process.

Despite these challenges, cross-border market access also presents opportunities for manufacturers to leverage regulatory convergence initiatives, mutual recognition agreements, and harmonization efforts to streamline the regulatory approval process. Collaborative approaches such as the International Medical Device Regulators Forum (IMDRF) and regional harmonization initiatives aim to align regulatory requirements, promote information sharing, and facilitate the acceptance of regulatory approvals across jurisdictions.

Furthermore, advancements in regulatory science, digital technologies, and real-world evidence generation offer opportunities to enhance regulatory efficiency, accelerate review processes, and improve decision-making in cross-border market access. Manufacturers can leverage innovative regulatory strategies, such as the use of predictive modeling, virtual simulations, and decentralized clinical trials, to generate robust data and streamline regulatory submissions.

6.6.2 Opportunities for Streamlining Regulatory Processes

Amidst the challenges of regulatory approvals, several opportunities exist for streamlining regulatory processes, enhancing efficiency, and accelerating market access for medical products. Proactive measures and strategic initiatives can capitalize on these opportunities to facilitate smoother regulatory pathways.

One significant opportunity lies in the adoption of innovative regulatory approaches and technologies. Embracing digital solutions such as electronic submissions, electronic health records, and electronic data capture systems can streamline documentation processes, reduce administrative burdens, and expedite regulatory reviews. Furthermore, the integration of artificial intelligence, machine learning, and predictive analytics holds promise for optimizing regulatory decision-making, identifying potential safety issues, and enhancing post-market surveillance.

Another opportunity for streamlining regulatory processes lies in the alignment of regulatory requirements and standards across jurisdictions. Collaborative initiatives such as the International Medical Device Regulators Forum (IMDRF) and regional harmonization efforts aim to harmonize regulatory frameworks, promote convergence of regulatory requirements, and facilitate the acceptance of regulatory approvals across borders. By leveraging mutual recognition agreements, harmonized standards, and common review procedures, manufacturers can navigate regulatory complexities more efficiently and expedite market access for their products.

Furthermore, the utilization of real-world evidence (RWE) offers opportunities to supplement traditional clinical trial data with real-world data from routine clinical practice, patient registries, and electronic health records. RWE can provide valuable insights into the safety, effectiveness, and performance of medical products in diverse patient populations and real-world settings, enhancing regulatory decision-making and expediting market access.

Additionally, regulatory agencies are increasingly adopting agile regulatory approaches, such as expedited pathways, breakthrough designations, and priority review programs, to accelerate the review and approval of innovative medical products. These initiatives prioritize the evaluation of products addressing unmet medical needs or demonstrating significant clinical benefit, allowing manufacturers to expedite market entry and address critical healthcare challenges more rapidly.

Moreover, proactive engagement with regulatory authorities, early dialogue meetings, and pre-submission consultations offer opportunities to clarify regulatory expectations, address potential issues upfront, and expedite the regulatory review process. By fostering open communication, collaboration, and transparency between manufacturers and regulators, these interactions can mitigate regulatory risks, streamline review timelines, and facilitate smoother market access pathways.

6.6.3 Importance of Regional Collaboration in Addressing Regulatory Challenges

Regional collaboration plays a pivotal role in addressing the complex regulatory challenges faced by manufacturers seeking market approvals for medical products. By fostering cooperation and alignment among regulatory authorities within a particular geographic region, regional collaboration initiatives offer several key benefits for both regulators and industry stakeholders.

First and foremost, regional collaboration enhances regulatory efficiency by promoting the harmonization of regulatory requirements, standards, and review processes across participating countries or jurisdictions. By aligning their regulatory frameworks, regulators can streamline documentation requirements, submission procedures, and evaluation criteria, reducing duplication of efforts and expediting market approvals for medical products. This harmonization facilitates a more predictable and transparent regulatory environment for manufacturers, enabling them to navigate regulatory complexities more efficiently and accelerate market access for their products.

Moreover, regional collaboration initiatives facilitate information sharing, capacity-building, and mutual learning among regulatory authorities, enabling them to leverage each other's expertise, resources, and best practices in medical product regulation. By exchanging regulatory insights, experiences, and challenges, regulators can enhance their regulatory capacity, strengthen regulatory oversight, and promote continuous improvement in regulatory practices. This collaboration fosters a culture of regulatory convergence and cooperation, ultimately benefiting patients by ensuring the timely availability of safe, effective, and high-quality medical products.

Furthermore, regional collaboration enables regulators to address common healthcare challenges, such as emerging public health threats, patient safety concerns, and access to essential medical products. By coordinating their regulatory responses and implementing harmonized approaches to address shared challenges, regulators can enhance their collective ability to safeguard public health, mitigate regulatory risks, and respond effectively to evolving healthcare needs. This collaborative approach fosters greater resilience and responsiveness in the regulatory system, ensuring that regulatory decisions are evidence-based, scientifically rigorous, and aligned with patient needs and preferences.

Additionally, regional collaboration initiatives promote stakeholder engagement and dialogue, facilitating communication and collaboration between regulators, industry stakeholders, healthcare professionals, and patient advocates. By involving all relevant stakeholders in the regulatory decision-making process, regional collaboration initiatives foster transparency, accountability, and trust in the regulatory system, enhancing public confidence in the safety, efficacy, and quality of medical products. This inclusive approach promotes shared responsibility and collective action in addressing regulatory challenges, ultimately benefiting all stakeholders involved in the medical product lifecycle.

6.6.4 Strategies for Navigating Complex Regulatory Landscapes in Asia

Navigating the complex regulatory landscapes in Asia requires strategic planning, meticulous attention to detail, and a comprehensive understanding of regulatory requirements and processes. Manufacturers seeking market approvals for medical products in Asia can employ several key strategies to effectively navigate regulatory complexities and expedite the approval process:

1. **Early Regulatory Planning:** Manufacturers should initiate regulatory planning early in the product development process to identify regulatory requirements, anticipate potential challenges, and develop a roadmap for regulatory submissions. By proactively engaging with regulatory authorities, manufacturers can gain insights into regulatory expectations, address potential issues upfront, and streamline the approval process.
2. **Localization of Regulatory Expertise:** Establishing a local regulatory team or partnering with regulatory consultants familiar with the regulatory landscape in each target market is essential for navigating regulatory complexities effectively. Local expertise enables manufacturers to navigate language barriers, cultural nuances, and regulatory intricacies, ensuring compliance with local regulations and streamlining the approval process.
3. **Tailored Regulatory Strategies:** Manufacturers should develop tailored regulatory strategies for each target market in Asia, taking into account variations in regulatory requirements, submission processes, and review timelines. By adapting regulatory strategies to align with specific market dynamics and regulatory frameworks, manufacturers can optimize their approach to market entry and accelerate the approval process.

4. **Harmonization Initiatives:** Leveraging regional harmonization initiatives, such as those promoted by the Association of Southeast Asian Nations (ASEAN), can facilitate market access across multiple countries in Asia. Manufacturers can capitalize on mutual recognition agreements, harmonized standards, and common submission procedures to streamline regulatory submissions and expedite approvals in participating countries.
5. **Engagement with Regulatory Authorities:** Establishing proactive and transparent communication channels with regulatory authorities is essential for building relationships, addressing regulatory queries, and expediting the approval process. Manufacturers should participate in regulatory meetings, workshops, and consultations to seek clarification on regulatory requirements, resolve issues, and demonstrate compliance with regulatory standards.
6. **Comprehensive Documentation:** Thorough preparation of regulatory submissions with comprehensive documentation is critical for demonstrating product safety, efficacy, and quality to regulatory authorities. Manufacturers should ensure that regulatory submissions are accurate, well-organized, and supported by robust scientific data, clinical evidence, and quality assurance documentation to facilitate regulatory review and approval.
7. **Risk Management and Mitigation:** Proactively identifying and addressing regulatory risks throughout the regulatory approval process is essential for minimizing delays and uncertainties. Manufacturers should conduct risk assessments, anticipate potential challenges, and implement mitigation strategies to address regulatory hurdles, compliance issues, and unforeseen obstacles that may arise during the approval process.
8. **Adaptation to Regulatory Changes:** Remaining vigilant and adaptable to evolving regulatory requirements, policy changes, and market dynamics is essential for navigating regulatory landscapes in Asia. Manufacturers should stay informed about regulatory updates, participate in industry forums, and engage with regulatory stakeholders to ensure compliance with changing regulations and maintain market access for their products.

By implementing these strategies, manufacturers can effectively navigate the complex regulatory landscapes in Asia, streamline the approval process, and accelerate market access for their medical products. Proactive regulatory planning, localization of expertise, tailored regulatory strategies, engagement with regulatory authorities, comprehensive documentation, risk management, and adaptation to regulatory changes are essential components of a successful regulatory strategy in Asia.

CHAPTER SEVEN

HARMONIZATION INITIATIVES AND FUTURE TRENDS

7.1 Harmonization Efforts

7.1.1 Introduction to Harmonization Initiatives

Harmonization initiatives in the realm of medical device regulation represent collaborative efforts among regulatory authorities, industry stakeholders, and other relevant entities to streamline and standardize regulatory requirements and processes across different jurisdictions. These initiatives aim to enhance patient safety, facilitate timely access to innovative medical technologies, and promote global trade by reducing redundant regulatory burdens and fostering mutual recognition of regulatory decisions. At the core of harmonization endeavors lie principles such as transparency, consistency, and convergence of regulatory standards. By aligning regulatory frameworks, harmonization initiatives seek to minimize unnecessary regulatory barriers while ensuring that the safety and effectiveness of medical devices remain paramount. Key aspects of harmonization efforts include the development of harmonized standards, guidelines, and regulatory pathways, as well as the establishment of mechanisms for information exchange and mutual reliance among regulatory authorities. Furthermore, harmonization initiatives often encompass capacity-building activities aimed at enhancing regulatory infrastructure and fostering regulatory convergence among participating jurisdictions. Overall, harmonization initiatives play a pivotal role in promoting regulatory efficiency, fostering innovation, and safeguarding public health on a global scale.

7.1.2 Historical Context of Harmonization Efforts

The historical evolution of harmonization efforts in medical device regulation can be traced back to the late 20th century, marked by an increasing recognition of the need for international cooperation to address the challenges posed by divergent regulatory requirements across different markets. The foundation of modern harmonization initiatives can be attributed to the establishment of organizations such as the International Medical Device Regulators Forum (IMDRF) and the Global Harmonization Task Force (GHTF), which laid the groundwork for collaboration among regulatory authorities from various regions. The GHTF, formed in 1992, played a significant role in harmonizing regulatory practices through the development of guidance documents, such as the Medical Device Single Audit Program (MDSAP), aimed at facilitating the mutual recognition of regulatory audits and inspections.

In the early 2000s, the transition from the GHTF to the IMDRF marked a shift towards broader international cooperation and standardization in medical device regulation. The IMDRF, established in 2011, expanded the scope of harmonization efforts by including additional regulatory authorities and stakeholders from across the globe. Through initiatives such as the harmonization of essential principles for medical device regulation and the development of regulatory guidance documents, the IMDRF has contributed to advancing regulatory convergence and facilitating the global harmonization of regulatory requirements.

Moreover, regional harmonization initiatives, such as those undertaken by the Association of Southeast Asian Nations (ASEAN) and the European Union (EU), have played a crucial role in promoting regulatory harmonization within specific geographic regions. The adoption of common regulatory frameworks, mutual recognition agreements, and convergence of technical standards have been key elements of these regional harmonization efforts, aimed at promoting trade facilitation and ensuring a high level of protection for public health and safety.

7.1.3 Importance of Harmonization in Medical Device Regulation

Harmonization in medical device regulation holds paramount importance due to its multifaceted benefits for global public health, innovation, and trade facilitation. At its core, harmonization seeks to streamline regulatory processes, align standards, and foster mutual recognition of regulatory decisions across jurisdictions, thereby reducing redundant regulatory burdens and promoting efficiency in the evaluation and approval of medical devices.

One of the primary benefits of harmonization is the enhancement of patient safety. By establishing common regulatory standards and requirements, harmonization ensures that medical devices meet consistent safety and performance criteria irrespective of the market in which they are introduced. This helps to mitigate risks associated with substandard or unsafe products, thereby safeguarding patients and healthcare professionals from potential harm.

Furthermore, harmonization fosters innovation by facilitating the timely introduction of new and advanced medical technologies into the market. By harmonizing regulatory requirements and streamlining approval processes, harmonization initiatives reduce the regulatory burden on manufacturers, enabling them to more efficiently navigate the pathway from product development to market access. This, in turn, incentivizes investment in research and development, accelerates the pace of technological advancement, and expands the availability of innovative medical devices for addressing unmet clinical needs.

From an economic perspective, harmonization promotes trade facilitation and market access by eliminating unnecessary regulatory barriers and fostering a level playing field for manufacturers operating in global markets. By aligning regulatory standards and facilitating mutual recognition of regulatory decisions, harmonization reduces duplicative testing, certification, and registration requirements, thereby lowering compliance costs and enhancing market competitiveness for manufacturers.

Moreover, harmonization enhances regulatory transparency, consistency, and predictability, thereby fostering public trust in regulatory decision-making processes. By promoting the adoption of internationally recognized standards and best practices, harmonization initiatives enhance regulatory coherence and facilitate information exchange among regulatory authorities, industry stakeholders, and other relevant entities. This contributes to a more efficient and effective regulatory ecosystem, wherein regulatory decisions are based on sound scientific principles and risk-based approaches.

7.2 Current Trends in Medical Device Regulation

7.2.1 Evolving Regulatory Landscape

The regulatory landscape governing medical devices is undergoing significant evolution in response to rapid technological advancements, emerging healthcare challenges, and evolving patient needs. One prominent trend is the increasing convergence of regulatory frameworks globally, driven by efforts to harmonize standards, streamline regulatory processes, and enhance patient safety. Regulatory authorities are increasingly adopting risk-based approaches to regulatory decision-making, focusing resources on high-risk devices while implementing proportionate regulatory requirements for low-risk devices to facilitate timely market access.

Additionally, there is growing recognition of the importance of post-market surveillance and vigilance in ensuring the ongoing safety and effectiveness of medical devices. Regulatory authorities are placing greater emphasis on real-world evidence and post-market data collection to monitor device performance, identify adverse events, and inform regulatory decision-making throughout the product lifecycle. This shift towards proactive surveillance reflects a broader trend towards evidence-based regulation and continuous improvement in regulatory oversight.

Furthermore, digital health technologies are reshaping the regulatory landscape by blurring the boundaries between traditional medical devices and software-based solutions. The proliferation of mobile health apps, wearable devices, and remote monitoring technologies presents new regulatory challenges related to data privacy, cybersecurity, and interoperability. Regulatory authorities are adapting their regulatory frameworks to accommodate these innovations while ensuring that appropriate safeguards are in place to protect patient safety and data integrity.

Another notable trend is the increasing emphasis on international collaboration and convergence in medical device regulation. Regulatory authorities are participating in initiatives such as the International Medical Device Regulators Forum (IMDRF) to harmonize regulatory standards, share best practices, and facilitate mutual recognition of regulatory decisions. This collaborative approach not only promotes regulatory efficiency and consistency but also fosters innovation and facilitates global market access for manufacturers.

Moreover, there is a growing focus on ensuring regulatory agility and responsiveness to address emerging public health challenges, such as pandemics and health emergencies. Regulatory authorities are adopting flexible regulatory pathways, expedited review processes, and accelerated approval mechanisms to facilitate the rapid development and deployment of medical devices to address urgent healthcare needs.

7.2.2 Impact of Technological Advancements on Regulation

Technological advancements are profoundly reshaping the landscape of medical device regulation, presenting both opportunities and challenges for regulatory authorities, industry stakeholders, and healthcare providers. One of the primary impacts of technological advancements is the proliferation of innovative medical devices incorporating cutting-edge technologies such as artificial intelligence (AI), machine learning (ML), robotics, and advanced materials. These advancements have the potential to revolutionize healthcare delivery, improve patient outcomes, and enhance the quality and efficiency of medical treatments.

However, the rapid pace of technological innovation also poses regulatory challenges related to the assessment of safety, effectiveness, and performance of novel medical devices. Regulatory authorities are tasked with evaluating the risks and benefits associated with new technologies, ensuring that regulatory frameworks remain flexible and adaptive to accommodate innovation while upholding rigorous standards for patient safety and product quality. Moreover, the interdisciplinary nature of many emerging technologies requires regulatory agencies to collaborate closely with experts in fields such as engineering, computer science, and data analytics to develop appropriate regulatory pathways and evaluation criteria.

Furthermore, the integration of digital health technologies, such as mobile health apps, wearable devices, and telemedicine platforms, into medical devices is blurring the lines between traditional medical devices and software-based solutions. This convergence presents unique regulatory challenges related to data privacy, cybersecurity, interoperability, and software validation. Regulatory authorities are grappling with the need to establish clear guidelines and standards for the development, validation, and regulation of digital health technologies, while ensuring that appropriate safeguards are in place to protect patient safety and data integrity.

Moreover, the globalization of the medical device industry and the increasing complexity of supply chains pose additional challenges for regulatory oversight. Regulatory authorities must contend with issues such as the outsourcing of manufacturing, the proliferation of contract manufacturing organizations (CMOs), and the globalization of clinical trials, which can complicate the assessment of product quality, traceability, and compliance with regulatory requirements. Efforts to enhance international collaboration and harmonization of regulatory standards are critical to addressing these challenges and ensuring consistent and effective regulation of medical devices across borders.

7.2.3 Globalization and its Effect on Regulatory Trends

The process of globalization has profoundly influenced regulatory trends in the field of medical devices, reshaping the landscape of regulatory oversight and decision-making on a global scale. As medical device markets become increasingly interconnected and integrated, regulatory authorities are faced with the challenge of harmonizing standards, streamlining processes, and ensuring consistent enforcement of regulatory requirements across diverse jurisdictions.

One of the primary effects of globalization on regulatory trends is the growing recognition of the need for international collaboration and convergence in regulatory standards. Regulatory authorities are actively engaging in initiatives such as the International Medical Device Regulators Forum (IMDRF) to harmonize regulatory frameworks, share best practices, and facilitate mutual recognition of regulatory decisions. This collaborative approach not only promotes regulatory efficiency and consistency but also fosters innovation and facilitates global market access for manufacturers.

Furthermore, globalization has led to the emergence of complex supply chains and global manufacturing networks in the medical device industry. Manufacturers often source components, raw materials, and finished products from multiple countries, leading to challenges related to product quality, traceability, and compliance with regulatory requirements. Regulatory authorities are adapting their oversight mechanisms to address these challenges by implementing risk-based approaches to inspection, strengthening post-market surveillance, and enhancing coordination with international counterparts to monitor and mitigate risks associated with global supply chains.

Moreover, the globalization of clinical trials and research activities presents additional challenges for regulatory oversight. Clinical trials are increasingly conducted across multiple countries and regions, necessitating coordination among regulatory authorities to ensure compliance with ethical standards, data integrity, and patient safety. Efforts to enhance mutual recognition of clinical trial data and harmonize requirements for regulatory submissions are critical to facilitating the efficient and timely approval of medical devices on a global scale.

Additionally, globalization has led to greater market access opportunities for manufacturers, enabling them to reach new markets and expand their global footprint. However, this expansion also poses challenges related to variations in regulatory requirements, cultural nuances, and market dynamics across different regions. Regulatory authorities are working to address these challenges by promoting transparency, consistency, and predictability in regulatory decision-making, fostering dialogue with industry stakeholders, and facilitating capacity-building efforts to strengthen regulatory infrastructure in emerging markets.

7.3 Future Outlook and Emerging Technologies

7.3.1 Shaping the Future of Medical Device Regulation

The future of medical device regulation is poised to be shaped by a confluence of emerging technologies, evolving healthcare needs, and regulatory imperatives. As advancements in medical technology continue to accelerate, regulatory authorities are faced with the challenge of adapting regulatory frameworks to accommodate innovation while ensuring patient safety, product quality, and public health.

One key aspect shaping the future of medical device regulation is the increasing integration of artificial intelligence (AI) and machine learning (ML) into medical devices. AI-powered medical devices have the potential to revolutionize diagnostics, treatment planning, and patient care by leveraging vast amounts of data to improve accuracy, efficiency, and outcomes. However, the complex and dynamic nature of AI algorithms presents regulatory challenges related to algorithm transparency, interpretability, validation, and ongoing monitoring. Regulatory authorities are working to develop guidelines and standards for the regulation of AI-based medical devices, balancing the need for innovation with the imperative of ensuring patient safety and regulatory compliance.

Moreover, the rise of personalized medicine and precision therapies is reshaping the landscape of medical device regulation. Personalized medical devices, such as implantable devices tailored to individual patient characteristics, genetic testing kits, and point-of-care diagnostic tools, hold the promise of delivering more targeted and effective treatments while minimizing adverse effects and improving patient outcomes. However, personalized medicine presents regulatory challenges related to data privacy, informed consent, data interoperability, and the validation of biomarkers and diagnostic assays. Regulatory authorities are exploring innovative regulatory pathways, such as adaptive licensing and real-world evidence frameworks, to facilitate the development and approval of personalized medical devices while ensuring patient safety and efficacy.

Furthermore, the proliferation of digital health technologies, including mobile health apps, wearable devices, and remote monitoring platforms, is transforming healthcare delivery and patient engagement. These technologies offer opportunities to improve access to healthcare, enhance patient empowerment, and optimize clinical workflows. However, they also raise regulatory challenges related to data privacy, cybersecurity, interoperability, and the validation of software algorithms. Regulatory authorities are working to develop regulatory frameworks that balance innovation with patient safety, ensuring that digital health technologies meet robust standards for data security, reliability, and effectiveness.

7.3.2 Incorporating Artificial Intelligence and Machine Learning

The incorporation of artificial intelligence (AI) and machine learning (ML) into medical devices represents a paradigm shift in healthcare delivery, offering unprecedented opportunities to improve diagnostics, treatment planning, and patient outcomes. AI and ML algorithms have the potential to analyze vast amounts of healthcare data, including medical images, electronic health records (EHRs), and genomic information, to identify patterns, predict outcomes, and optimize clinical decision-making. However, the integration of AI and ML into medical devices poses unique regulatory challenges that must be addressed to ensure patient safety, product quality, and regulatory compliance.

One of the primary challenges in incorporating AI and ML into medical devices is the validation and verification of algorithms to ensure their safety, effectiveness, and reliability. Unlike traditional medical devices with fixed algorithms and predictable behavior, AI and ML algorithms are dynamic, adaptive, and inherently complex, making traditional validation methods inadequate. Regulatory authorities are exploring innovative approaches to algorithm validation, such as the use of simulated data, real-world evidence, and continuous learning frameworks, to ensure that AI-based medical devices meet rigorous standards for performance and accuracy.

Moreover, the transparency and interpretability of AI and ML algorithms present additional challenges for regulatory oversight. Regulatory authorities are working to develop guidelines and standards for the documentation, explanation, and validation of AI algorithms to ensure transparency, accountability, and reproducibility. Additionally, efforts are underway to establish mechanisms for auditing and monitoring AI-based medical devices throughout their lifecycle to detect and mitigate potential biases, errors, and unintended consequences.

Furthermore, the integration of AI and ML into medical devices raises ethical and regulatory considerations related to data privacy, patient consent, and data governance. Regulatory authorities are developing frameworks for data protection, anonymization, and consent management to ensure that patient data used to train and validate AI algorithms are handled in a responsible and ethical manner. Additionally, efforts are underway to establish standards for the interoperability and exchange of healthcare data to facilitate the integration of AI-based medical devices into existing healthcare systems.

7.3.3 Nanotechnology and its Implications for Regulation

Nanotechnology, the manipulation of matter on an atomic and molecular scale, holds immense potential for revolutionizing the field of medical devices, offering opportunities to enhance diagnosis, treatment, and patient care. Nanotechnology-enabled medical devices, such as drug delivery systems, diagnostic sensors, and implantable devices, leverage the unique properties of nanomaterials to achieve unprecedented levels of precision, efficacy, and biocompatibility. However, the integration of nanotechnology into medical devices poses regulatory challenges that must be addressed to ensure patient safety, product quality, and regulatory compliance.

One of the primary challenges in regulating nanotechnology-enabled medical devices is the characterization and assessment of nanomaterials to determine their safety and biocompatibility. Nanomaterials exhibit unique physicochemical properties, such as size, shape, surface area, and reactivity, that can influence their biological interactions and potential health effects. Regulatory authorities are working to develop standardized methods for the characterization, risk assessment, and toxicological evaluation of nanomaterials to ensure that nanotechnology-enabled medical devices meet rigorous standards for safety and efficacy.

Moreover, the potential risks associated with the use of nanotechnology in medical devices, such as toxicity, biocompatibility, and environmental impact, raise ethical and regulatory considerations that must be addressed to safeguard public health and environmental sustainability. Regulatory authorities are developing guidelines and standards for the responsible design, manufacturing, and use of nanotechnology-enabled medical devices to minimize potential risks and ensure the ethical conduct of research and development activities.

Furthermore, the interdisciplinary nature of nanotechnology poses challenges for regulatory oversight, requiring collaboration among experts in fields such as materials science, engineering, biology, and toxicology. Regulatory authorities are working to foster interdisciplinary collaboration and communication to ensure that regulatory frameworks remain adaptive and responsive to the evolving landscape of nanotechnology-enabled medical devices.

Additionally, the globalization of the nanotechnology industry and the proliferation of nanotechnology-enabled medical devices across international markets present challenges for regulatory harmonization and coordination. Regulatory authorities are collaborating on initiatives such as the International Organization for Standardization (ISO) to develop harmonized standards and guidelines for the regulation of nanotechnology-enabled medical devices, facilitating market access and ensuring consistent regulatory oversight across borders.

7.3.4 Personalized Medicine and Regulatory Challenges

Personalized medicine, which tailors medical treatment to the individual characteristics of each patient, represents a paradigm shift in healthcare delivery, offering opportunities to optimize treatment outcomes, minimize adverse effects, and improve patient satisfaction. Personalized medical devices, such as genetic tests, implantable devices, and point-of-care diagnostic tools, are designed to deliver targeted and precise interventions based on the unique genetic, physiological, and environmental factors of each patient. However, the integration of personalized medicine into medical device regulation poses regulatory challenges that must be addressed to ensure patient safety, product quality, and regulatory compliance.

One of the primary challenges in regulating personalized medical devices is the validation and verification of biomarkers, diagnostic assays, and treatment algorithms to ensure their accuracy, reliability, and clinical utility. Personalized medical devices rely on biomarkers and diagnostic tests to identify patients who are likely to benefit from specific treatments, monitor treatment response, and adjust treatment plans accordingly. Regulatory authorities are working to develop guidelines and standards for the validation, clinical evaluation, and regulatory approval of personalized medical devices to ensure that they meet rigorous standards for safety, efficacy, and performance.

Moreover, the integration of personalized medicine into medical device regulation raises ethical and regulatory considerations related to data privacy, patient consent, and data governance. Personalized medical devices often rely on the collection, analysis, and interpretation of large volumes of patient data, including genetic information, medical history, and lifestyle factors. Regulatory authorities are developing frameworks for data protection, anonymization, and consent management to ensure that patient data used to inform personalized treatment decisions are handled in a responsible and ethical manner.

Furthermore, the complexity and variability of personalized medicine pose challenges for regulatory oversight, requiring adaptive and flexible regulatory approaches that can accommodate the dynamic nature of personalized treatments and technologies. Regulatory authorities are exploring innovative regulatory pathways, such as adaptive licensing and real-world evidence frameworks, to facilitate the development and approval of personalized medical devices while ensuring patient safety and regulatory compliance.

Additionally, the globalization of personalized medicine and the proliferation of personalized medical devices across international markets present challenges for regulatory harmonization and coordination. Regulatory authorities are collaborating on initiatives such as the International Medical Device Regulators Forum (IMDRF) to develop harmonized standards and guidelines for the regulation of personalized medical devices, facilitating market access and ensuring consistent regulatory oversight across borders.

7.3.5 Regulatory Considerations for 3D Printing in Medical Devices

The advent of 3D printing technology has revolutionized the field of medical device manufacturing, offering unprecedented opportunities to design and produce customized, patient-specific devices with enhanced functionality and performance. 3D printing, also known as additive manufacturing, enables the fabrication of complex geometric shapes, intricate structures, and personalized components that are difficult or impossible to achieve using traditional manufacturing methods. However, the integration of 3D printing into medical device regulation poses unique regulatory considerations that must be addressed to ensure patient safety, product quality, and regulatory compliance.

One of the primary regulatory considerations for 3D-printed medical devices is the validation and verification of manufacturing processes and materials to ensure their consistency, reproducibility, and reliability. 3D printing encompasses a wide range of technologies, materials, and processes, each of which may introduce variability and uncertainty into the manufacturing process. Regulatory authorities are working to develop guidelines and standards for the validation, qualification, and control of 3D printing processes and materials to ensure that 3D-printed medical devices meet rigorous standards for safety, efficacy, and performance.

Moreover, the customization and personalization capabilities of 3D printing raise regulatory challenges related to design control, risk management, and quality assurance. 3D-printed medical devices are often tailored to the specific anatomical characteristics and clinical needs of individual patients, requiring careful attention to design validation, patient-specific modeling, and post-market surveillance. Regulatory authorities are developing frameworks for design control, risk assessment, and post-market monitoring to ensure that 3D-printed medical devices meet regulatory requirements and deliver safe and effective outcomes for patients.

Furthermore, the use of novel materials in 3D printing, such as biocompatible polymers, ceramics, and metals, presents additional regulatory considerations related to material characterization, biocompatibility testing, and sterilization. Regulatory authorities are working to establish standards and guidelines for the assessment of material properties, biocompatibility, and sterility assurance to ensure that 3D-printed medical devices are safe, reliable, and suitable for their intended use.

Additionally, the globalization of 3D printing technology and the proliferation of 3D-printed medical devices across international markets present challenges for regulatory harmonization and coordination. Regulatory authorities are collaborating on initiatives such as the International Organization for Standardization (ISO) to develop harmonized standards and guidelines for the regulation of 3D-printed medical devices, facilitating market access and ensuring consistent regulatory oversight across borders.

7.4 Challenges in Harmonization Efforts

7.4.1 Divergent Regulatory Requirements

One of the most significant challenges in harmonization efforts in medical device regulation is the existence of divergent regulatory requirements across different jurisdictions. Regulatory authorities in various countries and regions often have distinct regulatory frameworks, standards, and processes for evaluating and approving medical devices, leading to inconsistencies, redundancies, and barriers to market access for manufacturers.

Divergent regulatory requirements arise from a variety of factors, including differences in legal systems, cultural norms, healthcare infrastructure, and risk tolerance. Regulatory authorities may have varying interpretations of international standards and guidelines, resulting in disparate regulatory expectations for manufacturers seeking approval for their medical devices in different markets. Additionally, differences in pre-market requirements, such as the documentation required for regulatory submissions, the scope of clinical evidence needed for approval, and the timelines for regulatory review, can create challenges for manufacturers navigating multiple regulatory pathways.

Moreover, divergent regulatory requirements may lead to inefficiencies and delays in the approval process, as manufacturers are required to navigate multiple regulatory frameworks and address varying regulatory expectations. This can result in increased costs, administrative burdens, and delays in bringing innovative medical devices to market, ultimately limiting patient access to new technologies and treatments.

Furthermore, divergent regulatory requirements can hinder international trade and collaboration in the medical device industry, as manufacturers may face barriers to market entry and difficulties in obtaining regulatory approvals for their products in different jurisdictions. This fragmentation of regulatory requirements can impede innovation and competition, as manufacturers may be deterred from investing in markets with complex or unpredictable regulatory environments.

Addressing the challenge of divergent regulatory requirements requires concerted efforts from regulatory authorities, industry stakeholders, and international organizations to promote harmonization, convergence, and mutual recognition of regulatory decisions. This may involve initiatives such as the development of harmonized standards and guidelines, the establishment of mutual recognition agreements, and the alignment of regulatory processes and requirements to facilitate the efficient and timely approval of medical devices across different markets.

7.4.2 Cultural and Socioeconomic Factors

Cultural and socioeconomic factors present significant challenges in harmonization efforts in medical device regulation. These factors encompass a wide range of cultural norms, values, and socioeconomic conditions that influence regulatory practices, patient preferences, and healthcare delivery systems across different countries and regions.

One of the challenges related to cultural factors is the diversity of healthcare practices and traditions among different cultures and societies. Cultural attitudes towards healthcare, medical treatment, and technology can vary significantly, leading to differences in patient expectations, acceptance of medical devices, and willingness to adopt new technologies. Regulatory authorities must consider these cultural factors when developing regulatory frameworks and standards to ensure that they are responsive to the needs and preferences of diverse patient populations.

Moreover, socioeconomic factors such as income levels, access to healthcare, and healthcare infrastructure can influence the adoption and regulation of medical devices. Socioeconomically disadvantaged populations may face barriers to accessing medical devices due to cost, geographic barriers, or lack of healthcare resources. Regulatory authorities must balance the need to promote innovation and access to medical devices with the imperative of ensuring affordability, accessibility, and equity in healthcare delivery.

Additionally, cultural and socioeconomic factors can impact the capacity of regulatory authorities to effectively regulate medical devices and enforce regulatory requirements. Regulatory agencies in low- and middle-income countries may have limited resources, expertise, and infrastructure for conducting regulatory assessments, inspections, and post-market surveillance activities. This can result in disparities in regulatory oversight and patient safety across different regions, posing challenges for manufacturers seeking to navigate diverse regulatory landscapes.

Addressing the challenges posed by cultural and socioeconomic factors requires collaborative efforts from regulatory authorities, industry stakeholders, and international organizations to promote equity, inclusivity, and patient-centered regulation. This may involve initiatives such as capacity-building programs, technology transfer initiatives, and public awareness campaigns to enhance regulatory capacity, improve patient access to medical devices, and foster trust in regulatory processes.

Furthermore, regulatory authorities must engage with diverse stakeholders, including patients, healthcare providers, advocacy groups, and community leaders, to understand and address cultural and socioeconomic barriers to the adoption and regulation of medical devices. By incorporating diverse perspectives and experiences into regulatory decision-making processes, regulatory authorities can develop more responsive, inclusive, and effective regulatory frameworks that promote patient safety, public health, and access to medical innovation for all populations.

7.4.3 Legal and Political Challenges

Harmonization efforts in medical device regulation face significant legal and political challenges that stem from the complex interplay of legal frameworks, political dynamics, and regulatory sovereignty across different countries and regions. These challenges can create barriers to regulatory convergence, hinder international collaboration, and impede progress towards harmonized regulatory standards and processes.

One of the primary legal challenges is the sovereignty of regulatory authorities and the divergent legal frameworks governing medical device regulation in different jurisdictions. Regulatory authorities are empowered by national laws and regulations to develop and enforce regulatory requirements tailored to the specific needs and priorities of their respective countries. This sovereignty can lead to differences in regulatory standards, processes, and enforcement mechanisms, complicating efforts to harmonize regulatory requirements and facilitate mutual recognition of regulatory decisions.

Moreover, legal barriers such as intellectual property rights, trade agreements, and liability laws can impact harmonization efforts by influencing market access, technology transfer, and collaboration among regulatory authorities. Intellectual property rights, including patents, trademarks, and copyrights, can create barriers to the sharing of proprietary information and technology transfer, hindering collaborative efforts to develop harmonized standards and guidelines. Trade agreements and international trade laws may also influence regulatory convergence by imposing restrictions on the recognition of foreign regulatory decisions and the acceptance of foreign standards and certifications.

Additionally, political factors such as geopolitical tensions, trade disputes, and national interests can affect harmonization efforts by shaping regulatory priorities, agendas, and decision-making processes. Political considerations may lead to divergent approaches to medical device regulation, with regulatory authorities prioritizing national interests, industry competitiveness, and public health concerns over international harmonization objectives. Geopolitical tensions and trade disputes can further exacerbate regulatory fragmentation by impeding cooperation and information sharing among regulatory authorities.

Addressing the legal and political challenges in harmonization efforts requires diplomatic engagement, policy coordination, and multilateral cooperation among regulatory authorities, industry stakeholders, and international organizations. This may involve initiatives such as diplomatic dialogues, bilateral and multilateral agreements, and mutual recognition arrangements aimed at promoting regulatory convergence, facilitating trade, and enhancing patient access to safe, effective, and innovative medical devices on a global scale.

Furthermore, regulatory authorities must navigate the complex legal and political landscape by adopting pragmatic and flexible approaches to harmonization, recognizing the diverse needs and priorities of different countries and regions. This may involve incremental steps towards regulatory convergence, pragmatic solutions to address legal and political barriers, and sustained efforts to build trust, transparency, and cooperation among regulatory authorities and stakeholders.

7.5 Strategies for Successful Harmonization

7.5.1 Strengthening International Collaboration

One of the key strategies for successful harmonization in medical device regulation is strengthening international collaboration among regulatory authorities, industry stakeholders, and international organizations. International collaboration fosters dialogue, information sharing, and mutual learning, facilitating the development of harmonized standards, guidelines, and regulatory processes that promote patient safety, product quality, and regulatory efficiency.

One aspect of strengthening international collaboration involves enhancing communication and coordination among regulatory authorities through forums, working groups, and collaborative initiatives. Regulatory authorities can participate in organizations such as the International Medical Device Regulators Forum (IMDRF) to exchange best practices, share regulatory experiences, and develop consensus-based approaches to regulatory challenges. These collaborative efforts enable regulatory authorities to align regulatory standards, streamline regulatory processes, and promote mutual recognition of regulatory decisions, ultimately enhancing patient access to safe, effective, and innovative medical devices on a global scale.

Moreover, international collaboration facilitates capacity-building and technical assistance initiatives aimed at enhancing regulatory expertise, infrastructure, and resources in low- and middle-income countries.

Regulatory authorities in developed countries can support their counterparts in developing countries through training programs, technology transfer initiatives, and regulatory harmonization projects. These capacity-building efforts empower regulatory authorities to fulfill their regulatory responsibilities effectively, promote regulatory convergence, and enhance patient access to medical devices in underserved regions.

Furthermore, international collaboration promotes transparency, accountability, and trust among regulatory authorities, industry stakeholders, and the public. Regulatory authorities can engage with industry stakeholders to develop industry standards, guidelines, and best practices that complement regulatory requirements and facilitate compliance with regulatory expectations. By fostering a collaborative regulatory environment, regulatory authorities can build confidence in regulatory processes, promote innovation, and facilitate market access for manufacturers while ensuring patient safety and public health.

7.5.2 Utilizing Regulatory Science and Research

Another vital strategy for successful harmonization in medical device regulation is the utilization of regulatory science and research to inform evidence-based decision-making, develop robust standards, and address emerging challenges in medical device regulation.

Regulatory science encompasses a multidisciplinary field that integrates scientific principles, methodologies, and technologies to inform regulatory decision-making and improve regulatory processes. By leveraging advances in fields such as biomedical engineering, data analytics, and clinical research, regulatory authorities can enhance their understanding of medical devices‘ safety, effectiveness, and performance, enabling them to develop evidence-based regulatory frameworks and standards that promote patient safety and public health.

One aspect of utilizing regulatory science involves conducting research to address knowledge gaps, identify areas of uncertainty, and develop scientific methodologies for evaluating medical devices' safety and efficacy. Regulatory authorities can collaborate with academic institutions, research organizations, and industry stakeholders to conduct studies, collect data, and generate evidence to support regulatory decision-making. This research may include studies on novel biomarkers, diagnostic assays, and clinical endpoints, as well as the development of innovative testing methodologies and computational modeling approaches to assess medical devices‘

performance and predict their long-term outcomes.

Moreover, regulatory science plays a critical role in advancing innovative regulatory approaches and methodologies to enhance regulatory efficiency, flexibility, and responsiveness. Regulatory authorities can explore new approaches such as adaptive licensing, real-world evidence frameworks, and modeling and simulation techniques to streamline regulatory processes, accelerate market access for innovative medical devices, and facilitate the development of personalized and digital health technologies. By embracing innovation and leveraging cutting-edge technologies, regulatory authorities can promote regulatory convergence, foster industry innovation, and enhance patient access to safe, effective, and high-quality medical devices on a global scale.

Furthermore, regulatory science enables regulatory authorities to address emerging challenges and opportunities in medical device regulation, such as the integration of artificial intelligence, nanotechnology, and 3D printing into medical devices. By staying abreast of technological advancements, conducting research on emerging technologies' safety and efficacy, and developing regulatory guidance and standards for their evaluation and approval, regulatory authorities can ensure that medical device regulation remains adaptive, responsive, and future-ready in the face of rapid technological innovation and market evolution.

7.5.3 Standardization of Regulatory Processes

Standardizing regulatory processes is a fundamental strategy for successful harmonization in medical device regulation. Standardization involves establishing uniform procedures, requirements, and guidelines for regulatory activities across different countries and regions, promoting consistency, predictability, and efficiency in regulatory decision-making.

One aspect of standardizing regulatory processes is the development of harmonized standards and guidelines for regulatory submissions, assessments, and approvals. Regulatory authorities can collaborate with international organizations such as the International Organization for Standardization (ISO) to develop standardized formats, terminology, and documentation requirements for regulatory submissions, facilitating the exchange of information and data between regulatory authorities and manufacturers. Harmonized standards and guidelines help streamline regulatory processes, reduce administrative burdens, and enhance transparency and predictability for manufacturers seeking regulatory approval for their medical devices in multiple markets.

Moreover, standardizing regulatory processes involves aligning regulatory requirements and timelines for regulatory submissions, reviews, and inspections across different countries and regions. Regulatory authorities can work together to harmonize pre-market requirements, such as the scope of clinical data needed for approval, the documentation required for regulatory submissions, and the timelines for regulatory review, to minimize duplicative efforts and streamline the regulatory pathway for manufacturers seeking market approval in multiple jurisdictions. By aligning regulatory requirements and timelines, regulatory authorities can enhance regulatory efficiency, reduce time to market, and promote patient access to safe, effective, and innovative medical devices on a global scale.

Furthermore, standardizing regulatory processes requires fostering collaboration and information sharing among regulatory authorities through platforms, networks, and working groups. Regulatory authorities can participate in initiatives such as the International Medical Device Regulators Forum (IMDRF) to exchange best practices, share regulatory experiences, and develop consensus-based approaches to regulatory challenges. Collaborative efforts to standardize regulatory processes promote mutual recognition of regulatory decisions, facilitate market access for manufacturers, and enhance patient access to safe, effective, and high-quality medical devices worldwide.

7.5.4 Public-Private Partnerships in Harmonization Efforts

Engaging in public-private partnerships (PPPs) is a strategic approach for successful harmonization in medical device regulation. PPPs involve collaboration between governmental regulatory agencies and private sector stakeholders, such as industry associations, academia, and non-profit organizations, to address common challenges, leverage resources, and advance shared objectives in medical device regulation.

One aspect of PPPs is facilitating knowledge exchange and capacity-building initiatives between regulatory authorities and private sector stakeholders. Regulatory authorities can collaborate with industry associations, professional societies, and academic institutions to develop training programs, workshops, and seminars aimed at enhancing regulatory expertise, fostering a better understanding of regulatory requirements, and promoting compliance with regulatory standards among medical device manufacturers. By sharing knowledge, best practices, and technical expertise, PPPs empower stakeholders to navigate regulatory processes more effectively, promote innovation, and enhance patient access to safe, effective, and high-quality medical devices.

Moreover, PPPs play a critical role in promoting innovation and advancing regulatory science in medical device regulation. Regulatory authorities can collaborate with industry stakeholders to support research and development initiatives, pilot projects, and demonstration studies aimed at advancing innovative technologies, methodologies, and regulatory approaches in medical device regulation. By leveraging industry expertise, resources, and infrastructure, regulatory authorities can accelerate the development and adoption of cutting-edge technologies, streamline regulatory processes, and promote regulatory convergence, ultimately enhancing patient access to innovative medical devices on a global scale.

Furthermore, PPPs facilitate stakeholder engagement and collaboration in the development of regulatory policies, standards, and guidelines. Regulatory authorities can establish public-private advisory committees, working groups, and task forces to engage with industry stakeholders, patient advocacy groups, and other relevant stakeholders in the development of regulatory frameworks and initiatives. By soliciting input, feedback, and expertise from diverse stakeholders, regulatory authorities can ensure that regulatory policies and standards are informed by stakeholder perspectives, reflect the latest scientific evidence, and are responsive to the needs and priorities of all stakeholders.

7.6 Ethical Considerations in Harmonization

Ethical considerations play a crucial role in harmonization efforts in medical device regulation, guiding regulatory decision-making, protecting patient rights, and promoting public trust in regulatory processes. Harmonization initiatives must prioritize ethical principles and values to ensure that regulatory frameworks and standards uphold the highest standards of integrity, transparency, and accountability.

One ethical consideration is the principle of beneficence, which emphasizes the obligation to promote the well-being and interests of patients and public health. Regulatory authorities must prioritize patient safety and welfare in their decision-making processes, ensuring that medical devices meet rigorous standards for safety, efficacy, and performance before they are approved for market access. Harmonized regulatory standards should prioritize the protection of vulnerable populations, such as children, the elderly, and individuals with disabilities, by requiring robust clinical evidence and post-market surveillance to monitor the safety and effectiveness of medical devices over time.

Moreover, the principle of justice requires that regulatory decisions be fair, equitable, and non-discriminatory, ensuring equal access to safe, effective, and innovative medical devices for all individuals, regardless of socioeconomic status, geographic location, or other demographic factors. Harmonization efforts should aim to reduce disparities in access to medical devices by promoting regulatory convergence, streamlining regulatory processes, and facilitating market access for manufacturers in underserved regions. Regulatory authorities should also consider the ethical implications of regulatory decisions on global health equity and strive to address inequities in access to healthcare technologies through collaborative initiatives and resource-sharing mechanisms.

Additionally, regulatory authorities must uphold the principles of autonomy and informed consent, respecting patients' rights to make autonomous decisions about their healthcare and ensuring that they have access to accurate, understandable, and unbiased information about medical devices. Harmonized regulatory standards should require transparent and accessible labeling, patient information materials, and consent forms to enable patients to make informed choices about the risks and benefits of medical devices. Regulatory authorities should also promote patient engagement and participation in regulatory processes, seeking input from patient advocacy groups, consumer organizations, and other stakeholders to incorporate patient perspectives into regulatory decision-making.

Furthermore, regulatory authorities must adhere to the principles of transparency and accountability, ensuring that regulatory processes are open, transparent, and subject to public scrutiny. Harmonization efforts should prioritize transparency in regulatory decision-making, including the disclosure of regulatory requirements, standards, and guidelines, as well as the rationale behind regulatory decisions. Regulatory authorities should also establish mechanisms for accountability and oversight to monitor regulatory compliance, address conflicts of interest, and investigate allegations of misconduct or wrongdoing.

7.6.1 Patient Safety and Ethical Standards

Patient safety is paramount in medical device regulation, and ensuring ethical standards is essential to uphold patient welfare. Harmonization efforts must prioritize patient safety by adhering to rigorous ethical standards throughout the regulatory process.

Ethical standards in medical device regulation encompass various aspects, including the design, development, manufacturing, marketing, and post-market surveillance of medical devices. Regulatory authorities must establish and enforce ethical guidelines that prioritize patient safety, efficacy, and well-being at every stage of the medical device lifecycle.

One crucial aspect of ethical standards is the requirement for robust clinical evidence to demonstrate the safety and efficacy of medical devices before they are approved for market access. Regulatory authorities must set high standards for clinical trials, ensuring that they are well-designed, adequately powered, and ethically conducted to generate reliable data on the safety and effectiveness of medical devices. Patients participating in clinical trials must be fully informed of the risks and benefits of the device under investigation and provide informed consent before enrolling in the study.

Moreover, ethical standards require transparent and honest communication between manufacturers, regulatory authorities, healthcare providers, and patients regarding the risks, benefits, and limitations of medical devices. Manufacturers must provide accurate and comprehensive information about their products, including indications for use, contraindications, warnings, and precautions, to enable healthcare providers and patients to make informed decisions about device selection, use, and management.

Furthermore, ethical standards necessitate robust post-market surveillance systems to monitor the safety and performance of medical devices once they are available on the market. Regulatory authorities must establish mechanisms for reporting adverse events, device malfunctions, and other safety concerns, enabling timely detection, investigation, and mitigation of potential risks to patient safety. Patients and healthcare providers must be encouraged and empowered to report adverse events and participate in post-market surveillance activities to enhance patient safety and public health.

Additionally, ethical standards require regulatory authorities to enforce strict enforcement measures against manufacturers that violate ethical principles or regulatory requirements. Regulatory authorities must conduct inspections, audits, and investigations to ensure compliance with ethical standards and take appropriate enforcement actions, such as product recalls, warning letters, fines, or sanctions, against manufacturers that fail to meet ethical and regulatory obligations.

7.6.2 Transparency and Accountability in Regulatory Decision-making

Transparency and accountability are foundational principles in regulatory decision-making, ensuring that regulatory processes are open, accessible, and subject to public scrutiny. In the context of harmonization efforts in medical device regulation, transparency and accountability are essential for building public trust, promoting stakeholder engagement, and upholding the integrity of regulatory systems.

Transparency in regulatory decision-making involves the disclosure of regulatory requirements, standards, guidelines, and the rationale behind regulatory decisions. Regulatory authorities must provide clear and accessible information to stakeholders, including medical device manufacturers, healthcare providers, patients, and the public, about regulatory processes, timelines, and expectations. This transparency enables stakeholders to understand regulatory requirements, navigate regulatory pathways, and make informed decisions about medical device development, approval, and use.

Moreover, transparency requires regulatory authorities to disclose information about the safety, efficacy, and performance of medical devices, including clinical trial data, adverse event reports, post-market surveillance findings, and regulatory decisions. Providing access to this information empowers healthcare providers and patients to make informed choices about device selection, use, and management, enhances public awareness of potential risks and benefits associated with medical devices, and fosters trust in regulatory processes.

Accountability in regulatory decision-making involves establishing mechanisms for oversight, review, and evaluation of regulatory actions and outcomes. Regulatory authorities must be accountable to the public, policymakers, and other stakeholders for their regulatory decisions, ensuring that decisions are made in accordance with ethical principles, regulatory requirements, and public health considerations. This accountability requires regulatory authorities to conduct regulatory assessments, inspections, and audits in a transparent and impartial manner, free from undue influence or conflicts of interest.

Furthermore, accountability involves responding promptly and effectively to concerns, complaints, and feedback from stakeholders regarding regulatory decisions or actions. Regulatory authorities must establish mechanisms for stakeholders to voice their concerns, provide feedback, and seek redress for grievances related to regulatory processes or outcomes. This responsiveness to stakeholder input promotes trust, confidence, and legitimacy in regulatory systems, enhancing public perception and acceptance of regulatory decisions.

7.6.3 Balancing Innovation with Regulatory Oversight

Balancing innovation with regulatory oversight is a critical ethical consideration in medical device regulation. While promoting innovation is essential for advancing healthcare and addressing unmet medical needs, regulatory authorities must ensure that innovative medical devices are safe, effective, and of high quality to protect patient safety and public health.

One aspect of balancing innovation with regulatory oversight involves adopting a risk-based approach to regulation that recognizes the potential risks and benefits associated with innovative medical devices. Regulatory authorities must assess the risks posed by new technologies, methodologies, and applications and tailor regulatory requirements accordingly to mitigate risks while facilitating innovation. This risk-based approach allows regulatory authorities to allocate resources effectively, prioritize regulatory activities, and focus oversight efforts on areas of highest risk, such as novel technologies, high-risk devices, and emerging threats to patient safety.

Moreover, regulatory authorities must foster a culture of innovation within regulatory frameworks by providing clear, predictable, and flexible pathways for the development, evaluation, and approval of innovative medical devices. This includes establishing expedited review programs, special access programs, and regulatory pathways for breakthrough technologies, orphan diseases, and unmet medical needs to accelerate patient access to innovative medical devices while maintaining robust regulatory oversight. Regulatory authorities must also engage with industry stakeholders, patient advocacy groups, and other stakeholders to identify regulatory barriers to innovation and develop strategies to address them collaboratively.

Furthermore, regulatory authorities must leverage innovative regulatory approaches and methodologies to keep pace with rapid technological advancements and evolving healthcare needs. This includes embracing novel technologies such as real-world evidence, modeling and simulation, and adaptive pathways to complement traditional clinical trial data and inform regulatory decision-making. By incorporating innovative regulatory approaches, regulatory authorities can enhance regulatory efficiency, flexibility, and responsiveness, while ensuring patient safety and public health.

However, regulatory authorities must also exercise caution and prudence in their approach to innovation, balancing the potential benefits of new technologies with the need to protect patient safety and public health. This requires regulatory authorities to conduct thorough assessments of the safety, efficacy, and performance of innovative medical devices, including consideration of potential long-term risks and uncertainties. Regulatory authorities must also monitor and evaluate the post-market safety and effectiveness of innovative medical devices through robust post-market surveillance systems to detect and mitigate emerging risks promptly.

CHAPTER EIGHT

RESOURCES AND REFERENCES

1. **Amitava Dasgupta**. *Regulatory and Clinical Aspects of In Vitro Diagnostics*. 2021, Elsevier Inc.

    - This book provides an extensive overview of the regulatory and clinical considerations for in vitro diagnostics, covering global standards and specific case studies.

1. **Sethu Vijayakumar**. *Global Harmonization of Regulatory Guidelines for Medical Devices*. 2019, Springer Nature.

    - Focuses on the efforts towards regulatory harmonization across different regions including IMDRF/GHTF standards, and discusses future trends in regulatory science.

3. **Marie B. Teixeira**. *Comprehensive Guide to Medical Device Regulations*. 2020, Wiley-Blackwell.

    - A thorough guide to medical device regulations in the USA, European Union, ASEAN, China, and Japan, providing a deep dive into the processes and ethical considerations in each region.

4. **Kim Trautman**. *Medical Device Quality Management Systems: Strategy and Techniques for Improving Efficiency and Effectiveness*. 2018, Academic Press.

- This book explores quality management systems in the medical device industry, focusing on regulatory compliance and operational efficiency.

5. **Stephanie Norris**. *Case Studies in Medical Device Regulatory Affairs*. 2022, CRC Press.

   - Contains practical applications and real-world case studies to illustrate the complexities and challenges of regulatory approvals in different jurisdictions.

6. **Sam Liao**. *Regulatory Affairs for Biomaterials and Medical Devices*. 2019, Woodhead Publishing.

   - All aspects of regulatory affairs for biomaterials and medical devices, with emphasis on ethical considerations and quality control.

7. **European Union Regulations**. *Official Journal of the European Union: Medical Devices Regulations*. Latest Edition, Publications Office of the European Union.

   - Provides the official text of the Medical Devices Regulations applicable in the European Union, detailing legislative frameworks and amendments.

8. **FDA Guidance Documents**. *Guidance for Industry and Food and Drug Administration Staff*. Updated Regularly, U.S. Food and Drug Administration.

   - A compilation of guidance documents from the FDA that provide comprehensive advice on regulatory processes for medical devices in the USA.

9. **Asia Pacific Medical Technology Association (APACMed)**. *Regulatory Affairs in Asia Pacific: Guidelines and Best Practices*. 2021, APACMed.

   - Offers insights into the regulatory landscapes in the Asia Pacific region, focusing on ASEAN, China, and Japan, and discusses best practices for compliance.

10. **International Medical Device Regulators Forum (IMDRF)**. *Technical Documents and Guidelines*. Accessed 2024, IMDRF.

    - A resource for global standards on medical device regulation, including technical and guidance documents developed by the IMDRF.

11. **Jeffrey K. Shapiro**. *How to Comply with FDA Regulations for Medical Devices and Software*. 2023, CRC Press.

    - This resource offers a detailed explanation of FDA regulations affecting medical devices and software, including compliance strategies and common pitfalls.

12. **Jonathan Kahan**. *Handbook of Medical Device Regulatory Affairs in Asia*. 2021, Pan Stanford.

    - A comprehensive guide on regulatory affairs in key Asian markets, offering detailed insights into the approval processes and regulatory requirements in these regions.

13. **Lisa Casavant and Robyn Meurant**. *International Medical Device Regulatory Monitor*. 2024, Wolters Kluwer.

    - A subscription-based newsletter providing up-to-date information on regulatory changes, guidelines, and global harmonization efforts.

14. **World Health Organization (WHO)**. *Medical Device Regulations: Global Overview and Guiding Principles*. 2022, WHO Press.

    - This publication offers a global overview of medical device regulations, providing guiding principles and frameworks used by regulatory bodies worldwide.

15. **John J. Tobin**. *European Union Medical Device Law*. 2023, LexisNexis.

- Detailed analysis of the EU Medical Device Regulation (MDR), exploring legal interpretations, compliance strategies, and the impact on medical device companies.

16. **Erik Vollebregt**. *Medical Devices Law and Regulation Answer Book*. 2022, Practising Law Institute.

    - Addresses frequently asked questions in medical device regulation, offering clear answers and practical advice on navigating complex regulatory landscapes.

17. **Susan Schniepp**. *Understanding Quality Systems Regulations in Pharmaceutical and Medical Device Manufacturing*. 2020, PDA/DHI.

    - Focuses on the quality systems regulations for medical devices and pharmaceuticals, discussing how to implement and maintain compliant systems.

18. **Anurag Rathore and Gail Sofer**. *The Regulatory Environment for Medical Devices and Pharmaceuticals: Global Approaches*. 2021, McGraw-Hill Education.

    - Compares regulatory environments across the globe, discussing differences and similarities in approaches to medical devices and pharmaceutical regulation.

19. **Health Canada**. *Guidance on Medical Device Compliance and Enforcement*. Latest Edition, Health Canada.

    - Official Canadian guidelines detailing compliance and enforcement actions in the medical device sector, including recent updates and amendments.

20. **Pharmaceuticals and Medical Devices Agency (PMDA) Japan**. *Guidelines for Medical Device Approval*. 2024, PMDA Publications.

    - Provides comprehensive guidelines for medical device approval in Japan, detailing the regulatory requirements and submission processes.

21. **Michael Cheng**. *Regulations for Medical Devices: Principles and Practices.* 2023, Springer.

    - An advanced textbook that delves into the principles and practices underpinning medical device regulations, with a focus on risk management and regulatory compliance.

22. **Bruce Vigon and Scott Rudge**. *Project Management in the Regulatory World: Best Practices for Medical Device Approval.* 2022, Elsevier.

    - A practical guide to project management within the regulatory framework, offering strategies for navigating complex approval processes in various jurisdictions.

23. **ISO 13485:2024**. *Medical Devices - Quality Management Systems - Requirements for Regulatory Purposes.* International Organization for Standardization.

    - The latest edition of ISO 13485, detailing requirements for quality management systems in the manufacture of medical devices to meet regulatory standards.

24. **Gert Bos** and **Bassil Akra**. *Clinical Evaluation of Medical Devices: Principles and Case Studies.* 2023, Springer.

    - Focuses on the clinical evaluation of medical devices, providing principles and real-world case studies that illustrate regulatory challenges and solutions.

25. **U.S. Food and Drug Administration (FDA)**. *Comprehensive Planning for the Pre-Market Application Review Process.* 2024, FDA Publications.

    - A detailed guide from the FDA outlining the strategic planning necessary for the pre-market application review process for medical devices.

26. **European Medicines Agency (EMA).** *European Regulatory Guidelines for Medical Devices*. 2023, EMA Publications.

    - Comprehensive guidelines issued by the EMA that cover regulatory policies, procedures, and approval processes for medical devices in the European Union.

27. **Simon Turner and Frank Agbogbo**. *Medical Device Regulations in Emerging Markets*. 2023, Wiley.

    - Examines medical device regulations in emerging markets, including specific challenges, opportunities, and strategic considerations for market entry and compliance.

28. **Asia-Pacific Economic Cooperation (APEC).** *Harmonization of Regulatory Standards for Medical Devices in the Asia-Pacific Region*. 2022, APEC Publications.

    - Discusses efforts towards harmonization of regulatory standards across the Asia-Pacific region, providing a synthesis of current standards and future directions.

29. **Suzanne Schwartz** and **Mark Kramer**. *FDA Device Regulations: Case Studies and Lessons Learned*. 2023, Academic Press.

    - A collection of case studies from the FDA's device approval process, providing insights into common regulatory hurdles and the lessons learned from each case.

30. **Michael Mortimer and Sheila Barry**. *Global Compliance for Medical Devices: Strategies and Techniques*. 2024, McGraw-Hill.

    - Provides strategies and techniques for achieving global compliance in the medical device industry, focusing on harmonization and adherence to international standards.

www.ingramcontent.com/pod-product-compliance
Ingram Content Group UK Ltd.
Pitfield, Milton Keynes, MK11 3LW, UK
UKHW062310290726
14090UKWH00018B/994